BOOKS BY BENJAMIN KEEN

David Curtis DeForest and the Revolution of Buenos Aires, 1947

Readings in Latin-American Civilization, 1954

The Life of the Admiral Christopher Columbus by His Son Ferdinand, 1959

The Spain of Ferdinand and Isabella, 1961

Life and Labor in Ancient Mexico: *The Brief and Summary Relation of the Lords of New Spain,* 1963

Americans All: *The Story of Our Latin American Neighbors,* 1966

LIFE *and* LABOR *in*
ANCIENT MEXICO

THE *Brief and Summary Relation of the Lords of*
New Spain

BY

Alonso de Zorita

TRANSLATED AND WITH AN INTRODUCTION BY
BENJAMIN KEEN

RUTGERS UNIVERSITY PRESS
New Brunswick, New Jersey

This book has been published
with the assistance of the
Ford Foundation.

Illustrations in this volume are from the Codex
Telleriano Remensis and the Codex Borbonicus.

Contents

✣

Editor's Introduction

AT THE OPENING of the sixteenth century most of Central Mexico, from the fringes of the arid northern plateau southward to the lowlands of Tehuantepec, paid tribute to the Aztecs[1] of the Valley of Mexico. These Aztecs were latecomers in an ancient, intensely civilized land. Little more than two centuries before, they had been an obscure barbarian tribe, one of a number of such tribes who broke into the valley when the Toltec Empire, with its seat at Tula, collapsed at the end of the twelfth century. These invaders, some of whom may have served as mercenaries guarding the marches of Toltec civilization, felt much respect for the superior Toltec culture and claimed for themselves the prestige attached to the Toltec name. Five succession states, all parading real or assumed Toltec origins, soon arose in the Valley of Mexico.

Last to arrive in the valley, much later than the others, were the Aztecs. Their picture chronicles give the date 1168 as the date of their departure from their homeland somewhere in the North. Led by four chiefs and a woman who carried a medicine bundle housing the spirit of their tribal god, Huitzilopochtli, who guided their steps speaking in the strange twittering voice of a hummingbird, the Aztecs wandered for many years before they entered the valley, probably at the end of the thirteenth century. They were unwelcome to the claimants of the densely populated valley. Buffeted about and finally driven into the marshy waters of Lake Texcoco, where they lived miserably on a sandy islet, the early Aztecs showed no sign of their future greatness. Not until 1344 or 1345 did they found the town of Tenochtitlán-México, the future capital of their empire.

They made their first mark as vassals or mercenaries in the armies of the town of Atzcapotzalco, the dominant power in the lake country in the late fourteenth and early fifteenth centuries. In 1427 came a turning point in Aztec history. The Aztecs joined with the rebellious city-state of Texcoco to destroy the tyranny of Atzcapotzalco. This triumph led to the formation of a Triple Alliance uniting Tenochtitlán, Texcoco, and the much smaller town of Tlacopan. The alliance became an Aztec instrument for conquest, first of the valley, then of much of the Middle American world. The strong position of their island redoubt, practically impregnable to the attack of rival tribes, together with a shrewd policy of forming alliances and sharing the spoils of conquest with strategic mainland towns, which the Aztecs later reduced to satellites, helps to explain Aztec success in gaining control of the Valley of Mexico. Control of the valley in turn offered a key to the conquest of Middle America. "The valley possessed all the advantages of short internal lines of communication, surrounded by a mountainous perimeter of defense. Yet, through gateways leading to the north, east, west, and south, its traders and soldiers had easy access to adjacent valleys." [2]

Like all imperialist peoples, the Aztecs had an ideology that served to justify their career of conquest. The Aztecs believed themselves to be the People of the Sun, destined by Huitzilopochtli to become masters of the world and instruments for the fulfillment of his will. The Aztec repaid the sun for his favors by nourishing the god with the blood of sacrificial victims, the magic substance of life, without which he would succumb in his daily cosmic struggle with the forces of darkness, the moon and the stars. Thus the Aztecs assumed the sacred duty of providing the sun and the other gods with food so that they in turn would continue to lavish on mankind their gifts of sunlight, wind, and rain. Human sacrifice on a monumental scale marred the last decades of Aztec rule.

Yet the Aztecs loved beauty. Their Nahuatl language is very expressive and plastic; even everyday Aztec speech appears to have been ornate and musical. Aztec poetry abounds in references to the scent and loveliness of flowers, to the flashing beauty of gems, to the brevity of life and its uncertain joys. The same tragic sense of life appears in the severe Aztec sculpture. All the Aztec people shared in a rich heritage of poetry, music, and the dance.

If Tenochtitlán was the military center of the Triple Alliance, the mainland town of Texcoco was its cultural center. Texcoco had its finest hour under the philosopher-king Nezahualcoyotl (1418-1472), perhaps the most remarkable figure to emerge from the mists of ancient America. In Texcoco the processes of conquest and political centralization were accompanied by "intellectual developments which issued in the enactment of a great legal code, in the growth of a philosophy of monotheism, and in the disavowal of human sacrifice." [3] Nezahualcoyotl presided over this movement of intellectual advance.

He did more. He was a patron of art and literature, inviting the finest craftsmen and artists of the valley to his capital. He established a commission on arts and letters which met regularly to gather information and to award prizes for outstanding achievements and administer punishments for poor craftsmanship to musicians, poets, goldsmiths, sculptors, and featherworkers. He was himself a poet, and his verse sounds the characteristic Aztec note of pathos: "The pleasures which our lives present—earth's scepters, and its wealth—are lent, are shadows fleeting by." Yet this sensitive king joined the rulers of Tenochtitlán and Tlacopan in predatory wars and presided over mass killings of slaves and war prisoners. In Nezahualcoyotl the paradoxes of Aztec civilization find a distinctive expression.

By the opening of the sixteenth century major changes had taken place in Aztec society. The growth of war and trade had created a highly stratified social order topped by ruling castes of warrior nobility, priests, and merchants, with a mass of humble free commoners, serfs, and slaves below. Tribal democracy had virtually disappeared, for political power was now concentrated in a hereditary ruler advised by a council of great nobles who were his own close relatives. The ancient unit of tribal organization and landholding, the *calpulli* or clan, had lost much of its autonomy and all voice in the conduct of general tribal affairs. Private property in land was increasing, as was the number of slaves and serfs.

The Triple Alliance had reached a peak of pride and power; more than two hundred and seventy towns poured tribute of the most varied kinds into the allied capitals and especially into the island redoubt of Tenochtitlán. Yet the Aztec leaders lived in fear; the Aztec chronicles register a pervasive mood of insecurity. The mounting demands of Aztec tribute collectors caused revolts on the part of tributary towns; though repressed, they broke out afresh. The exploitative tactics and arrogance of Aztec merchants, used as spies and *agents provocateurs* by the war lords of Tenochtitlán, produced hostility that flamed into open war. The haunted Aztec imagination saw portents of evil on earth and in the troubled air. A child was born with two heads; the volcano Popocatepetl became unusually active; a comet streamed across the sky. The year

1519 approached, the year in which according to Aztec lore the Toltec god-king Quetzalcoatl might return to reclaim the realm from which he had been driven centuries before by the forces of evil.

By coincidence, there appeared on the shores of Mexico, in the same year, Hernando Cortés and some six hundred comrades. In the ensuing crisis the luckless Moctezuma displayed an irresolution that suggests a decline in the quality of Aztec leadership. The king's pathetic efforts to bribe or cajole the Spaniards to leave Mexico were fruitless. As the Aztecs' doom approached, their own gods turned against them; a group of sorcerers and soothsayers sent by Moctezuma to cast spells over the Spaniards were halted by the young god Tezcatlipoca, who conjured up before their horrified eyes a vision of Tenochtitlán-México burning to the ground. The handful of Spaniards owed their victory, however, neither to Aztec superstition nor to their superior arms but to the aid of masses of Indians eager to throw off the Aztec yoke. On August 23, 1521, after a final siege in which the Aztecs had fought for three months with a splendid valor and fortitude, their last king, Cuauhtemoc, surrendered amid the laments of his starving people, and Cortés took possession of the ruins that had been the magnificent city of Tenochtitlán.

Now a common doom came upon the Indians of Mexico, both the Aztecs and their former subjects. The agony of the siege and fall of Tenochtitlán was succeeded by a prolonged ordeal as the Indians struggled to adjust to the whims and ways of their conquerors. More than a century elapsed before new patterns of life and labor took shape and a precarious stability was attained.

Gold was the symbol and object of the conquistadores' lust for wealth. "Like monkeys they seized upon the gold," bitterly commented an Aztec chronicler, "they thirsted mightily for gold; they stuffed themselves with it, and hungered and lusted for it like pigs." [4] Of gold, however, the Spaniards found but little, and they soon turned to exploit its equivalents in the form of Indian tribute and labor. To satisfy the clamor of his hard-bitten soldiers, Cortés established in New Spain the encomienda system, already tried in the West Indies with disastrous results to the native population. A royal order forbidding the assignment of any more encomiendas in New Spain, and commanding the revocation of those already granted, went for naught. Cortés argued so persuasively in favor of the encomienda system as necessary for the security and welfare of the colony that the order was withdrawn.

Under this system a conquistador received from the royal governor an allotment of Indians who were to serve him with tribute and labor. The encomendero, in turn, assumed the feudal obligation of defending the country for the emperor Charles V, of protecting his Indian charges, and of instructing them in the Christian religion. The encomienda did not involve an award of land, but along with the distribution of Indians often went a grant of land to the conquistador.

The collective tribute and labor demands of the Spanish settlers, the Crown, and the Church far exceeded the relatively puny exactions of the Aztec rulers, nobility, and priesthood. The more advanced European economy demanded a large increase in the supply of labor; the conquistadores or their sons became capitalist entrepreneurs with visions of limitless wealth to be obtained through silver mines, sugar and cacao plantations, cattle ranches, wheat farms. The intensity of exploitation of Indian labor became intolerable. And the Indians, their bodies enfeebled by excessive toil, malnutrition, and the hardships of long journeys to distant mines and plantations, their spirits broken by the loss of ancient tribal purposes and beliefs that gave meaning to life, became easy prey to disease, both endemic and epidemic, to maladies with which they were familiar and to scourges imported by the Europeans: smallpox, influenza, measles, typhoid, malaria. A demographic tragedy of frightful proportions resulted. The Indian population of Mexico, according to a recent estimate based on published tribute records, declined from approximately 16,-871,408 in 1532 to 2,649,573 in 1568, 1,372,228 in 1595, and 1,069,255 in 1608.[5]

Technological changes of Spanish origin contributed to this disaster. A horde of Spanish-imported cattle and sheep swarmed over the Mexican land, often invading not only the land vacated by the declining Indian population but also the reserves of land needed by the Indian system of field rotation. The introduction of plow agriculture, less productive than Indian hoe agriculture per unit of land, and Spanish diversion of scarce water resources from Indian fields to their own fields, cattle ranches, and flour mills, also tended to upset the critical balance between land and people in Indian Mexico. "In a population ravaged by disease, such loss of land and water must have had a snowballing effect; it condemned a large percentage of the population to obsolescence and decay." [6]

The catastrophic decline of the Indian population posed a grave dilemma before all Spanish parties to the colonial process: the encomenderos, the Crown, and the Church. The Crown faced a problem of harmonizing the demand of the colonists for cheap Indian labor, frequently employed in a wasteful and destructive manner, with its own interest in the preservation of a large tribute-paying Indian population. There was a political issue as well: Excessive concentration of land and Indians in the hands of the encomenderos might lead to the rise of a class of great feudal lords independent of royal authority, a development the Spanish monarchs were determined to prevent. The Church had a vital interest in the Indian problem. If the Indians perished, the great task of saving pagan souls would be left incomplete and the good name of the Church would suffer; besides, who then would construct monasteries and churches and support the servants of God in the Indies?

The evolution of Spain's Indian policy reflected a complex clash of interests and opinions. A handful of uncompromisingly pro-Indian reformers of the school of Bartolomé de Las Casas demanded suppression of the encomiendas, liberation of the Indians from all forms of servitude, and administration of the native population by the religious. The encomenderos recalled their services in the Conquest, threatened the Crown with loss of its American empire through Indian revolt or foreign invasion if they quit the country because their privileges had been revoked, and pleaded that their encomiendas be made perpetual. Perhaps a majority of Crown officials and most of the clergy, including the orders, took a "realist" middle-of-the-road position; they argued that the encomienda, regulated to safeguard Indian welfare, was necessary for the prosperity and security of the land. "There could be no permanence in the land without rich men," said a spokesman for this point of view, "and there could be no rich men without encomiendas, because all industry was carried on with Indian labor, and only those with Indians could engage in commerce." [7]

Slowly and cautiously the Crown moved to bring order out of chaos, curb the power of the encomenderos, and arrest the decline of the Indian population. The efforts of the first bishop of Mexico, Juan de Zumárraga, who came with the title of "Protector of the Indians," to enforce the laws against abuse of the Indians, were largely ineffective. The second Audiencia or high court of New Spain, established in 1527, took the first steps in the direction of a solution of the Indian problem: It moderated the tribute paid by many Indian towns, provided for the registration with the Audiencia of all tribute assessments, and forbade, in principle, the use of Indians as carriers without their consent.

The climax of royal intervention in the Indian question came with the New Laws of the Indies (1542). These laws looked to the ultimate extinction of the encomienda. They prohibited the enslavement of Indians in the future, ordered the release of slaves to whom title could not be proved, abolished compulsory personal services by Indians, regulated tribute, and provided that existing encomiendas were to lapse on the death of the holder.

The New Laws provoked a great revolt in Peru; in New Spain they caused a storm of protest by the encomenderos and a large part of the clergy. Under this pressure the Crown retreated and finally agreed to a compromise. The laws forbidding enslavement and forced personal service were reaffirmed, but the right of inheritance by the heir of an encomendero was recognized and was extended by stages to a third, fourth, and sometimes even a fifth life. Thereafter, or earlier in the absence of an heir, the encomienda reverted to the Crown. In the natural course of events, the number of private encomiendas steadily diminished and that of Crown towns increased.

By 1560, then, royal intervention had curbed the power of the encomenderos and had partially stabilized the once chaotic tribute and labor situation in New Spain. Tribute was now almost everywhere assessed by the Audiencia, which made a continuing effort to adjust tribute to the fluctuation of population and harvests on appeal from the Indians. The institution of *visita* and *cuenta* was employed to make such adjustment. The visita, or inspection of a town, yielded information concerning its resources or capacity to pay, which was needed to determine the per capita quota. The cuenta, or count, made at the same time, gave the number of tribute-payers. The quota multiplied by the number of tribute-payers gave the assessment. About 1560 the per capita yearly tribute paid to the king or to an encomendero tended to be about 1 peso and half a fanega of maize, or its equivalents in other products.[8]

This mechanism of assessment and a copious related legislation failed to bring any significant or enduring relief to the Indians. Alonso de Zorita, in the account which follows, vividly documents, on the basis of a decade (1556-1566) of observation and administrative experience in New Spain, such abuses as the padding of population counts by encomenderos and other persons for their own ends. Of more importance is the fact that the recounts and reassessments consistently lagged behind the rapid shrinkage in the number of tribute-payers, with the result that the survivors had to bear the tribute burdens of those who had died or fled. Moreover, from the accession to the throne of Philip II (1556), the dominant motive in Spain's Indian policy was that of augmenting the royal revenues in order to overcome the Crown's desperate financial crisis. As a result of the visita (1536-1564) of Jerónimo de Valderrama, the royal commissioner whose insistence on squeezing more tribute out of the Indians gained him the title of *afligidor de los indios*, towns that had previously been totally or partly exempt from civil tribute because of their services in the Conquest (Tlaxcala) or because of their special duties in the way of construction, repair, and servicing of Spanish towns (the Indian barrios or wards of San Juan and Tlatelolco in Mexico City) lost their favored position. The number of categories of persons exempt from payment was steadily reduced, and the tribute quota was progressively raised. As a result of these measures and the gradual escheat of encomiendas to the Crown, between 1550 and the close of the eighteenth century the amount of royal tribute collected annually in New Spain rose from about 100,000 pesos to well over 1 million pesos.[9]

If the role of the encomendero as a recipient of Indian tribute diminished in importance after 1550, the same was not true of two other privileged groups, the Indian nobility and the clergy. The native aristocracy, itself under attack from Spaniards who sought to acquire its lands and perquisites, intensified its exploitation of the Indian commoners in what Charles Gibson interprets as "a response to strain, an effort to maintain position and security." The legal privilege of the Indian chiefs and other *principales* or native nobility of collecting and delivering tribute to the Spaniards offered large opportunities for taking advantage of the commoners. The Indian nobility also exploited fully its right to collect tribute for its own support. Gibson observes that "in mid-sixteenth century a community paying 1,000 pesos in tribute to the king might be paying up to 4,000 pesos to its own Indian upper class." [10]

The clergy, despite their fame as protectors of the Indians, added materially to the tribute burdens of the natives, often in extralegal ways. A common complaint was that parish priests extorted excessive fees for marriages, funerals, and other services of the Church. As the high religious excitement of the first strenuous decades after the Conquest dissolved, the orders lost much of their apostolic fervor and devotion to Indian welfare. Viceroy Juan de Mendoza, Marqués de Montesclaros, in a report to Philip III of August 1607, assured the monarch, doubtless with some exaggeration, that the Indians suffered the heaviest oppression at the hands of the friars and that one Indian paid more tribute to his parish priest than twenty paid to His Majesty.[11]

Matters stood no better in what concerns Indian forced labor. "The laws forbidding forced personal service were

entirely without effect. The Indians, whether held in encomienda or not, were in practice held to all sorts of exactions." [12]
The proverb, *plus ça change, plus c'est la même chose*, could
be fairly applied to Spain's Indian policy. Indian forced labor,
legally separated from the encomienda under the New Laws,
appeared in another guise. The labor needs of the colonists
and the Crown were to be satisfied by the *repartimiento*, a
system under which all adult male Indians were required to
give a certain amount of their time to work in mines and factories, on farms and ranches, and on public works. They were
to receive a small wage for their labor. Like the encomienda,
the repartimiento or *cuatequil* offered many loopholes for
abuses, and the Crown's efforts to regulate it seem to have
been largely ineffective. The Indian nobility and the clergy
shared with the colonists and Crown officials in intense exploitation of Indian labor. The caciques or chiefs "forced
maceguales to plant their fields and build their houses, to run
their errands, to labor for them and serve them in unprecedented ways." [13] Indians built the countless churches and
monasteries of New Spain and provided for the wants of the
numerous clergy. In one convent alone, "and that not the
largest," the visitador Valderrama found more than one hundred and ninety Indian servants.[14]

Even as the mountain of legislation designed to lighten the
burdens of the Indians grew higher, the decline of the Indian
population continued at an accelerating pace. This decline had
calamitous economic consequences for New Spain. Shortages
of labor caused a steady decline in food production, leading
to serious difficulties in supplying the Spanish cities with
foodstuffs. Shortages of labor also contributed to a steady decline in mining output and to the decay of the cacao and silk
industries. The contraction in mining activity injured the
stock-raising industry, which had expanded to satisfy the demand of the new mining centers. After 1575 Spain herself

entered on a period of economic and demographic decline that curtailed her ability to provide the colony with manufactures at relatively low prices and to absorb colonial exports of wool, hides, and dye. Under the impact of these factors the sixteenth-century boom lost its impetus and gave way to "New Spain's Century of Depression." [15] From large-scale commercial enterprise the Spanish settlers turned increasingly to production for subsistence purposes. The reduced tempo of economic activity probably lessened the intensity of exploitation of Indian labor and may have helped to initiate the painfully slow Indian demographic recovery that began in the last quarter of the seventeenth century.

As the Spanish colonists retreated from the sixteenth-century dream of limitless wealth, Mexican society was reintegrated about two rural centers, with a corresponding decline in the relative importance of the city. One was the hacienda, the Spanish landed estate, which had grown in number and size since the Conquest, largely at the expense of Indian lands. The other was the Indian pueblo or town, reconstructed to conform to Spanish ideals, with its government, privileges, and obligations carefully defined in Spanish law. In the last half of the sixteenth and the first half of the seventeenth centuries the Crown made an energetic effort to collect the dispersed Indian population and resettle it in new towns called "reductions" or "congregations." Much violence and great hardships to the Indians accompanied this process. Yet "the thousands of congregations still listed in the Mexican census and the indelible Spanish stamp of the great majority of villages testify to the magnitude of the revolution wrought by the Spanish town-builders." [16]

Since the repartimiento failed to provide a dependable and continuing supply of labor, the hacendado in the seventeenth century turned increasingly to the use of so-called free labor. From the first such labor had been closely associated with the system of debt peonage, a system that helped to bind and hold workers in a time of rapid population decrease. The heavy weight of tribute and repartimiento burdens on a steadily shrinking population and the narrowing boundaries of Indian town lands because of Spanish encroachments were among the factors that induced Indians to accept the hacendado's invitation to settle on or near his estate as farm laborers working for wages, usually in kind. An advance of money or goods bound the peon to work for his employer until the debt was paid, a miracle that rarely occurred. The hacienda grew at the expense of the pueblo, leaving the Indian town without enough land for its people; the hacienda lured laborers from the pueblo, making it difficult for the Indian town to meet its tribute and repartimiento obligations. Between the two *repúblicas*, the *república de indios* and the *república de españoles*, stretched a gulf of hostility and distrust.

Semifeudal, semicapitalist, operated with an archaic technology, typically producing below capacity in terms of available labor and capital, the hacienda represented an adjustment to the economic stagnation of the seventeenth century. When that long depression gave way to the economic revival of the eighteenth century, the flexible hacienda possessed the reserves of land and labor needed to make the best of its opportunities. The hacienda easily survived the Wars of Independence; indeed, it improved its position after independence as creole hacendados took advantage of the lapse of Spanish protective legislation to acquire by various means the lands of neighboring Indian communities. The land reform ushered in by the great Revolution of 1910 dealt the hacienda a heavy but not mortal blow. The drowsy semifeudal hacienda of the past survives only in out-of-the-way regions of the Republic. But a new hacienda has arisen, technically efficient and arrayed in modern corporate guise, which plays a dominant role in Mexico's agricultural life. Meanwhile Indian and mestizo small landholders, lacking machinery and often without access to irrigation, struggle to gain a bare living from a heavily eroded soil, while landlessness again increases. The Indian problem, fused with the general problem of transition from a colonial to a modern economy, remains part of Mexico's unfinished business in the third quarter of the twentieth century.

This book makes available for the first time in English translation a major source on life and labor in Mexico both under Aztec rule and in the critical half-century after the Conquest. The *Brief and Summary Relation of the Lords of New Spain* (*Breve y sumaria relación de los señores de la Nueva España*) of Alonso de Zorita is no academic treatise smelling of the lamp. Its style is unadorned and unaffected, its tone urgent and sometimes agonized as befits a work telling of a social catastrophe. Its freedom from pedantry reflects its prac-

tical purpose. The *Brief Relation* offers an idealized portrait of life in Mexico before the Conquest, contrasts that
pagan Golden Age with the miserable state of the Mexican
Indian under Spanish rule, and searches for solutions to the insoluble problems of Spain's Indian policy.

The author of the *Brief Relation* was a Spanish judge of
massive integrity and wide experience in colonial affairs. His
description of the contemporary Mexican scene was based on
a decade of observation and administrative activity in New
Spain. The honorable poverty to which he retired in 1566
after nineteen years of officeholding in the Indies testifies to
the purity of his official life and to the disinterested spirit in
which he wrote his book.

Students of ancient Mexico have used and rendered tribute
to Zorita's *Brief Relation* ever since its first publication. Prescott commended Zorita's "sound and discriminating judgment," observing that "he is very rarely betrayed into the
extravagances of expression so visible in the writers of the
time." Prescott went on to affirm that "this temperance, combined with his uncommon sources of information, makes his
work one of highest authority on the limited topics within
its range." A modern French scholar speaks of the *Brief
Relation* as "indispensable." And a recent German writer on
Aztec social and economic life notes that Zorita had a
true ethnological sense. "He describes institutions which
were in the main foreign to the Spaniards, such as the calpulli
or the Aztec nobility, with an extreme precision, without
introducing Spanish conceptions into his account, as was the
practice of many chroniclers." [17] The great factual value of
Zorita's work more than compensates for the distortion of
Aztec reality caused by his idealized view of the Indian past.

We owe most of our knowledge of Zorita's life to his official letters and memorials, some of which were discovered and
published in Madrid in 1909 by the Spanish historian Manuel

Serrano y Sanz.[18] Alonso de Zorita[19] was born in 1511 or 1512, probably in the city of Córdoba, where his father still lived in 1547. We know almost nothing of the elder Zorita. We may speculate that he belonged to the numerous lower nobility of Spain and was not without means, since he was able to give his son money and goods to the value of 1,000 ducats to defray the cost of his passage to the Indies and equip his household in the New World.

Alonso de Zorita was born into a Spain soaring toward a peak of political and military grandeur abroad and artistic and literary splendor within. The constructive work of Ferdinand and Isabella paved the way for the dazzling successes of their Hapsburg grandson, Charles V. If Charles squandered the inheritance of the Catholic Sovereigns in unprofitable foreign wars, if he allowed foreign merchant princes to dominate the finances of Spain, if he established a heavy-handed Oriental despotism, the full implications of his acts were not immediately apparent. The Spanish people of the first half of the sixteenth century began to receive rapturous accounts of the exploits of Spanish knights in the New World, as wonderful as the adventures told of in the romances of chivalry; they gloated over the victories of the invincible Spanish infantry in Europe. Spaniards left off grumbling about Hapsburg folly and extravagance, and set to dreaming of El Dorados, universal empires, and a universal church:

> One Fold, one Shepherd only on the earth. . . .
> One Monarch, one Empire, and one Sword.[20]

Reports reaching Spain during Zorita's childhood and youth appeared to erase the line between dream and reality. An hidalgo named Balboa, who had escaped from his debts on Española and hidden in an empty provision cask, crossed the Isthmus of Panama and discovered a vast uncharted sea. Another gentleman-adventurer, the devious, masterful Cortés, landed on the shores of Mexico and overthrew the great Aztec Empire. An illiterate soldier of fortune, Francisco Pizarro, seeking a golden kingdom reputed to lie beyond the "South Sea" found by Balboa, landed on the coast of Peru and added another empire to the long list of Spain's possessions.

Countless projects, one more wonderful than the other, were hatched in the fevered brains of the impresarios of conquest. Spain sent to America its best and its worst: adventurers with pasts that they preferred to forget, as well as young, high-spirited hidalgos, "men of good family who were not reared behind the plow," who proposed to win gold and glory by serving God and King.

The young Zorita was not one of this number. A studious disposition, a deep-rooted love of books and learning, manifests itself in his writings. He was not the stuff of which conquerors are made. His father evidently drew the appropriate conclusions: The boy went to Salamanca to study law. The career of law was then a highroad to success for ambitious sons of the middle class and the lower nobility. The growth of the royal power, the expansion of the Spanish Empire, created an ever-growing demand for *letrados* or civil lawyers as administrators, judges, officials of every kind.

We do not know the precise dates of Zorita's attendance at the University of Salamanca. From a reference in one of his writings it is clear that he was there from 1537 to 1540, but he doubtless had come some years before. Salamanca, a city of fifty thousand inhabitants, "the nurse of scholars and gentlemen," as the Italian humanist Lucius Marineus Siculus called it, was dominated by its university, one of the great seats of learning of Christendom. In 1552 its matriculation roll showed a total of 6,328 persons. The professors taught all the liberal arts and sciences; and the school graduated "jurisconsults, theologians, physicians, doctors of science of every kind." Almost alone among European universities, it admitted women to its courses of study and degrees.

Having completed his studies and passed his examination, Zorita received the degree of *licenciado* or bachelor of law, probably in 1540. The young lawyer then established himself in the city of Granada, where he practiced before the Audiencia of Granada, the supreme court of southern Castile. About two years later Zorita was married. Of his wife we know only that she bore with him the rigors of a voyage to the New World and the great hardships of a journey overland from Guatemala to Mexico, and that she suffered much from ill health. We also know that the couple was childless; in a memorial dated July 20, 1562, Zorita wistfully noted, "Our Lord has not been pleased to give me children."

Perhaps the young lawyer's skill and seriousness in pleading came to the ears of high Crown officials. A royal order of May 21, 1547, issued in Madrid, appointed Zorita one of the four *oidores* or judges of the Audiencia of Santo Domingo on Española. He was then about thirty-five years old. His legal practice had not made him wealthy, for he had to apply for an advance of 400 ducats on his salary to cover the costs of the voyage to America. This was in addition to the 1,000 ducats in money and goods that he received from his father. Zorita also secured exemption from the payment of export duties on household goods and merchandise to the value of 1,000 pesos for himself and 500 pesos for his wife; he secured similar exemption from payment of duties on four Negro slaves who accompanied the *oidor* and his wife.

We do not know the exact date of Zorita's departure for the New World, but almost certainly he sailed in the spring fleet of 1548. The sailing of vessels in semiannual, protected fleets, one scheduled to sail in March, the other in September, had been obligatory practice since 1543. Sailings were made from Seville or its seaport, San Lúcar de Barrameda.

Danger and hardship attended each long voyage to the Indies. Shipwrecks were appallingly common, and French corsairs infested the sea routes. Even the most uneventful crossing was filled with trials. Zorita left no record of his experiences, but Fray Tomás de la Torre, one of a number of Dominican friars who accompanied Bishop Bartolomé de Las Casas to Mexico in 1544, wrote this impression of a voyage from Seville to Santo Domingo:

"The heat, the stuffiness, and the sense of confinement are sometimes overpowering. The bed is ordinarily the floor. . . . Add to this the general nausea and poor health; most passengers go about as if out of their minds and in great torment—some longer than others, and a few for the entire voyage. There is very little desire to eat, and sweet things do not go down well; there is an incredible thirst, sharpened by a diet of hardtack and salt beef. The water ration is half a liter daily; if you want wine you must bring your own. There are infinite numbers of lice, which eat men alive, and you cannot wash clothing because the sea water shrinks it. There is an evil stink, especially below deck, that becomes intolerable throughout the ship when the pump is working—and it is going more or less constantly, depending on how the ship sails. On a good day the pump runs four or five times, to drain the foul-smelling bilge water." [21]

From Zorita's papers we learn only that he arrived at Santo Domingo in the first days of June 1548.

Major changes had taken place on Española since its stormy beginnings as a colony under the rule of Christopher Columbus. The frenzied search for gold had subsided; sugar cane and cattle were now the foundations of the island's prosperity. Some settlers owned as many as thirty-two thousand head of cattle. Wild cattle were so plentiful that men killed them for their hides only, leaving the flesh to rot. More than twenty large sugar mills processed cane into sugar, which was shipped in great quantities to Spain. The rapid decline of the Indian population had led to the importation of large numbers of Negro slaves. These slaves sometimes joined rebellious Indians of the interior in such uprisings as that of 1533, led by the cacique Enriquillo, which took ten years to suppress.

Santo Domingo was already a beautiful town, according to the Spanish chronicler Gonzalo Fernández de Oviedo, who lived there during a part of Zorita's tenure as oidor on the island. "So well built is it," he wrote, "that there is no town in Spain better constructed, all things considered, leaving aside the illustrious and very noble city of Barcelona." It possessed a cathedral, "made of beautiful and strong stonework," "many fine houses belonging to prominent men, in which any lord or grandee could lodge," "beautiful streets well planned and wide," and even a *colegio* or school. Yet Fernández de Oviedo found that the town of Santo Domingo had a smaller population in 1547 than in 1525. He explained this by the fact that settlers who had made a fortune had returned to Spain, while others had gone to settle in other islands or on the mainland, "this island being the head and mother and nurse of all the other parts of this empire." [22]

The Audiencia of Santo Domingo, founded in 1511, was the oldest high court of Spain in the New World. The subsequent establishment of the Audiencias of Mexico (1527) and Lima (1542) deprived it of authority over most of the mainland, but at the time of Zorita's coming it still had jurisdiction over the provinces comprising the present-day republics of Colombia and Venezuela.

A memorial written by Zorita in 1562 in which he related his services to the king illustrates the variety of his duties as oidor on Española. As judge, he dealt out justice "with all the probity and rectitude of which he was capable." In those days, he recalled with nostalgia, he enjoyed the affection of the whole island, for he had no cases involving Indians, which cause Spaniards to hate the honest judge who does his duty. One of the oidor's duties was to maintain peace and order in Santo Domingo by patrolling the city at night. Zorita had become such a terror to rowdies, bullies, and drunkards that these troublemakers took care to ascertain when the Licentiate Zorita made his nocturnal rounds that they might be safely indoors when he appeared on the streets. When a scare ran through the town because French corsairs had been seen off the coast, Zorita changed his judge's robes for the warrior's sword and cuirass. Appointed captain of the cavalry by the Audiencia, he summoned a thousand men to horse and arms, instructed them in their duties, reviewed them. He looked to the defenses of the city, visited the fortress, ordered construction of a new fort for the better defense of the approaches to the city, and transferred part of the artillery to the new structure. To the relief of all, the danger of a French invasion soon evaporated.

Zorita had not been a year and a half on Española when the Audiencia ordered him to the mainland on a mission that was to prove the most difficult and frustrating of his life. The land that we now call Colombia then consisted of the coastal settlements of Santa Marta, Cartagena, and Río de la Hacha, and the interior provinces of New Granada, conquered by Gonzalo Jiménez de Quesada, and Popayán, conquered by Pizarro's lieutenant, Sebastián de Benalcázar. The work of conquest had barely ended when there broke out a confusion of disputes over lands, Indians, and titles. A "greedy and daring adventurer," Alonso Luis de Lugo, had used his influence at court to secure appointment as *adelantado* or governor of New Granada in place of its conqueror, Jiménez de Quesada. After a brief but profitable career of robbery and violence, Lugo returned to Spain, where his wealth cleared him of all charges.

Lugo's successor was the Licentiate Miguel Díez de Armendáriz, sent out as *visitador* in 1546 with orders to hold a *residencia*, or judicial inquest, of officials, proclaim the New Laws for the protection of the Indians, and report to the king on the state of affairs in the colony. Armendáriz, a Navarrese of arbitrary temper, soon became embroiled in fresh quarrels. If he won the affection of some by lavish gifts of lands, Indians, and offices, he won the enmity of others by stripping them of their spoils. Meanwhile the New Laws regulating treatment of the Indians were proclaimed but remained a dead letter; Armendáriz, complying with the wishes of the encomenderos, appears to have invoked the solemn formula, *obedezco pero no cumplo* ("I obey but do not carry out").

Armendáriz's enemies sent charges against him to the Audiencia of Santo Domingo; they sent similar charges to the Royal Council of the Indies in Spain. The Audiencia of Santo Domingo named Zorita as judge and governor empowered to hold a residencia of Armendáriz and other officials cited in the charges. The Council of the Indies, which had supreme control over affairs in Spain's New World, had meantime determined to provide a remedy for the troubles of New Granada by establishing a new Audiencia at Santa Fe de Bogotá. The Licentiate Gutierre de Mercado was named president of the tribunal, with instructions to hold a residencia of Armendáriz.

When the Council learned that the Audiencia of Santo Domingo had appointed Zorita as judge to try Armendáriz, it revoked Mercado's title of *juez de residencia*. In confirming Zorita's appointment, the Council also charged him with responsibility for investigating and punishing offenses against the Indians. However, the Council withdrew from Zorita the title of governor and vested governmental powers in the new Audiencia of New Granada. At the same time it forbade

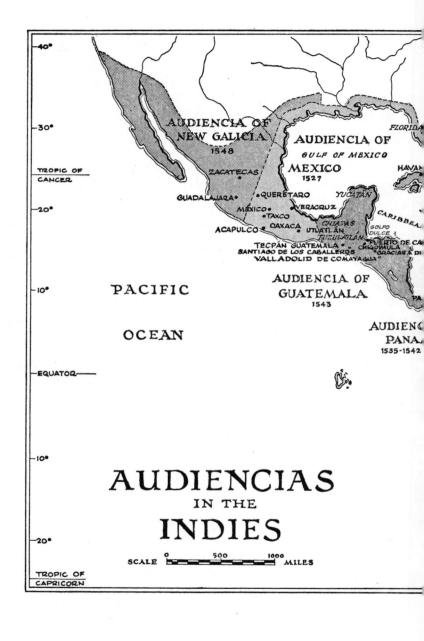

AUDIENCIAS
IN THE
INDIES

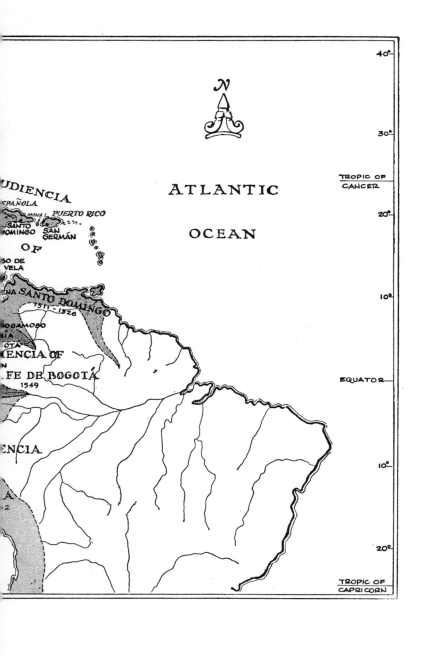

this tribunal to receive appeals from Zorita's verdicts. The resulting division of authority between Zorita and the Audiencia of New Granada, so characteristic of Spain's colonial policy, seriously impaired the prospects of success of Zorita's mission.

When it became known in Santo Domingo that Zorita was about to leave the island, the civil and ecclesiastical corporations of the city expressed their regrets and displeasure to the Audiencia, "for all were happy and content with his equal justice and mode of governance." Zorita attempted to quiet these remonstrances by promising that he would petition the king to reassign him to the Audiencia of Santo Domingo on completion of his mission. On January 17, 1550, he sailed in a chartered ship for the mainland port of Cabo de la Vela.

On arrival at this place, Zorita discovered that the Spanish settlers treated the Indians very harshly; they bought and sold them as if they were slaves and neglected to teach them Christian doctrine. Zorita ordered all encomenderos to prove the legitimacy of their titles and freed from personal service or subjection Indians who were not rightfully held in encomienda.

From Cabo de la Vela, Zorita sailed to Santa Marta. There he sought to persuade the settlers not to depend on the miserable tribute they received from the Indians, but to cultivate fields of maize and cassava, and to build houses of stone as recommended in a royal order. Zorita passed several days in securing and outfitting canoes for the ascent of the Magdalena to Santa Fe de Bogotá. Everywhere he encountered hostility and derision from the friends of Armendáriz. At Mompós his enemies untied some of his boats and sent them drifting down the river. Part of the journey had to be made on foot through trackless wastes, over high mountains, under an almost continuous deluge of rain. At last Zorita and his party attained the upper reaches of the river and took the Indian trail leading up a steep escarpment of the Andes to the capital of New Granada.

News of his coming had preceded Zorita, and the town buzzed with mockery and resentment for the royal commissioner. "Almost all the Spaniards rose up against me," recalled Zorita, "for all but a very few were parties to the cruelties that had been done to the Indians. When I began to proceed against them and seize the guilty parties, each and every one expected the same treatment. Accordingly they decided that by acting as one against me they could cover up their unheard-of crimes and cruelties against the Indians."

The new Audiencia, already installed at Santa Fe, did all in its power to frustrate Zorita's mission. The president of the tribunal, Gutierre de Mercado, had died before reaching his post; another oidor, Francisco Briceño, had journeyed on to look into the affairs of Popayán. One of the two remaining judges, Beltrán de Góngora, was a Navarrese and a kinsman of Armendáriz, according to Zorita; the other, Juan López de Galarza, was "obligated to him for many great favors." The oidores flaunted their partiality for Armendáriz and his friends. When Zorita ordered the arrest of some Spaniards who had committed crimes against the Indians, the judges personally ordered their release; they intimidated witnesses that they might not give testimony; they claimed jurisdiction for themselves in certain cases of mistreatment of Indians and let the offenders off with light sentences. They would not allow Zorita to hold a residencia of Armendáriz; instead they defied the royal instructions by giving Armendáriz a year's grace to take the case directly to the Council of the Indies.

Checkmated at every step by the legal maneuvers of the Audiencia, boycotted by the settlers, reduced to desperate financial plight because the royal coffers from which he was supposed to draw his salary were empty, Zorita abandoned

Santa Fe at the end of the ninety days allotted for the residencia in that city. His mission was an almost total failure. The
descent of the Magdalena was even more difficult and hazard-
ous than the journey upstream. Hostile Indians shooting poisoned arrows followed the boats on the banks of the river;
Zorita and his men could not drive them off because financial
need had forced him to sell his arms and even part of his clothing in Santa Fe. For two days they were under fire. The hail
of arrows confused and unnerved the oarsmen and helmsmen
of the boats; as they passed through a difficult place called the
Salto, filled with many large stones, one boat struck a rock,
opening a breach more than six feet long. Water poured in and
ruined Zorita's precious books, clothes, and bed linen.

Zorita had to hold a residencia of Armendáriz in the principal town of each province or district of which he had been
governor. On arrival at Santa Marta, Zorita held a residencia
of Armendáriz and his lieutenants in that town and province,
after which he journeyed on to do the same in Cartagena. "In
all those parts," Zorita records, "he [Zorita] was well loved
by the Indians because of the great favor he showed them. But
the Spaniards hated him for this reason and because he proceeded against them in many cases in which he found them
guilty and punished them."

News of the fiasco of the residencia in Santa Fe, so dam-
aging to the royal prestige, at last reached Spain. Swift retri-
bution followed. In June 1553, there arrived at Santa Fe a
stern new juez de residencia, Juan Montaño. He suspended
the oidores Galarza and Góngora from office, clapped them
in chains, and sent them to Spain for trial before the Council
of the Indies. The ship carrying the prisoners went down in a
storm off the coast of Spain, and the oidores, wrote Zorita,
"went to the true residencia and accounting for the things
they had done." Armendáriz, who had fled to Santo Domingo,
was imprisoned there, with difficulty secured his release, and

finally made his way to Spain, where he managed to clear himself before the Council of the Indies. He ended his days as a canon in a church at Sigüenza.

One of Zorita's instructions ordered him to see that clergy were assigned to the Indian towns and that the natives were instructed in the Faith. On his travels through the mainland provinces Zorita discovered that a tepid piety and strong fleshly appetites were characteristics of the secular clergy. The curates lived in splendid style at the expense of the miserable Indians. They compelled the Indians to provide great quantities of food for the support of their relatives, guests, and slaves; they made the Indians guard their cattle, and paid them no other wage than a sound thrashing. The ecclesiastical vicar of Popayán neglected the duties of his office; he spent his time roaming the country in search of ancient Indian tombs containing gold ornaments. Although lame, he sped about as swiftly as "a soul borne by the demon of greed," supporting himself on the shoulders of two Indians. It was said in the country that "other clergy buried the dead, but the vicar dug them up." In Popayán was another clergyman who gave his whelps to be trained in the barbarous sport of hunting down Indians with dogs, which were fed on the bodies of their victims.

This immorality strengthened Zorita's affection for the friars, Franciscans and Dominicans, who almost alone had supported his efforts in behalf of the Indians of the mainland. Zorita's subsequent experiences in Guatemala and Mexico confirmed his high opinion of the regulars. In retirement he wrote a *Parecer sobre la enseñanza de los indios* ("Opinion Concerning the Religious Instruction of the Indians") in which he recommended that Indian parishes be intrusted to the friars alone, and preferably to members of the Franciscan Order.

On May 10, 1552, Zorita took ship from Cartagena for Santo Domingo. The record of his homeward voyage is a catalogue of woes. First the wind fell, with the result that it required many days to reach the port of Havana in Cuba. There the ship's master suddenly determined to sail for Castile, so Zorita had to board another ship, bound for Puerto Rico for a cargo of wine and cloth, and intending to return to Havana by way of Santo Domingo.

In Puerto Rico, Zorita learned that there was a great plenty of cloth and other Spanish wares in the island because two ships bound for New Spain with these goods had been stranded on the coast. Because he knew these things were in short supply in Santo Domingo, the prudent Zorita purchased on credit a large quantity of woolen and linen cloth, silk, wine, olive oil, and vinegar for the use of his household. Since the vessel in which he came from Havana was freighted to capacity, he sent his purchases in a caravel also bound for Santo Domingo, and transferred to this ship some of his servants and personal possessions.

On August 20, 1552, the two ships set out together for Santo Domingo. The next morning, as they were off the island of Mona, near Española, they sighted three large ships lying there at anchor. The strange vessels hoisted sails and began to give chase to Zorita's ship and her companion. Zorita and his people were convinced their pursuers were French corsairs who had recently pillaged the town of San Germán on Puerto Rico and were believed to be prowling among the islands, so the two ships fled out to sea.

The strange ships were actually Spanish craft of the armada of Santo Domingo, in search of French pirates; they, too, were sure they had come on the pillagers of San Germán. All that day they followed Zorita's ship and the caravel in hot pursuit; they finally let the caravel go because she turned in to land and so reached Santo Domingo a day earlier than Zorita.

In the afternoon, perceiving that their pursuers were drawing near, Zorita and his people made signs of peace; they broke out a Castilian flag, lowered all sails except the foresail, which was needed to steer the ship, and lowered and raised their main topsail. Still the strange craft came relentlessly on, firing heavy shot; as they drew even nearer they began firing harquebuses, crossbows, and stones. Toward nightfall the attackers approached with the evident intention of sending Zorita's ship to the bottom.

By this time Zorita and his people had become aware that their pursuers were Spaniards and began to call out: "España! España!" and "Zorita! Zorita!" At last came recognition, and the firing stopped. Officers of the warships came aboard to explain and make excuses for their error. Then Zorita's ship continued on its way.

On Sunday, August 28, 1552, they reached the mouth of the Ozama River, on which Santo Domingo lay. The sea was running high and they had trouble entering the river. Meanwhile the caravel had arrived the previous day and had reported Zorita's coming. As soon as his ship was sighted, boats were sent out to row Zorita and his people to the city, while others began towing in the heavily loaded ship. Now came a reaction to the hardships that Zorita had endured by land and sea; no sooner had he come ashore than he fell ill with a high fever. Meanwhile the winds blew up, turning into a hurricane that snapped the moorings of five ships and drove them down the river and out to sea. One was the caravel that Zorita had freighted with the goods he purchased in Puerto Rico on credit. This ship struck on a rocky coast with the loss of all hands and her cargo, a loss to Zorita of 1,500 ducats.

Zorita had little time to rest from his ordeals. Within six months of his return to Santo Domingo he received orders from the Council of the Indies naming him oidor in the Audiencia of Guatemala. He was being dispatched to another battlefield of the tense struggle between the Crown and the settlers over the Indian question. The New Laws of the Indies of 1542 had established the Audiencia of Guatemala, or Audiencia de los Confines (so called because it was first set up on the boundary of Nicaragua and Guatemala, without a definite place of residence), with jurisdiction over all Central America and the provinces of Chiapas and Yucatán in modern Mexico. At the time of Zorita's appointment its seat was the town of Santiago de los Caballeros de Guatemala (modern La Antigua). Since one of the principal aims of the new Audiencia was to implement the provisions of the New Laws for the protection of the Indians, its work met with the bitter opposition of the Spanish settlers.

Accompanied by his wife and household, in the spring of 1553 Zorita sailed from Santo Domingo for Puerto de Caballos, on the shore of Honduras. Another ship took him and his party from Puerto de Caballos into Golfo Dulce, on the coast of Guatemala, the point of disembarkation for passengers and wares bound for Santiago de Guatemala and other Central American towns. At Golfo Dulce, Zorita chartered a mule train to convey his baggage, while he and his party mounted horses. They traversed more than 50 leagues of wild unpopulated country, under almost incessant fall of rain, to reach the town of Santiago de Guatemala.

The president of the Audiencia of Guatemala during the greater part of Zorita's tenure as oidor was Dr. Antonio Rodríguez de Quesada, former oidor of the Audiencia of Mexico, and reputed as a man of learning and ability. Like his predecessor, Alonso López de Cerrato, Rodríguez de Quesada made a serious effort to enforce the New Laws for the protection of the Indians. In Zorita he found a capable and devoted agent. The historian Hubert H. Bancroft, whose sources of information on this episode included the manuscript correspondence of the Dominicans in the province, declares that "the carrying into effect of Quesada's plans was in great part due to the efforts of Zorita, who was commissioned for this purpose." [23]

At the beginning of March 1555, Zorita set out on his first visita or tour of inspection through the province of Guatemala. "During six months," writes Bancroft, "he visited on foot the most rugged portions of the province, moderated tributes, and corrected abuses." [24] Zorita made three such tours during his stay in Guatemala. He traveled through regions never before visited by a Spanish judge and inhabited by no Spaniards other than a few encomenderos. "He journeyed in rain, on foot, without sleeping in a bed, for horses were needed to carry a bed, and he toured regions where horses could not ascend with packs. Because he traveled on foot, through country where there are great variations in climate, he lost the skin from his face, hands, and feet. In some places they must build bridges and had to cut rafters to make them, and he helped with his own hands, for he had no Indians to assist him, only his own people, and they even lacked sufficient food."

Zorita gave much attention to the extirpation of pagan rites among the Indians, many of whom secretly continued to worship their ancient gods. In the course of his *visitas* he seized a great number of idols from the natives. In a memorial he recalled that "the Bishop of Guatemala and the friars used to say that he had done more in those visitas than they had done in many years before him. When he came to a town, the Indians brought out their idols, because he had sent warnings that they must bring them out before he came or suffer severe punishment."

In Guatemala, as in New Granada, the encomenderos reacted to Zorita's efforts in behalf of the Indians with intense hostility. "Finding him incorruptible," says Bancroft, "they had recourse as usual to false reports; and since he would not yield, the Spaniards determined to drive him from the province." [25] Zorita asserts that he suffered greatly at the hands of the settlers, who made false and infamous charges against him before the Audiencia. He also complains that his colleagues allowed his foes to read and display these charges in public with complete impunity ("sin irse a la mano en cosa alguna los Oidores").

The encomenderos ultimately gained most of what they sought, first by the transfer of Zorita to the Audiencia of Mexico in 1556, second by the appointment in 1559 of a new president who was satisfactory to the great landowners. "The colonists were jubilant that the humane measures of Cerrato and of Zorita . . . were now certain of defeat. Dr. Mejía, one of the oidores, was ordered to make an official tour of the provinces, as Zorita had been under the former administration. His measures counteracted the benefits of Zorita's labors. The regulation of tribute was entrusted to the encomenderos and caciques, and as these latter were often but the creatures of the former, the result may be readily inferred." [26]

We can only speculate as to whether Zorita's appointment in 1556 as oidor of the Audiencia of Mexico represented a royal yielding to reactionary pressure or a reward to a loyal servant for his services to the Crown. The Audiencia of Mexico was, after that of Lima, the most important and prestigious body of its kind in the New World, and an appointment to its bench was greatly cherished. Although the appointment found both Zorita and his wife in poor health, they promptly prepared to set out for their new home, leaving on April 25, 1556. Two hundred and forty leagues of mountain, forest, and swamp lay between them and the capital of New Spain. Since the mule trains plying between Guatemala and Mexico carried only cacao, Zorita had to buy saddle and pack horses and equipment for the journey. This involved assuming a mass of new debts on top of old ones.

The day or even the month on which Zorita's cavalcade filed into the capital of New Spain is unknown. Thirty-five years after the Conquest the Aztec metropolis had been rebuilt by the labor of thousands of Indians into a Spanish city. Riding down the long Tacuba street, very straight and level, with an open canal down the middle, Zorita could view on either side the imposing homes of wealthy citizens, "built so regularly and evenly that none varies a finger's breadth from another." [27] They were so strongly built that they seemed fortresses rather than houses; they had been so built to offer protection against attack by Indians in the first uncertain years after the Conquest. Over the lintel of each house appeared the armorial insignia of its owner.

Mexico City, into which flowed most of the wealth produced by the mines, plantations, and cattle ranches of the country, was already acquiring fame for the beauty of its women, horses, and streets, the riches of its shops, and the reckless spending and generosity of its aristocracy. In the words of the poet Bernardo de Balbuena, some decades later:

> That prodigal giving of every ilk,
> Without a care how great the cost,
> Of pearls, of gold, of silver, and of silk.[28]

The heart of the city was the broad central square, filled by day with a multitude of people, on foot and on horseback, making a great din. On the east side of the square stood the viceregal palace, where the Audiencia held its sessions. A throng of litigants, attorneys, notaries, and idlers milled in the corridors of the palace during the Audiencia's working hours. So great was the hubbub that Fray Gerónimo de Mendieta, of the Franciscan Order, wrote in 1562 that "the traffic and arguments in the Audiencia of New Spain resemble nothing more than the image and picture of hell." [29]

The courtroom, which must be entered with uncovered head, silently and respectfully, was large and very ornate, and "one that commands a certain respect in those who enter it." Zorita and his colleagues, dressed in their judge's robes, sat around the viceroy and president of the Audiencia, Don Luis de Velasco, on an elevated platform. None spoke save the judge whose duty it was that week to issue decrees and mete out justice. The presiding judge spoke briefly and seldom, "for silence increases the dignity of the court." His colleagues broke in only when the case was very controversial or if they wished to clarify some point. At the rear of the courtroom, separated by a wooden grating, stood the general public and the common people, who were not permitted to enter and sit, "because they are entirely unworthy of that honor." [30]

Another building facing the central square housed the city's pride, the Royal and Pontifical University of Mexico, installed with great pomp and ceremony by Viceroy Velasco and the Audiencia in January 1553. On an ordinary school day its halls resounded with lectures by the learned professors and disputations between the students, dressed in cassocks, long cloaks, and brimless caps pulled down to their ears. Here, just as at Salamanca, the seven pillars of learning were theology, scripture, canon and civil law, the decretals, rhetoric, and the arts, all taught in Latin. Again, just as at Salamanca, students and teachers formed a corporation with immunity from the civil authorities in all but specified cases.

Between the university and the Audiencia existed an intimate connection, for the first rector and two professors were members of the high court. In the *Crónica de la Universidad de México* of Cristóbal de la Plaza appears the notation that on November 20, 1556, the "magnífico señor," Alonso de Zorita, was admitted with the degree of doctor of laws to the cloister or governing body of the university, composed of

the faculties and the doctors and masters residing in or near the university city.

The years of Zorita's residence in Mexico (1556-1566) formed a crucial decade in the history of New Spain. The Indian question, with which all others were involved, dominated the agenda of politics. The Crown, having beaten a tacti-

cal retreat as a result of the storm raised by the first promulga-
tion of the New Laws, renewed its offensive against the
encomienda and the abuses connected with it. "You are to do
justice in all things," affirmed a royal order to Viceroy Luis de
Velasco, who came out in 1550, "and you will see that the
Indians are not abused and that the tributes are made very moderate." [31] More tentatively, the Crown raised again the question of the inheritability of the encomienda. Even the suggestion of a lapse of their rights caused uneasiness among the
encomenderos. Their determination to make the encomienda
perpetual lay behind the abortive plot (1565) to kill the viceroy and the judges of the Audiencia and establish an independent Mexican monarchy headed by the Marqués Don Martín
Cortés, son and heir of the Conqueror.

Zorita, whose dislike and contempt for the encomenderos
clearly emerge from the pages of the *Brief Relation*, zealously
collaborated with the Crown in its efforts to weaken the economic base of its great vassals. Don Martín Cortés, with an
income from tributes in 1560 of about 86,000 pesos a year,
contributed by some sixty thousand tributaries, was the greatest encomendero in New Spain. In 1529 Charles V had
granted to Hernando Cortés as a perpetual fief the immense
Marquesado del Valle de Oaxaca, about five times the area
of Connecticut, with twenty-three thousand vassals. The
Crown had almost immediately repented of its generosity and
attempted to pare down its grant, rightly suspecting that the
Marquesado contained many more than twenty-three thousand
tributaries. The second Audiencia made a partly successful
effort to reduce the Marquesado, apparently removing sixteen
towns and almost thirty thousand tributaries.

In Zorita's time the effort was renewed. According to Bancroft, a statement placing Don Martín's income at a very high
figure reached the ears of the king, "who thought the revenue almost too royal for a subject, and directed the solicitor

general to notify Cortés that the Crown had been deceived with regard to the value of his encomiendas." Bancroft adds that the Audiencia assigned Zorita to make a count of the Indians held by Cortés in encomienda, and that Zorita's report was adverse to the holder.[32] However, no action was taken upon the report; Don Martín survived this crisis as he survived the greater crisis of the abortive conspiracy of 1565. At the opening of the nineteenth century the Cortés holdings, still in the possession of the Conqueror's heirs, composed an immense domain occupied by some one hundred fifty thousand inhabitants.

Zorita's name is linked with Don Martín in another connection. An entry in the record of the tribute assessments made by the Audiencia of Mexico, dated April 28, 1564, notes the action of the court following a cuenta and visita made by the oidor Alonso de Zorita of the town of Guatepecque[33] and its subject towns, belonging to the encomienda of the Marqués del Valle, Don Martín Cortés. I cite the Audiencia's decision as typical of the work of Zorita and his colleagues in the area of tribute assessment.

On the basis of the information provided by Zorita concerning the resources and population of these towns, the Audiencia ordered the following: The Indians are to pay the Marqués each year 3,679 pesos and 4 tomines, and 1,834 fanegas and 9 almudes of maize. They are to deposit this tribute in the provincial capital of Guatepecque and are to give the Marqués no other service or tribute of any kind. The quota for each married tributary is set at 1 peso and half a fanega of maize each year; widows, widowers, and unmarried landholders are to pay half as much. The Indians are to cultivate the maize field that they are accustomed to cultivate, placing the proceeds in a strong box in the *casa de la comunidad* to be applied to the salaries of the Indian officials and other communal needs. The Marqués is to provide for the support of the friars who reside in a monastery in Guatepecque and have charge of the religious instruction of the natives; he is to deposit 100 pesos and 50 fanegas of maize for the maintenance of each friar in the said casa de communidad.[34]

Consistent in his pro-Indian position, Zorita opposed certain royal initiatives to increase Indian tribute burdens. In various orders[35] the king asked the viceroy, Audiencia, and other royal officials of New Spain to consider the question of whether the Indian barrios of Mexico City, hitherto exempt from taxation because of their special services of construction and maintenance of public works, should pay tribute like other pueblos. A sharply divided opinion and vote revealed the perplexity of the viceroy and oidores.

In the main, Zorita's arguments echoed those of Viceroy Velasco, who voted in the negative. The viceroy advanced three major points. First, if the Indians of Mexico City were to pay tribute, they could not be expected to perform gratis their customary and most necessary labor of constructing public works, repairing bridges, fountains, and streets, and the like. Second, such imposition of tribute would go against one of the New Laws which provided that the Indians should pay less tribute than when they were pagans. (At that time, affirmed Velasco, most of the Indians of Tenochtitlán were warriors, civil servants, and other privileged folk, who paid Moctezuma no other tribute than some slight tokens of fealty.) Third, the Indians could not pay tribute in grain as did the Tlaxcalans, for the Spaniards had left them so little land that the Indian quarters were hedged in by the waters of the lake and the pastures, fields, and gardens of the Spaniards.

To these points Zorita added a remarkable argument that cited the Aztec law of war and peace as precedent for exempting the Indian quarters of Mexico City from payment of tribute. When some town or province peacefully submitted to Moctezuma, Zorita observed, it paid no other tribute than some presents or the harvest from a field set aside for that purpose. Now, when Moctezuma learned of the coming of the Spaniards, he promptly sent messengers to greet them with food and other gifts as tokens of peace and friendship. He did this along the whole line of their march to Tenochtitlán, where he and all his people received them peacefully. In token thereof he placed a large gold chain about Cortés' neck, received him and the other Spaniards as brothers, and lodged them in his own houses. However, the Spaniards, greedy for Moctezuma's gold and jewels, seized him, although neither he nor his people had given cause for such action. If the Indians later rose in revolt, they did so because the Spaniards had imprisoned Moctezuma, and because Pedro de Alvarado and his soldiers had killed Moctezuma's nobles and other principales as they danced in the courtyard of the house where Moctezuma was held, to assuage the grief of their unhappy king.[36]

Zorita's citation of Aztec international law injected a novel element into the controversy over Indian tribute. All arguments nevertheless yielded to the pressing financial needs of the Crown. Soon after the arrival in New Spain of the visitador Valderrama, a royal decree ordered taxation of all Indian towns hitherto exempt from tribute. The oidor Vasco de Puga made the visita and cuenta of these towns (October 1563-February 1564); assessment was made by the visitador and the Audiencia. A quota of 1 peso and half a fanega of maize was assigned to the tributaries of Mexico City.[37]

An episode from Zorita's life in Mexico presents him in the unfamiliar light of a stern judge passing sentence on Indian offenders. In 1557 the Indians of San Juan Teotihuacán, dissatisfied with the tutelage of the Augustinian friars to whom their religious instruction had been assigned, began to riot and demanded the return of the Franciscans who had previously governed them. The Augustinians complained to the viceroy and Audiencia, who decided to send Zorita to the scene of the disturbance because he was well liked by the Indians.

Accompanied by a number of Spaniards, Zorita rode out to the Indian town. When he was still 2 leagues away, the cacique Don Francisco Verdugo came out with all the Indians to greet him. They welcomed the oidor with roses, among which were some gilded leaves that glistened like gold. "Some claimed that the Indians had given him roses made of gold as a bribe that he might not do justice. The oidor learned what was being said, and sent the roses to the Fathers that they might see what these things were." On arrival in the town, Zorita assembled the Indians and sought to take testimony from them. All in vain. Like the townspeople in Lope de Vega's play, *Fuente Ovejuna*, the Indians claimed collective responsibility for their misdeed. Zorita could not find one more guilty than another. "Just so that it might not be said that he had come for nothing, he ordered about sixty Indians seized, sent twenty of them to forced labor for six months in workshops, as a lesson and warning to the others, ordered the rest set free, and therewith returned to Mexico City." [38] The stubborn Indians of San Juan Teotihuacán finally gained their point, however; the Augustinians soon departed, and the Franciscans returned to the town.

A Spanish scholar taxes Zorita with being harsh and even unjust to the Indians in this affair.[39] A Mexican writer, on the other hand, sees Zorita's action as "a graceful way of defending the prestige of authority with the least possible severity." [40] The episode did not injure Zorita's fame as a sincere friend of the Indians.

A letter from Fray Gerónimo de Mendieta to Fray Francisco de Bustamante, written in 1561, shows the high regard that Zorita continued to enjoy among the regular clergy. In this letter Mendieta expressed concern about the ruinous passion of the natives for litigation. He thought the evil could be checked by appointing a special tribunal composed of three persons "excelling all others in the land in Christian piety, goodness, and wisdom." This tribunal should tour the Indian towns and decide on the spot, simply and without the right of appeal, all disputes relating to land boundaries. In Mendieta's opinion, one of the three persons possessing the necessary qualities was Dr. Alonso de Zorita.[41]

Even as Zorita busied himself with the administration of justice, with visitas and cuentas, with inquiries into encomiendas, and with countless other duties, the shadow of disabling illness fell upon him. Shortly after his arrival in Mexico he discovered that he was losing his hearing. With the medical naïveté of his time, Zorita ascribed his condition to "the very bad night dews" of the capital, aggravated by the fact that the Audiencia almost never ended its sessions before nightfall, and to the fact that "this city is very unhealthy for the head." He also complained that the official lodgings to which he had been assigned were so damp that he had found it necessary to lease another dwelling. Since his growing deafness was not only a source of embarrassment but a serious impediment to his work as judge, as early as January 1558, Zorita petitioned the Council of the Indies to allow him to resign his office and return to Spain.

The Council responded with its customary lack of alacrity. Not until Christmas of 1561 did Zorita receive official permission to quit his post and return to Spain at a time of his own choosing, with a grant of one year's salary to help defray his travel expenses. By that time Zorita had recovered much of his hearing, and his health in general had improved.

News of Zorita's impending departure had meantime caused dismay among the regular clergy and others of the pro-Indian party. In a letter to the king the provincials of the three orders in New Spain requested the monarch to revoke Zorita's permission to quit the country, because he had regained his hearing and because the land and the Indians needed his presence. Citing his great services, the provincials noted that Zorita was a poor man without other means of support than his salary—perhaps a suggestion that not all judges were in his hard case—and urged the king to grant Zorita some special recompense for these services.[42] From Fray Tomás Casilla, bishop of Chiapas and colleague of Las Casas, came a letter rebuking Zorita for seeking to leave the field in which he had labored; he must stay, wrote Fray Tomás, for it was a question of conscience. Viceroy Velasco joined the chorus of voices opposing Zorita's departure. Velasco evidently communicated to the Council of the Indies the improvement in Zorita's hearing and the strong objections to his retirement. On August 31, 1561, the Council revoked the permission given to Zorita to return to Spain.

Even before this turn of events, Zorita had had a change of mind. His health and hearing had improved, and he was fired with an idea worthy of a disciple of Las Casas. Zorita knew that the great Dominican had entered among the warlike Indians of the province of Tuzulatlán in Guatemala, and that he had applied his doctrine of conquest by persuasion so successfully that the province was renamed Vera Paz to commemorate its peaceful conquest. Could Zorita not do the same in the vast untamed regions to the north, as far as the distant lands visited by Francisco Vásquez de Coronado and the indefinite expanse that men vaguely called Florida?

Zorita's project was rooted in a concrete and urgent problem. Ever since the great silver strike at Zacatecas in 1546 chronic warfare had raged between the Spaniards and the Chichimeca, the nomadic Indians of the region between the east and west sierras and north of a line between Querétaro and Guadalajara. Indian raids on traffic along the routes running between Mexico City and Zacatecas threatened to cut off the southward flow of silver and ruin the precious new industry. Efforts to defeat the tough and elusive northern warriors had failed; efforts to conciliate them had been rebuffed.

On July 20, 1561, a religious named Fray Jacinto de San Francisco sent the king a report in which he proposed a plan for the pacification of the Chichimeca on the way to Zacatecas and in the great interior beyond, using the Lascasian method of conquest by persuasion. As will appear, this report must have been prepared with the knowledge of and probably in consultation with Zorita. In his letter Fray Jacinto related that he was one of the first discoverers of New Spain, having come there before Hernando Cortés. He had returned thither with the Marqués and had served in the Conquest from beginning to end. Cortés had rewarded him with the grant of certain Indian towns and slaves who mined gold for him. But God illuminated his spirit and showed him that his encomiendas and slaves were putting him in the way of perdition. He had abandoned his encomiendas and freed his slaves and had assumed the Franciscan habit, which he had now worn more than thirty-three years.

"Being as I am, the first Spaniard who ever saw and journeyed through these lands," wrote the friar, "and recalling the large populations that once lived here, and the marvelous fertility of the land, and how all has been lost and destroyed in so short a time, I weep tears of blood that I should have been the first discoverer of these people, for I see how all have perished from excessive labor, without receiving instruction in the Faith or baptism, all to the end of augmenting the revenues of Your Majesty and the Royal Crown of Spain. They would have increased much more, in my poor judgment, if matters had been so ordered that the natives of this land had been preserved and had multiplied for the glory of Our Lord and Your Majesty. True that they had great and continuous wars and human sacrifices in their time, but the Spaniards have made even greater wars and sacrifices among them."

Two years before Fray Jacinto had set out for New Mexico in the company of two other religious; their hope was to launch as great a conversion among the heathen tribes of the north as that achieved by the Franciscans in New Spain. They had penetrated 150 leagues into the interior and had baptized many, for the Indians accorded the friars a friendly welcome, although they were at war with the Spaniards. Fray Jacinto and his companions had been recalled by the viceroy of New Spain and by their own provincial because the viceroy could not provide the men who were needed to carry forward the great enterprise. Now Fray Jacinto appealed to the king to give him the necessary assistance.

His plan envisaged sending a force of one hundred Spanish soldiers to aid the friars in the campaign of peaceful conquest. There was to be no war, no killings; the sole duty of these soldiers would be to quiet the Indians so that they might listen to the religious. There were to be no encomiendas, those snares of the Devil to lead men to Hell, and no enslavement of Indians. The Spanish settlers were to be content with royal grants of land or the mines to be discovered in those regions. Since the Franciscans assumed responsibility for the pacification effort, they should have the right to name the captain who would lead the force of one hundred Spaniards. He must be a man of tested virtue and zeal for the Faith and the conversion of the natives. Fray Jacinto declared that the religious of New Spain knew only one person who combined the necessary qualifications: He was Dr. Alonso de Zorita, oidor of the Audiencia of Mexico.[43]

Simultaneously, and by obvious arrangement with Fray Jacinto and his Franciscan brethren, Zorita addressed a memorial to Philip II in which he offered to lead an expedition of the kind proposed by Fray Jacinto into the land of the Chichimeca and the mysterious interior beyond. At least twenty Franciscans and one hundred lay Spaniards would compose the expeditionary force.

Zorita proposed to win the Indians to Christianity and civilization by the methods of Las Casas, by kindness, good works, and good example. Messengers of their own nation would be sent to invite the Indians to settle in towns; from these all lay Spaniards would be barred. A religious would have charge of the conversion and religious instruction of the natives in each Indian town. Zorita was convinced that the Indians were disposed to pursue a peaceful agricultural life, were it not for their fear of the Spaniards, from whom they had received much injury. There should be no encomiendas; the Indians were to be subjects in perpetuity of the Crown, and should be exempt from tribute for a number of years.

For himself Zorita asked the title of governor and captain general of New Galicia, a frontier province extending west and northwest of Michoacán, which he proposed to use as his base of operations, and an annual salary of 10,000 pesos de minas (12,000 ducats of Castile) for a term of ten years. To ensure independence of action Zorita also asked for suppression of the Audiencia of New Galicia, with its seat at Guadalajara. For his soldiers he requested an annual salary of 300 ducats of Castile. Two years was time enough to test the value of Zorita's project. In that time His Majesty would risk no more than 50,000 or 60,000 ducats; he could hope to win many thousands of souls for Heaven, many thousands of ducats in revenue for his royal treasury, and many great kingdoms and provinces for himself.[44]

The Council of the Indies evidently found the projects of Fray Jacinto and Zorita fanciful, and Zorita's demands excessive. The official reply to Zorita authorized him to make an incursion of the kind he planned into the land of the Chichimeca, but at his own expense. The Spanish authorities chose not the method of peaceful persuasion but the policy of "war by the sword" (*guerra a fuego y sangre*) as their solution for the Chichimeca problem. They applied this policy without marked success from 1570 to 1585. Only after the military approach had clearly failed did a new design emerge, a design of attracting the Indians to peaceful settlement by promises of food, clothing, agricultural implements, and religious administration, combined with a program of colonizing the Chichimeca territory with Indian farmers from settled portions of the viceroyalty. These policies, which closely resembled the projects of Fray Jacinto and Zorita, were to bring peace to the "middle corridor" between the great sierras by the early 1600's.[45]

Official rejection of his project collapsed Zorita's dream. The exaltation inspired by Fray Jacinto's fervor, by the prospect of leading a great crusade for the material and spiritual salvation of a world of Indians, quickly left him. He was again an aging official of fifty-odd years, harassed by chronic illness and poverty, weighed down not only by his own sorrows but by the griefs of countless Indians. His deafness had returned. He renewed his pleas to the Council of the Indies for permission to retire, with a grant of three years' salary, and there was a doleful and querulous tone in his letters.

In May 1565, the Council acceded to Zorita's request for permission to retire to Spain, but with a grant of only one year's salary to help defray the costs of his return home. Zorita found this subsidy most inadequate. He estimated that his official transfers in the Indies had cost him 8,000 pesos de minas. He complained that after selling all his books and clothing, and all his household furnishings, he was was returning to Spain after nineteen years of service in the Indies with some 8,000 ducats, a sum less than the value of his personal and household goods when he had departed for America.

Zorita sailed for home in the fleet that reached Seville in September 1566. On arrival at Seville he ran into unexpected difficulties. So chronic and acute had become the Crown's financial troubles that the practice of seizing gold and silver remittances from the colonies to Spain as forced loans to the king had become a highly lucrative abuse.[46] Small as well as large fish fell into the royal net: the Casa de Contratación, the administrative agency controlling all trade and navigation with the Indies, sequestered the 8,000 ducats Zorita had brought with him. Zorita vainly pleaded for release of his money, complaining that he and his household were being detained at Seville with great expense to himself. At last a settlement was reached. Zorita lent 7,000 ducats to His Majesty and received in exchange an annuity bearing a certain rate of interest; he was allowed 1,000 ducats to pay freight charges, duties, and other costs. This business detained Zorita in Seville for two months, after which he left for his house Granada.

In this city Zorita passed his remaining years, years of pinching poverty which appeals to the king for financial assistance did nothing to relieve. In the affairs of the Indies, and especially in the welfare of the Indians, he continued to take a deep and anxious interest. He maintained a correspondence with friends of the regular clergy in New Spain, men like himself of the pro-Indian party. From Mexico City, Fray Gerónimo de Mendieta wrote that by order of his prelates he was writing a history—the great *Historia eclesiástica indiana;* would Zorita send him a certain manuscript work of Fray Toribio de Motolinía on the Indians of New Spain? Zorita cheerfully complied with the request. Fray Domingo de la Anunciación, he of such exemplary piety that he never ate flesh, wore linen, or rode on horseback, wrote from Mexico that he and Fray Vicente de Las Casas were writing a history of the Dominican Order in New Spain; both men were Zorita's old friends.

Seeking information on matters close to his heart, Zorita invited to his home men of long residence in the Indies. One such old-timer was Gonzalo de Las Casas, citizen of Trujillo in Spain, and author of a work on the Chichimeca Indians, who visited Zorita during a stay in Granada, "whither he came on very weighty business."

We do not know the date of Zorita's death, but we may assume that it came not long after his completion of the "Relación de las cosas notables de la Nueva España" (1585). With his death the Spanish scene lost a most attractive figure. Modest, unpretentious, Zorita employed his considerable juridical talents and knowledge in defense of the oppressed Indians of America, at no small cost to himself. That exalted Spanish humanism and *Indianismo* whose dominating personality was Fray Bartolomé de Las Casas found in Zorita a worthy representative.

We may assume that Zorita's motive in writing his *Brief Relation* was to dispose the Spanish king and his counselors to effective remedial action on the tragedy that was unfolding in the Indies, to delineate the issues of the Indian problem with a fullness, an unsparing candor, and a vehemence that might have been inappropriate in the formal communication of a judge who still held office. However, the occasion for his work had been provided earlier by a royal cedula of December 20, 1553. This order, cast in the form of a questionnaire and addressed to the viceroys and Audiencias of the Indies, requested an exhaustive review of the elements of the tribute problem, past and present. The Crown wished to know what tribute the Indians paid their rulers and lords before the Conquest, and what tribute they now paid the Spaniards; who were the tribute-payers; what was the method of making assessments; what was the capacity of the Indians to pay; and a host of related matters. The viceroys and Audiencias were to seek the assistance of the religious, of aged Indians, and of other informed parties in answering these questions. The Crown, it appears, sought the information in order to evolve a general solution of the Indian problem that would eliminate remaining abuses, stabilize the Indian tribute and labor system, and halt the progressive decline of the Indian population.

We know that Zorita wrote his *Brief Relation* in retirement, for he himself explains the circumstances that prevented him from joining in the official replies of the Audiencias of which he had been a member to the cedula of December 20, 1553, and the factors that delayed his preparation of the work until his return to Spain. He writes that at the time the royal cedula was received by the Audiencia of Guatemala, in which he served as oidor, he left for Mexico City to serve as oidor in the Audiencia of that capital. By the time he arrived in Mexico City the Audiencia there had already completed its inquiry and dispatched its report and opinion. Zorita further explains in his preface that because of the press of work during his remaining years in New

Spain, "I found it impossible to write this relation, as I greatly wished to do." We know that in preparation for his task Zorita collected material on Indian tribute and on the manners and customs of the Indians for many years. Precisely when he completed the *Brief Relation* is not known, but there is some internal evidence that it was written before 1570.

Zorita's work was presumably read by one or more members of the Council of the Indies, to which it was sent; it is more doubtful that it ever met the eyes of Philip II. One can only speculate as to what influence, if any, the *Brief Relation* had on the course of Spain's Indian policy. In a time of acute financial crisis for the Crown, the royal counselors could hardly have taken seriously Zorita's sweeping proposal that Indian money tribute be ended and that the Indians pay tribute in the form of labor on designated fields, as in pre-Conquest times.

On the other hand, two contemporary pieces of royal legislation conform generally with Zorita's recommendations. Zorita proposed to do away with the repartimiento or labor draft, replacing it with a system under which each Indian town would send to a neighboring Spanish town a certain number of laborers who could sell their labor to all comers at whatever wages they could get. A decree of Philip III, embodying this principle of a free choice of employer by Indian workers, was issued on November 24, 1601. The new code was only partially enforced, however, and by a supplementary decree of 1609 the repartimiento was restored in agriculture and cattle-raising and for certain tasks in the mines. Another proposal of Zorita's, limiting the annual income from an encomienda to 3,000 ducats, resembles a royal order of 1568 limiting large encomiendas to an income of 2,000 pesos.[47] There is apparently no evidence, however, that these measures were inspired by a reading of the *Brief Relation*.

I find no mention of Zorita's manuscript for more than a century after the book was written. In 1683, according to a note at the end of a manuscript copy of the *Brief Relation* in the Manuscripts Division of the New York Public Library, the presumed original fell into the hands of a Licentiate Pensado, no indication being given of how or where. Joaquín García Icazbalceta states that Fray Agustín de Vetancurt, in his *Teatro mexicano* (1698), was the first to mention Zorita's work, citing a text in the possession of the Mexican scientist, writer, and student of Indian antiquities, Carlos de Sigüenza y Góngora (1645-1700). How the Mexican savant acquired this manuscript, believed to be the original, remains a mystery.

From the collection of Sigüenza y Góngora, a member of the Society of Jesus, the manuscript found its way into the library of the Jesuit Colegio de San Pedro y San Pablo in Mexico City. Here an Italian scholar-adventurer, the Cavaliere Lorenzo Boturini Benaduci (1702-c. 1751), discovered it in the course of his search for sources on the ancient Indian civilizations of Mexico. Boturini recognized the importance of his find and made a copy of the manuscript with his own hand. The presumed original later came into the possession of the Mexican scholar and bibliophile José F. Ramírez; from this García Icazbalceta made another copy "with all care" in 1867 and used it to prepare the first reliable edition (1891) of the *Brief Relation*. The modern Mexican scholar Joaquín Ramírez Cabañas believes that a manuscript of Zorita's work acquired some decades ago by the Biblioteca Nacional de México may be this same copy.

The manuscript copy in the New York Public Library appears to be a transcript of Boturini's copy of the presumed original. The document is bound together in one volume with an unrelated Spanish manuscript. This volume formed part of the Obadiah Rich Collection acquired by purchase by the New York Public Library. No information is available concerning the identity of the copyist of this transcript of the *Brief Relation* or of its previous owners.

In the introduction to his edition of the *Brief Relation,* García Icazbalceta noted that in addition to the Boturini copy and the copies made therefrom,. there existed another family of defective copies that exhibit large textual gaps. García Icazbalceta believed that the father copy of this family of defective texts was one made from the Boturini copy by or for a certain Don Diego Panes, an officer in the Spanish army. Panes or his scribe must have been responsible for the omissions from Zorita's work. One of these defective texts was used to prepare the first Spanish edition (1864) of the *Brief Relation.*

This proliferation of manuscript copies of Zorita's relation indicates that students of ancient and colonial Mexico recognized the book's worth and importance long before its first publication.

Four editions of the *Brief Relation,* one French and three Spanish, have been published to date. I list these editions in order of their appearance.

Alonzo de Zurita. *Rapport sur les différentes classes de chefs de la Nouvelle-Espagne,* Vol. XI (1840), in Henri Ternaux-Compans, ed., *Voyages, relations, et mémoires originaux pour servir a l'histoire de la découverte de l'Amérique, publiés pour la première fois en français* (Paris, 20 vols., 1837-1851). This French version was made from a transcript of the Boturini copy of the presumed original. The translation, generally unreliable, sometimes verges on the absurd; the scanty annotation is not very helpful.

Alonso de Zurita. *Breve y sumaria relación de los señores de la Nueva España,* Vol. II (1864), pp. 1-126, in *Colección de documentos inéditos relativos al descubrimiento, conquista y colonización de las posesiones españolas en América y Oceanía* (Madrid, 42 vols., 1864-1884). This edition, based on a defective transcript of the copy made by Boturini, is completely unacceptable.

Alonso de Çorita. *Breve y sumaria relación de los señores y maneras y diferencias que había de ellos en la Nueva España, y en otras provincias sus comarcanas, y de sus leyes, usos, y costumbres, y de la forma que tenían en les tributar sus vasallos en tiempo de su gentilidad y la que después de conquistados se ha tenido y tiene en los tributos que pagan a S. M., y a otros en su Real Nombre, y en el imponerlos y repartirlos, y de la orden que se podría tener para cumplir con el precepto de los diezmos, sin que lo tengan por nueva imposición y carga los naturales de aquellas partes,* Vol. III (1891), *Pomar y Zurita (Siglo XVI),* pp. 71-227, in Joaquín García Icazbalceta, ed., *Nueva colección de documentos para la historia de México* (Mexico, 5 vols., 1886-1892). This edition, I have noted, utilized a copy of Zorita's work personally made by García Icazbalceta from the original in the possession of José F. Ramírez. García Icazbalceta entered in the text a few notes or suppressions made by Zorita, as well as some marginal comments in a different hand. The editor's preface briefly told Zorita's life, traced the history of the original and its copies, and described earlier editions. Unfortunately, the work is without annotation.

Alonso de Zorita. *Breve y sumaria relación de los señores de la Nueva España,* Joaquín Ramírez Cabañas, ed. (Mexico, 1942). This is a volume in the Biblioteca del Estudiante Universitario, published by the Universidad Nacional Autónoma de México. For his edition Ramírez Cabañas chiefly relied on that of García Icazbalceta, but omitted some of the notes appearing in the latter text. In his brief but well-written preface Ramírez Cabañas summarizes Zorita's life and the importance of his work, and makes a spirited rejoinder to the criticisms leveled at Zorita by Serrano y Sanz. This edition is very thinly annotated.

In addition to the *Brief Relation*, Zorita wrote or compiled at least three other large-scale works during the years of his retirement. The titles and contents of these works, in the presumed order of their writing, follow:

I. "Suma de los tributos." This work, now lost, is cited several times in the *Brief Relation*. Serrano y Sanz suggests that its contents in large part probably duplicated the material on the subject of tribute in the *Brief Relation*.

II. "Leyes y Ordenanzas reales de las Indias del mar Océano por las cuales primeramente se han de librar todos los pleitos civiles y criminales de aquellas partes y lo que por ellas no estuviere determinado se ha de librar por las leyes y Ordenanzas de los reinos de Castilla" (1574). In his dedication to King Philip, Zorita explained that his inspiration for this work had been the monarch's project for an official compilation of the Laws of the Indies. Zorita's collection was based on materials which he had begun to assemble when he was an oidor in the Audiencias of Guatemala and Mexico. Serrano y Sanz found this manuscript work of 367 folio pages in the Biblioteca del Real Palacio de Madrid. He intended to publish this compilation in the same series in which appeared Zorita's *Historia de la Nueva España,* but did not carry out his project.

III. "Relación de las cosas notables de la Nueva España y de la conquista y pacificación della y de la doctrina y conversión de los naturales" (1585). This major work of 633 folio pages remained in manuscript until Serrano y Sanz, who discovered it in the Biblioteca del Real Palacio in Madrid, published Part 1 as Volume 10 of the series, *Colección de libros y documentos referentes a la historia de América,* under the title, *Historia de la Nueva España por el doctor Alonso de Zorita (siglo XVI),* Vol. I (Madrid, 1909). No other parts were published. The original consists of four parts. Part 1 treats of the geography and ancient history of New Spain. According to Serrano y Sanz, the greater portion of Part 2 is a reproduction of what Alonso de Zorita wrote concerning Indian laws, customs, and tribute in his *Brief Relation.* Part 3 treats of the Conquest of Mexico and also has some account of developments in Guatemala and Nicaragua. Part 4 tells of the conversion of the Indians of New Spain to Christianity.

Serrano y Sanz, whose useful biographical introduction to the *Historia de la Nueva España* is marred by his evident antipathy to Zorita as a "do-gooder" of the Las Casas school, complained that Zorita "copied freely and without the slightest scruple from the works of others, whence follows a capital defect: the small originality of the work." Serrano y Sanz grudgingly conceded a certain value to the book, noting that Zorita drew on various sources that are now lost.

I am inclined to protest against the severity of Serrano y Sanz's judgment on Zorita's work. To be sure, the *Historia* suffers from some fashionable vices of contemporary Spanish historiography: pedantry, the inclusion of irrelevant material, and the use of such puerile devices as a listing of all the fine things of New Spain that began with C. The work is indeed highly derivative, being in the main a compilation of borrowings from other writers. But Zorita, with characteristic honesty, made no effort to conceal this derivative character of his work. In a valuable bibliographical introduction, entitled "Catálogo de los autores que han escrito historias de Indias, o tratado algo de ellos," Zorita listed all the authors and titles on the subject of the Indies of which he had any knowledge. In each case he carefully indicated whether he only knew of the source, or whether he had actually used it in the preparation of his book. Some typical comments follow:

"I made use of the published writings of the very learned and studious Bartolomé de Las Casas. . . . I made use of some other writings of his that I have in manuscript and remain unpublished."

"Fray Bernardino de Sahagún, of the Franciscan Order, long resident in New Spain, where I knew him when I was oidor there, has spent many years in instruction of the natives. He has written a treatise on the manners and customs of those people, of their rites and ceremonies, and of their mode of government. I have not seen it, but have heard it praised; I have also heard that it contains many interesting things in our Castilian tongue and in Mexican [Nahuatl], and that it is in manuscript in the library of the convent of San Francisco de México."

"Bernaldo Díaz del Castillo, citizen of Guatemala City, where he has a good repartimiento. He was a conquistador in that land and in New Spain and Guacigualco.[48] When I was oidor in the Royal Audiencia de los Confines, which sits in the city of Santiago de Guatemala, he told me that he was writing a history of that country, and showed me part of what he had written. I do not know if he has finished it, or if it has seen the light." [49]

In the body of the *Historia*, Zorita frequently introduces statements with the words: "Fray Toribio says," or, "Fray Andrés relates." Such scrupulous acknowledgment of sources of information was not universal in Zorita's time. I may cite the case of the royal chronicler of the Indies, Antonio de Herrera y Tordesillas (1549-1625), who in his *Historia de los hechos de los Castellanos en las islas y Tierra Firme del mar Océano* "carried to an extreme the abusive privilege claimed by contemporary historians of pillaging the works of others without indicating the source." [50]

In his seventy-third year, as Zorita himself informs us in the dedication of the *Historia*, he began to write a philosophical and devotional work entitled "Discursos de la vida humana." We do not know if he lived to complete this work or if the manuscript survives. Very likely, as Serrano y Sanz suggests, we need not mourn its loss, for Zorita's writing reveals no particular flair for speculation or metaphysics.

Few of Zorita's contemporaries possessed such a formidable equipment of experience, observation, and learning as he brought to the writing of the *Brief Relation*. Nineteen years of service as oidor in the Audiencias of Santo Domingo, Guatemala, and Mexico, and as juez de residencia in northern

South America, give his descriptions of the contemporary colonial scene an immense authority. To his first-hand knowledge of local conditions Zorita joined a trained lawyer's knowledge of the law and of the innumerable shifts and expedients by which judges, encomenderos, and principales evaded the law. None knew better than he the gap between Spanish colonial theory and practice.

For his description of pre-Conquest Indian society, Zorita drew on the materials accumulated by his friends among the regular clergy, avid students of Indian culture, and on oral and written accounts of their past supplied by Indian elders and principales. In the introduction to his *Historia de la Nueva España*, Zorita mentions some of his sources of information. He names Fray Toribio de Motolinía, Fray Andrés de Olmos, and Fray Francisco de Las Navas, among the friars; he cites Don Pablo Nazareo, among the principales.

Zorita states that he used a book on the *cosas* of New Spain by Motolinía; I have noted that Zorita lent this book to Fray Gerónimo de Mendieta to assist him in writing his great *Historia eclesiástica indiana*. Collation of Zorita's citations with Motolinía's published works reveals that some of the citations appear in the latter's *Historia de los indios de la Nueva España* but not in Motolinía's *Memoriales;* others appear in the *Memoriales* but not in the *Historia de los indios;* in still other cases parallel passages are found in both works, but they differ from each other and from Zorita's citation in details of phrasing. Mendieta's citations from Motolinía reveal similar discrepancies. Robert Ricard has offered a convincing solution to the problem: Zorita and Mendieta used neither the *Historia de los indios de la Nueva España*, nor the *Memoriales*, nor a draft of either, but a third work, now lost, that may have been the crowning effort of the Franciscan scholar.[51]

Zorita also mentions that he consulted a smaller work on

the same subject by Fray Andrés de Olmos, but gives no title. He also had access to Spanish versions of some of a set of Indian "Speeches of the Ancients" (*huehuetlatolli*), compiled by Olmos between 1540 and 1545 and appended to the manuscript of his Nahuatl *Arte* or grammar, now in the Library of Congress.[52]

We do not know the title of the writing that Fray Francisco de Las Navas made available to Zorita; it evidently dealt with the rules of succession among the Indians. Zorita mentions that he consulted other *memoriales*, based on Indian picture writings, given to him by a principal of the town of Xaltocan. This principal, named Don Pablo Nazareo, was "very virtuous and a good Christian, a good Latinist, rhetorician, logician, and philosopher," and had been for many years rector and teacher in the famous colegio of Santa Cruz in Tlatelolco, founded for the education of Indian youth by the Franciscans.

Two closely related questions remain to be answered. First, how well does Zorita's somber assessment of the condition of the Mexican Indians in the period under discussion (about 1550-1570) agree with the testimony of other observers? Second, how well does Zorita's idyllic picture of Indian pre-Conquest society agree with the available data on this subject?

It may safely be said that Zorita's assessment of the condition of the Indians in his time conforms with the majority view of the matter among his contemporaries. A Mexican writer on the tribute question observes that Zorita's stress on the extreme poverty of the Indians represents the most widely held opinion, especially in clerical circles.[53] The optimistic statements of Motolinía and the venerable oidor Francisco de Ceynos,[54] on which L. B. Simpson leans heavily to support his thesis that "the encomenderos had been sufficiently chastised and were not pushing their Indian tributaries beyond endurance," [55] cannot be regarded as typical.

An appendix to this book, summarizing other replies to the royal cedula of December 20, 1553, presents pessimistic comments on the status of the Indian by Fray Nicolás de Witte and Fray Domingo de la Anunciación, and a joint comment by Motolinía and Fray Diego de Olarte which is much more restrained in its optimism than Motolinía's more famous letter to Charles V. Among the other witnesses who support Zorita's thesis of intolerable Indian misery three may be cited here. All three were ecclesiastics or civil officials of high reputation and authority.

Fray Pedro de Gante (Peter of Ghent), a lay brother of the Franciscan Order and near relative of Charles V, and a great missionary educator of long residence in Mexico, wrote a letter to the Emperor Charles on February 15, 1552. Fray Pedro informed the emperor that the Indians were dying out from excessive labor and from hunger, for they were not left even enough time to get their food. His Majesty's cedulas in favor of the Indians were good and beneficial in intent, but the governors and judges evaded them. His Majesty must secure enforcement of the laws against compulsory personal service by the Indians, for this was one of the chief causes of their destruction. Fray Pedro knew of cases of Indians who were called from their towns and who were gone from home for a month; this was especially true of Indians who lived in towns some distance from Mexico. These towns had to serve their encomendero in Mexico City, supplying him with household servants and with vegetables, fuel, chickens, fodder, and other commodities. If a town could not supply the en-comendero's demands, the poor Indians had to toil day and night to find the means of purchasing them elsewhere.

"For the love of Our Lord," pleaded Fray Pedro, "let Your Majesty take pity on the poor Indian woman who is alone in her hut and has no one to support her and her chil-dren because her husband could stand no more the burdens of his tribute obligations. . . . If Your Majesty does not pro-vide that the Indians pay tribute as is done in Spain, giving of what the land produces, and that they be not treated as slaves, the land will be ruined, and thirty years hence these regions will be as depopulated as the West Indies, with a loss of ever so many souls, and a stain on Your Majesty's con-science."

Fray Pedro also called attention to the evils of the emerg-ing institution of repartimiento or labor draft. The Indians from towns within a distance of ten leagues around Mexico City had to come to the capital to be hired by Spanish em-ployers. A common laborer received a wage of 12 maravedís a day. An Indian might spend two days in travel to the capi-tal, and then might have to wait for three or four days for some Spaniard to hire him; during this time he must sell the clothes off his back to keep alive. After being hired he got his 12 maravedís a day, of which 10 or all had to go for food, and so he had served for nothing and had lost his clothing in the bargain.[56]

Eleven years later the provincials of the three orders in New Spain wrote the king that the Indians lived in anguish, for they felt that new tributes were daily being imposed on them. The prelates complained that the tribute quota of 1 peso and half a fanega of maize was excessive, for the Indians were so poor that some did not harvest even half a fanega of maize. Moreover, the entire tribute went to the encomendero or the Crown, leaving nothing for the expenses of the community. As a result, the principales had to levy extra assessments on the Indians, publicly or in secret.[57]

We have also the brief testimony of an able viceroy, Martín Enríquez, addressing his successor in 1580: "The Indians are so miserable a people that no Christian heart can fail to feel pity for them. . . . The majority could not raise a real without selling themselves." [58]

In recent decades it has been common to regard epidemic diseases of European origin as the major causal factor in the catastrophic decline of the native population of Mexico in the sixteenth century, and to ascribe a secondary role at best to Spanish mistreatment and overwork of the Indians. A recent study[59] of population trends in New Spain between 1550 and 1570 casts doubt on this familiar thesis. Noting that these years fall between the two great epidemics of 1544-1546 and 1575-1579, the authors conclude that "the asssertion seems warranted from the published taxation records that the population of New Spain was diminishing in the decade from 1550 to 1570 at a rate of 2 to 4 per cent a year, and that such decrease indicates a relatively high rate of decrease in these decades caused by factors other than the great epidemics." They suggest that factors of importance were "endemic diseases, social dislocation, increasing demands upon the Indian population for labor, and deterioration in nutrition." They further conclude that "it seems likely that such factors have hitherto been given less weight than they deserve relative to the massive inroads of the major epidemics." These conclusions give strong support to Zorita's argument that Spanish tribute and labor policies were primarily responsible for the catastrophic decline of the Indian population of New Spain.

The idealized role that Zorita assigns to the Indian aristocracy, or *señores naturales*, in the period after the Conquest is much more open to question. José Miranda dryly observes that Zorita did not seem to know the history of the tribute question very well when he proposed to entrust the assignment of tribute to these señores naturales. "The documents of the period show that the assignment of tribute by the caciques gave rise to infinite abuses." [60] Collusion between the Indian lords and encomenderos grew so scandalous that a royal cedula of December 18, 1552, forbade assessment of tribute by way of agreements between principales and encomenderos, "because it redounds to the destruction of the Indians, since the caciques and the encomenderos combine to enrich themselves and plunder the poor macehuales." [61]

Charles Gibson and François Chevalier document the great abuses committed by the Indian lords in the post-Conquest era: They usurped the calpulli or communal lands, imposed excessive rents on their *mayeques* or serfs, and on their tenants, levied illegal tribute, and forced the commoners to labor for them and give them service in unprecedented ways.[62] Zorita, to be sure, puts the shoe on the other foot; he asserts that such "tyrants" were not the old señores naturales but commoners who had usurped their places; he also complains of mayeques who rose up against their lords, threw off their hereditary obligations, and proclaimed that the land they worked was their own. No doubt incidents of this kind did occur in the disordered times following the Conquest.

If Zorita was guilty of embellishing the role of the Indian aristocracy in the post-Conquest era, his contention that the position of the native nobility deteriorated sharply in the same period is well supported by facts. Under the new order of things the principales were made responsible for the collection of tribute from the commoners. When the number of tribute-payers in a town declined because of an epidemic or other circumstances, the Indian lords had to make up the arrears or go to jail. Meanwhile Spanish encomenderos encroached on the private lands of the native nobility and appropriated for themselves the various sources of revenue enjoyed by the principales. As a result, by the end of the century the old Indian aristocracy was in full decline. "The Indian nobility gained little from the lands it had managed to occupy; its recent acquisitions and its ancient domains alike soon passed for very small amounts of money into the hands of the conquerors." [63]

Zorita's tendency to idealize the role of the Indian nobility both in the pre- and post-Conquest era is of a piece with his general tendency to embellish the Indian past. His frequent contrast of an idealized past with a somber present makes the *Brief Relation* a study in unrelieved whites and blacks, augmenting the dramatic force of the work. The *Brief Relation* offers to our view a pagan Golden Age in which obedient commoners lived happily under the mild sway of enlightened rulers. A nostalgic tone pervades Zorita's description of this Lost Paradise:

"In the old days they performed their communal labor in their own towns. Their labor was lighter, and they were well treated. They did not have to leave their homes and families, and they ate food they were accustomed to eat and at the usual hours. They did their work together and with much merriment. . . . They returned to their houses, which, being very small, were cozy and took the place of clothing. Their wives had a fire ready and laid out food; and they took pleasure in the company of their wives and children. There was never any question of payment for this communal labor."

Zorita's romanticism offered an easy target to critics. Serrano y Sanz declared that Zorita's false picture of Mexican society was a major defect. With heavy sarcasm, Serrano y Sanz commented: "Those Indians, so cultured, so honorable, so pious, and even so philosophical in their discourses and counsels; that impeccable administration of justice; that paternal government of kings and lords; that mild assignment of public labors—all is as stylized and conventional as the picture Garcilaso de la Vega left us of the Quichuas and their Incas in his *Royal Commentaries,* or the fantasies drawn by Father Las Casas in his *Apologetical History of the Indies.*" [64]

With more restraint, García Icazbalceta wrote that "Zorita's compassion for the sufferings of the natives caused him to overlook the possibility of exaggeration in the picture that they themselves drew of their former felicity." Like Serrano y Sanz, García Icazbalceta sounded the Social Darwinist theme of the historical necessity of the subjugation of the weaker race by a stronger, all in the name of progress. He observed that in itself Zorita's account of the delicate constitutions and small stamina of the natives proved that on the arrival on the scene of a new race, "a race destined to develop the material resources already known, and to create new sources of wealth of which the native never dreamed, they must inevitably be forced to do the labor that they shunned, a situation doubtless aggravated, perhaps unnecessarily, by the greed and harsh tempers of those Spaniards." [65]

Zorita's palpable exaggerations, and the ardent, polemical tone with which he defended the Indian character and intelligence become understandable when viewed in the context of his time and the problems faced by Zorita, Las Casas, and other champions of the Indian. The decades following the Conquest saw a great debate over Indian policy in which questions of the capacity and cultural level of the natives assumed a capital theoretical and practical importance.[66] The conquistadores and their apologists developed a typical "colonialist" position that would sanction a virtual free hand for the settlers in dealing with the Indians. Listen to the learned Juan Ginés de Sepúlveda, debating with Las Casas in 1550.

What, he asked, could one expect of "these little men in whom you will scarcely find even vestiges of humanity; who not only are devoid of learning but do not even have a written language; who preserve no mementos of their history, aside from some vague and obscure reminiscence of past events, represented by means of certain paintings; and who have no written laws but only barbaric customs and institutions. And if we are to speak of virtues, what moderation or mildness can you expect of men who are given to all kinds of intemperance and wicked lusts, and who eat human flesh?

"And do not believe that before the coming of the Christians they lived in that peaceful reign of Saturn that the poets describe; on the contrary, they waged continuous and ferocious war against each other with such fury that they considered a victory hardly worth while if they did not glut their monstrous hunger with the flesh of their enemies. . . . For the rest, these Indians are so cowardly that they almost run at the sight of our settlers, and frequently thousands of them have run like women before a very few Spaniards, numbering less than a hundred." [67]

In Mexico City, in Zorita's time, resided a learned detractor of Indians; he was Francisco Cervantes de Salazar, professor at the University of Mexico and official chronicler of the Ayuntamiento or city council of the capital. Zorita knew him well. From a potpourri of defamatory statements directed against the Mexican Indians in his *Crónica de la Nueva España,* I offer a selection in paraphrase:

The Indians are cowardly and have no sense of honor. They are extremely vindictive and cannot keep a secret.

They are ungrateful and changeable. They are so lazy that if necessity did not force them to work, they would squat the whole day on their haunches, never speaking to each other. They are false swearers and even in confession rarely tell the truth. They have plenty of land, yet prefer to sow right next to Spanish pastures, in order that the cattle may damage their crops and give them a pretext for complaining to the judges and getting the land away from the Spaniards. There is nothing they will not steal, given the chance.[68]

In the light of these charges of Indian inferiority and wickedness, made by men of high standing in the world of sixteenth-century Spanish scholarship, such as Juan Ginés de Sepúlveda and Francisco Cervantes de Salazar, the vehemence with which Zorita defended the moral and intellectual character of the Indian becomes understandable and pardonable.

Another source of Zorita's idealized image of the Indian past is "the Noble Savage Convention," [69] so prominent in Renaissance thought and literature. In a Europe swept by storms of change, in which the familiar landmarks were rapidly disappearing, sensitive spirits began to question the value of civilization and learning, to eulogize pastoral simplicity and innocence. The discovery of America and its primitive peoples gave a stimulus to this "disillusioned recoil from the civilized world." Some confusion crept into the thought of these critics of Europe as a result of reports of the advanced civilizations of the Incas and Aztecs. As H. N. Fairchild shrewdly observes, "they are uncertain whether to admire the Indian because he is so civilized or because he is so savage." [70] Zorita, a true son of the Renaissance, reflects both the disillusionment of many Humanists with the fruits of civilization and their somewhat discordant ideas about the American Indians: Now Zorita eulogizes the rustic simplicity and innocence of the natives, now he compliments them on being "so intelligent that they can present their plea or petition to the very viceroy or the entire Audiencia, without flutter or nervousness, and all so well phrased that one might think they had lived all their lives in the press of affairs and amid very well-informed people."

It would be a mistake to suppose that Zorita's positive assessment of pre-Conquest Mexican society had no basis in fact, that it was merely a figment of an overgenerous imagination or a reflection of a prevailing Humanist mood of disillusionment with European civilization. In spite of the many evils that darkened the life of ancient Mexico, it may be affirmed that Indian morale and living standards were higher before the Conquest than after that event. All the available data on population trends and the history of the tribute question in the post-Conquest period force that conclusion on the student of the subject.

George C. Vaillant doubtless exaggerated when he wrote, in the spirit of Zorita, that the Indians of ancient Mexico "worked together for their common good, and no sacrifice was too great for their corporate well-being." [71] Yet Vaillant's sweeping statement had its element of truth. At the coming of the Spaniards the tribal foundations of Indian society still survived, although greatly weakened, especially in Tenochtitlán, by the growth of war, trade, and the state. The calpulli or clan, based on kinship, communal land tenure, and mutual assistance, remained the basic unit of social organization, uniting all the free commoners. Patriarchal relations between the rulers and the ruled doubtless still prevailed in many localities. Tribute demands were still limited by custom and the relatively modest appetites of the rulers, nobility, and priesthood. Even the asperity of relations between Indian conquerors and conquered was somewhat mitigated by the sway of custom, which demanded respect for the principle of autonomy, and by the possession by the victors and the vanquished of a common world outlook and a common stock of culture.

After all necessary concessions to Zorita's point of view are made, it must be said that his portrait of ancient Mexican society omits its most serious blemishes and failures.

Chronic warfare was a deadly scourge of ancient Mexico. The loss of life and attendant destruction from this source must have been very heavy. War joined hands with religion to promote human sacrifice in monstrous numbers. During the reign of Moctezuma alone, between twenty-five thousand and sixty thousand prisoners of war were sacrificed. Members of the Aztec tribe were also sacrificed on the altars of Tenochtitlán.

Granted that Spanish tribute demands were considerably greater than those of the Indian authorities, the condition of pre-Conquest Indian commoners was less favorable than Zorita would have us believe. In addition to paying tribute to the rulers of Tenochtitlán, Texcoco, or Tlacopan, the subjects of the Triple Alliance had to support their own lords and priesthood. Even the Aztec commoner, who shared in the tribute exacted from conquered peoples, must have had difficulty meeting his obligations. In addition to communal labor for the support of clan leaders and priests, he had to labor on construction and maintenance of dikes, fortifications, temples, and other public works.

Compulsory offerings to the gods placed a heavy burden on the commoners of Tenochtitlán. In Book XII of his *Historia general de las cosas de Nueva España*, Fray Bernardino de Sahagún offers a vivid example in connection with the worship of the tribal god Huitzilopochtli. For one whole year the families of two neighborhoods or subdivisions of a clan were responsible for providing the enormous quantities of wood burned each night in honor of the god. The next year two new neighborhoods succeeded to the responsibility. To pay its share of the cost, each family had to contribute one large mantle and four small mantles, one small basket of kernels of dried maize, and one hundred dried ears of maize. A Nahuatl passage, based on the oral accounts of native informants, describes the plight of the commoner overwhelmed by the burdens of this religious tribute. "This gave rise to much distress; it caused much anguish; it affected them. And some therefore fled; they went elsewhere. And many flung themselves in the midst of war, they cast themselves to their deaths." [72]

Little is known about the condition in the pre-Conquest era of the mayeques or serfs, who apparently were not organized in *calpullis;* or of the people whom the Spaniards called *terrazgueros* or tenant farmers. The Spanish chronicler Fernández de Oviedo, who obtained his information from Spanish veterans of the Conquest, draws an unvarnished picture of the poverty and oppression endured by these people.

According to Fernández de Oviedo, each Indian lord assigned a specific piece of land to each of his tenants. The majority of these tenants lived on the lord's domain; a *tequitlato* or tribute collector had charge of from twenty to fifty households. At harvest time this tequitlato left each household enough maize or other produce to satisfy its needs for the coming year, and took all the rest. In addition, each tenant had to pay tribute in mantles, gold, silver, honey, wax, lime, wood, or whatever was the customary tribute in that region. He had to pay this tribute every forty, sixty, seventy, or ninety days, according to the terms of the agreement. If an Indian could not pay his tribute because of ill health or poverty, the lord instructed his tribute collector to take the tenant to a *tianguis* or market, which was held every five days in all the towns of the land, and there sell him into slavery, applying the proceeds to the payment of his tribute.[73]

Such caprices of nature as drought, hailstones, and blight added to the difficulties of the common people. When crops failed, as happened from 1451 to 1456, and all reserves were exhausted, the unhappy commoner must beg for charity or even sell himself and his children into slavery to wealthy merchants. In time of famine, we read in Sahagún's work, the houses of the merchants were filled with the victims of economic disaster. "At this time one sold oneself. . . . Or else one sold and delivered into bondage his beloved son, his dear child. . . . Already they wielded the hoe, already they used the tump line,[74] already they were as someone else's dog, someone else's turkeys." Great economic differences and even class hatred had crept into Zorita's well-ordered Indian state. "The merchants were those who had plenty, who prospered; the greedy, the well-fed man, the covetous, the niggardly, the man who controlled wealth and family." [75]

Whatever reservations one may have concerning Zorita's embellishment of the social order of ancient Mexico, they do not significantly affect the value of his account. We owe to Zorita a rather full and precise description of the structure and workings of the calpulli or clan, the only such description available. He sketches with equal precision the various types of Indian nobility and land tenure, and the operations of the native tribute system. We obtain a glimpse, though all too brief, of the round of Indian existence from birth to death, of life in the royal palace and the peasant's hut, of the administration of justice, of the education of the young. The delightful "Speeches of the Ancients" reveal some tampering by pious hands, but they have a genuine indigenous flavor; they afford some notion of the imagery and coloring of Nahuatl speech and poetry, and offer insight into Aztec psychology and social relations.

In short, the work is a mine of information on ancient and colonial Mexico, presented for the most part in a spirited and attractive way, although hampered by the form of a reply to the eighteen articles of a royal cedula in which it is cast. I have made it available in English translation in the belief that its merits deserve a larger reading public than the small circle of specialists acquainted with the original.

In preparing this translation I have used the Spanish editions of García Icazbalceta and Ramírez Cabañas. The paragraphing is mine. I have omitted in translation redundant material and long-winded phrases without substantive content. I have altered Zorita's spelling of some personal and place names to make it conform to standard usage.

In my Glossary of Spanish and Nahuatl terms I have defined the monetary units mentioned in this book, giving their value in terms of a theoretical unit, the Castilian maravedí. Here a few words on the complex monetary situation in sixteenth-century Mexico may be in order. During the first decades after the Conquest, in the absence of facilities for coining money, the settlers resorted to uncoined gold and silver units reckoned by weight and fineness in pesos de minas of 450 maravedís. Other means of exchange included the peso de oro común, valued at about 300 maravedís, and the peso de oro de tipuzque, a kind of gold mixed with copper, valued at about 272 maravedís. As a unit of account, the colonists also employed the ducado or ducat, whose value was fixed at 375 maravedís.

Very few coins minted in Europe reached New Spain in this early period, and these coins were quickly hoarded. As a result of complaints of the circulation of falsified money and generally chaotic conditions, the Emperor Charles V in 1535 ordered the establishment of the first Mexican mint, coining silver and copper coins. After 1536 the silver peso of 8 reals or 272 maravedís (real de á ocho) gradually superseded the uncoined units cited above in cities and commercial regions, but the process was a slow one.

Some notion of the purchasing power of the peso in Zorita's time may be gained from the following data, supplied by Indian informants in 1554: A *manta* (a piece of cotton cloth about 1 yard wide and 4 yards long), cost 4 pesos; a fanega (about 1.60 bushels) of maize, 4 reals "at the lowest"; a fanega of kidney beans, 1 peso; a *huipil*, or woman's blouse, 4 pesos.

BENJAMIN KEEN

Upper Montclair, New Jersey
December 1962

The Brief and Summary Relation of the Lords of New Spain

Catholic Royal Majesty:

VARIUS GEMINUS, wishing one day to speak to Julius Caesar about an important matter, began his discourse with these words: "Whoever dares speak before thee, O Caesar, knows not thy greatness; whoever dares not speak before thee, knows not thy goodness." [1] With much more reason, most Christian and very powerful lord and king, could this be said of Your Majesty, for Your Majesty holds sway more securely and with better title than did Caesar when Varius Geminus spoke with him. Omnipotent God has made Your Majesty ruler over many very great and powerful realms and lordships in Europe, part of Africa and Asia, and universal king and supreme lord of all the Indies of the Ocean Sea, where Your Majesty holds and possesses more realms and provinces than any other prince in the world. Not a day passes but multitudes of peoples and many spacious lands, filled with such abundant riches that the most powerful kings tremble with fright to hear of it, are discovered and brought to your royal service.

I, being Your Majesty's servant and loyal vassal, wished to dedicate to Your Majesty this *Summary and Brief Relation of the Lords and Lordships of New Spain.* It treats of the rules of succession among the Indian lords, of the manner in which their vassals paid tribute to them in the time of their heathendom, and of how they have done this since the land was conquered. It also treats of the tribute that they pay to Your Majesty and to private persons in your royal name, of how this tribute is imposed and apportioned, and considers whether it is proper for the natives of New Spain to pay tithes at the present time.

When I reflected on Your Majesty's awe-inspiring grandeur and my own low and humble state, I shrank from presenting this relation to Your Majesty. Considering, however, that God has endowed Your Majesty with those same qualities of benevolence and clemency which Varius found in Caesar, I am encouraged to proceed with my design.

I humbly pray Your Majesty, then, to accept this small work, for I undertook it to satisfy Your Majesty's wish to be informed about the matters touched on in the royal cedula to which this relation is a reply. Your Majesty's acceptance of this writing will make happy this your servant, who expended much labor to learn what is contained therein. Such acceptance will also enhance the book's worth and will encourage others to do the same for other provinces, for Your Majesty's provinces in those parts are so numerous and diverse in habits and customs that many persons could usefully occupy themselves with their description. May Our Lord preserve the Catholic, royal person of Your Majesty and cause Your Majesty to prosper for many years in His holy service, to the benefit of the Universe.

To the Very Illustrious Señores, the president and oidores *of His Majesty's Royal Council of the Indies, Dr. Alonso de Zorita, onetime* oidor *of the royal Audiencia that resides in the very famous and great city of Mexico in New Spain:*

It was the opinion, very illustrious Sirs, of that great philosopher Plato, whom Cicero and the glorious St. Jerome call divine, that it would be a very serious matter if God thought more of our offerings and sacrifices than of the spirit in which they are offered. Our Lord and Master confirmed this opinion when He praised that poor widow who cast her mite into the coffer, saying He preferred the poor offering of that good woman to the much greater offerings of rich and powerful men who gave of their abundance.

Reflecting upon this, very illustrious Sirs, I have dared offer His Majesty this poor untidy little work. It treats of the lords and lordships and tributes of New Spain, of the rules of succession and government the Indians had in the time of their heathendom, with other matters relating thereto. It also proposes a way whereby the precept of tithing may be observed without making it appear a new burden to the Indians. I am confident that His Majesty, imitating the King of Heaven, will consider not the value of the work but the spirit in which it is offered, and will receive it with a benign aspect.

In his royal name, therefore, I pray Your Lordships to accept this relation, to order that it be examined, and to give it such endorsement that I may dare lay it before His Majesty.

Surely it behooves such illustrious persons as yourselves to receive with equal kindness the services of those who give much and those who give little, that the latter may feel rewarded for their labors and that others be inspired to do greater things. Should I merit such a signal favor, it will encourage me to complete some other things that I have begun and still others that I have projected. Our Lord grant the very illustrious persons of Your Lordships the good fortune they deserve, and at the end of very long lives may He grant Your Lordships the eternal reward and glory.

How this relation came to be written, and why it was not written until now:

In December 1553, there was issued at Valladolid a royal cedula[2] that commanded the Audiencias of the Indies to make inquiry into certain matters about which His Majesty wished to be informed. They were to inquire who were the lords of the land, what tribute the natives paid them in the time of their heathendom, and what tribute they have been paying since they came under the Royal Crown of Castile. When the Audiencias had gathered this information, they were to send it together with their opinions to His Majesty.

At the time this royal cedula was received by the Audiencia

de los Confines,[3] in which I served as oidor, I left for Mexico City, whither His Majesty sent me to serve as oidor in the Audiencia of that capital. When I arrived in Mexico City, the Audiencia there had already completed its inquiry and had dispatched its report and opinion. The Audiencia de los Confines, on the other hand, made its inquiry after I had left. Since I was in His Majesty's service when his royal cedula was issued and when the inquiries were made and the reports sent, and since it does not excuse me that I was absent from both Audiencias when the matter was under discussion, I feel an obligation to say what I think about it.

I wish to relate what I learned in the nineteen years I served His Majesty in those parts. The first two I passed as oidor in the town of Santo Domingo, and the next three in the New Kingdom of Granada, in Santa Marta, Cartagena, and Cabo de la Vela, where by His Majesty's order I went to hold a *residencia* of the governor of those provinces. On my return to Santo Domingo to resume my office, I received His Majesty's instructions ordering me to go to serve him as oidor in the Audiencia de los Confines. There I passed three years during which I visited almost every part of the province of Guatemala. The rest of the time I resided in Mexico City. Because of the press of work, I found it impossible to write this relation, as I greatly wished. Now that I am unoccupied, having returned to Spain with His Majesty's permission because the state of my health prevented me from serving him with my wonted diligence and care, I have determined to put in finished form the material I kept for many years in my notebooks and papers. I have done this by putting in the form of a reply to each article of the royal cedula the material relating to that article.

In traveling through the Indies, I always sought to learn the habits and customs of the natives, for I always intended to provide the information requested in this cedula when I had

the opportunity. When I lived in Mexico City, I made a special
effort to gather information on the topics listed in His Majesty's
cedula from learned friars who had resided many years in that
country and among the Indians, for the friars are the persons
who have made the most careful study of these and related
matters. Much of what I write down here was communicated
to these friars in my presence. I also obtained information
from aged Indian *principales* who could be regarded as trustworthy.

I must say at the outset, however, that it is impossible to
state a general rule as concerns any part of Indian government
and customs, for there are great differences in almost every
province. Indeed, two or three different languages are spoken
in many towns, and there is almost no contact or acquaintance
between the groups speaking these different languages. I have
heard this is general in the Indies, and from what I have seen
in my travels, I can affirm it to be true. Consequently, if
what I say here appears to contradict some other information,
the cause must be the diversity that exists in all things in every
province and not any lack of diligence on my part in seeking
the truth. Nor should we wonder that some divergencies appear in the Indian accounts. To begin with, in the majority of
cases the versions of the interpreters are faulty. In the second
place, the Indians lacked an alphabet and writing and preserved all their past history in the form of pictures,[4] most of
which have been lost or damaged. Add to this that the memory of men is frail, and that most of the aged Indians who
were knowledgeable about these matters are dead. These are
the reasons why there are different accounts about everything. Yet another reason is the small value that men attach to
the study of Indian antiquity, which they regard as something
from which little or no profit can be derived.

I can affirm that what I have written here is true, because my
chief sources of information were three Franciscan friars[5] (as

well as religious of other Orders), who had lived a long time in that land, having come there a few years after it was conquered. Among them was one of the first twelve friars to come to that land, and they were all great servants of Our Lord who were always among the Indians and worked for their instruction and conversion throughout New Spain, in Michoacán, Jalisco or New Galicia, and in Pánuco. They always took particular care to inform themselves of the habits and customs of these people, and they could do this better than is now possible, for they knew aged Indians who could help them, and the picture writings were still sound and whole. They obtained much accurate information from these pictures, for they were aided by aged Indian principales who knew how to interpret them and who had seen and heard their elders do the same. I took from each friar what he had learned and wrote down in my notebooks the material relating to the contents of the royal cedula, ordering all as well as I could. Moreover, I checked the accuracy of all my notes with aged Indians. In this I was aided by some aged friars, members of the three orders[6] active in New Spain, who were very good interpreters.

I shall not speak of each province separately, but shall tell what applies generally to the most important provinces of New Spain or the greater part of it. Because the cedula sent to the Audiencia de los Confines is somewhat more detailed than the one sent to Mexico City, I shall set down and comment on the articles individually, but not in the order in which they appear in the cedula. I shall begin with the ninth, which reads as follows:

ARTICLE 9

Item: You will inform yourselves which lords held their lordship by succession, and which were elected by their subjects. You will also inform yourselves what power and jurisdiction these caciques exercised over their subjects in the time of their heathendom, what power and jurisdiction they exercise now, and what advantage their subjects derive from this rule as concerns their government and way of life.

This article contains four questions, and in the interests of clarity I shall reply to each individually.

These natives commonly had and still have (where the Indian lords have not been done away with) three supreme lords in each province. In some provinces, however, as in Tlaxcala and Tepeaca, there were four. Each of these lords had his recognized lordship and jurisdiction apart from the others. There were also inferior lords, whom they commonly call caciques, a word borrowed from the island of Española.

I found the same arrangement in the important province of Utlatlán, which borders on Guatemala, while visiting there on official business as Your Majesty's oidor. The same rule prevailed in the Valley of Matlalcinco and Ixtlahuaca, which border on the province of Mexico, when I was there on Your Majesty's business.

In Mexico City and its province there were three principal lords. They were the ruler of Mexico,[7] the ruler of Texcoco, and the ruler of Tlacopan, now called Tacuba. All the other inferior lords served and obeyed these three rulers. Since they were confederates, they divided all the land they conquered among themselves.

The rulers of Texcoco and Tacuba obeyed the ruler of Mexico in matters of war. They were equals in all the rest, for none could meddle in the affairs of another. They held some towns in common, however, dividing among themselves the tribute paid by these towns. In some cases they divided the tribute equally. In others they divided the tribute into five parts: Two fell to the share of the ruler of Mexico, two to the ruler of Texcoco, and one to the ruler of Tacuba.

In what concerns the rules of succession to the supreme lordship, practices and customs varied from province to province. However, Mexico and the cities allied to it, and Tlaxcala, had almost the same mode of succession.

The most common succession was from father to son. Daughters could not succeed. The son chosen was the eldest son born of the ruler's principal wife, acknowledged by him as such and respected as such by all his other wives and all his vassals. If one of the ruler's wives was of the royal house of Mexico, she was the principal wife, and her son succeeded to the rule if he was qualified. This was the rule in Texcoco and Tacuba and all the provinces subject to them.

If the eldest son was not qualified to rule, his father selected from his other sons the one who seemed the most competent to succeed, always giving preference to the sons of his principal wife in this and all else.

If the ruler had no male heir, but had daughters, and one of them had sons, the ruler chose as his successor that grandson whom he regarded as best qualified to rule. If he had grandsons by his sons, however, he preferred them to grandsons by daughters, always giving preference to descendants of the principal wife if they were qualified; he followed this rule if he had no sons or if they were disqualified to govern.

If none of the ruler's sons or grandsons was capable of governing, he left the choice of a successor to the principales of the realm, whose responsibility it was to choose the ruler in default of a successor. In performing this duty they followed an order that will be described below.

Thus, like the great Alexander, the rulers were more concerned with leaving a successor capable of governing their lands and vassals than with leaving their inheritance to sons or grandsons. They had the same rule of succession with regard to their patrimonial lands and the vassals (called *mayeques*) living on these lands; the rulers distributed such lands and vassals as they thought best among their sons or heirs.

If a ruler had no sons or grandsons, or if they were not qualified to rule, a brother succeeded. And just as the ruler chose from among his sons or grandsons the one who was most fit to govern, so the principales chose from among his brothers the one who was best qualified.

In default of brothers or of a brother competent to rule, they chose the best qualified kinsman of the ruler, and in default of such they chose some other *principal*. But they never chose a *macehual*, that is, a man of the common people. They always tried to choose one of the line or kindred of the ruler, if one was eligible, but in default of such they chose others.

If the ruler of Mexico failed to appoint a successor, the lords and principales of the realm chose the new ruler, and he was confirmed in office by the rulers of Texcoco and Tacuba. If either Texcoco or Tacuba lacked a successor, the selection in each case was made by the principales of the land, and confirmation was made by the ruler of Mexico. The rulers informed themselves whether the election had been made in proper form, and in the contrary case they ordered that the election should be made anew.

The same order was observed in the succession and election of the rulers subject to the rulers of Mexico, Texcoco, and Tacuba, each of the latter confirming the election of the rulers who were his vassals. Each of these subject rulers, however, had his own recognized and separate lordship, with civil and criminal jurisdiction. These rulers in turn confirmed the election of other lesser lords. The same system, with slight variations, prevailed throughout New Spain.

The same order of things was found in the kingdom of Michoacán, with some small variations. During his lifetime the ruler named the son or grandson who should succeed him, and from that time on this heir presumptive began to govern and have some part in administration, for this was the custom and will of the ruler. This arrangement existed only in the kingdom of Michoacán.

If the ruler of Michoacán had not appointed the son or grandson who should succeed him, in his last days he was asked what were his wishes, and the person he named succeeded. As a rule, however, the ruler made his selection while he still enjoyed good health. In connection with this appointment the Indians held a special feast with appropriate ceremonies, and from that time on the person chosen was recognized as successor.

In some places, especially in Mexico, even if there were eligible sons, brothers succeeded in order of seniority if they were qualified to reign. They said that being sons of one father, they should be equal in rights. When the line of brothers was exhausted, the succession returned to the ruler's sons in the order described above. In Mexico, Moctezuma succeeded two of his brothers who had ruled before him.[8] In Tecpán Guatemala, which is a very important town near Guatemala City, I knew a lord who had succeeded his brother. The son of the deceased lord was living, and I knew him well. He held the patrimonial lands and mayeques, but his uncle had the lordship. It was said this had been done because the ruler's son was blind, and so the ruler gave the chieftainship to his brother.

If a son or any other of those who had a right to succeed showed himself ambitious to rule, or sought preference or advantage for himself in dress, or meddled in government or rule ahead of time, the people would not let him succeed even though the ruler had designated him as the eldest and most competent; nor would the ruler who had the right of confirmation consent to it. This act of confirmation took place after the ruler's death, and in such case as I told of above the Indians waited for a few days before deciding which son or grandson or other individual who had a right to succeed was best qualified to reign and govern. They chose him in the manner I have described, and the appropriate ruler confirmed his election.

Since wars were so continuous among them, in the succession and election of rulers the Indians were very careful to select one who was very valiant, if with this he combined ability to govern. A ruler who had not performed certain feats and had not shown himself warlike and spirited lacked certain distinguishing insignia and ornaments in his apparel.

Some declare that the most common mode of succession was from brother to brother, followed by the sons of the deceased lord in order of seniority, but I have described what I found to be the most general practice and usage in this matter. What I have written conforms with an account of this subject that Fray Francisco de Las Navas gave me.

It is unnecessary for me to describe the ceremonies they performed when a new ruler was elected or succeeded. I shall say only that he was escorted to the temple and was accompanied by a multitude of people, all keeping silence.[9] Two principales supported him by the arms as he mounted the numerous steps. When he reached the summit, the high priest of the temple vested him with the royal insignia and greeted him with a few words. Then he clothed him with two mantles, one blue and the other black, on which were painted many skulls and bones to remind him that he must die like all other men. When the ceremonies were over, the high priest addressed him as follows:

My Lord: Consider the honor your vassals have done you. Now that you are confirmed as ruler you must take great care of them and regard them as your sons; you must see to it that they be not offended and that the greater do not mistreat the lesser. You see that the lords of your country, your vassals, are all here with their people. You are their father and mother, and as such you must protect and defend them and treat them justly; for the eyes of all are upon you, and you are the one who must govern them and keep order among them. You must be very diligent in affairs of war. You must watch over and punish the wicked, lords

as well as commoners, and correct and reform the disobedient.
You must give special care to the service of God and his temples,
so that there will be no lack of what is needed for the sacrifices.
Thus all your affairs will flourish and God will watch over you.[10]

After hearing this speech, the ruler promised to do all that
was asked of him and thanked the high priest for his counsel.
Then he descended to the courtyard, where all the other lords
were waiting to make their pledges of fealty. As a mark
thereof, having done their homage, they presented him with
jewels and rich mantles. Then they accompanied him to a
room that was in the same courtyard. He did not emerge
from this room for four days, during which time he fasted
and thanked his idols, and for this he went to the temple at the
appointed hours. At the end of these four days all the lords
came and escorted him with great pomp and rejoicing to his
palaces, where they held high festivities and celebrations.
Thenceforth he reigned as ruler, and was so obeyed and
feared that none dared raise his eyes to look him in the face,
save when he was amusing himself in the company of some
lords or intimates.

In Tlaxcala and Huexotcingo and Cholula, the man who
was to succeed the ruler was first promoted to a dignity or
title called *tecuitli*, which was the greatest dignity they had,
and for this the Indians held certain ceremonies in their temple. When these ceremonies were over, the common people
hurled insults at the ruler-elect and even pushed him about to
try his patience. So great was his endurance that he spoke not
a word, nor even turned around to see who insulted or mistreated him.

These people are by nature very long-suffering, and nothing
will excite or anger them. They are very obedient and teachable; if you blame or scold them for some negligence or vice,
they display great humility and attention, and their only re-

ply is, "I have sinned." The more noble they are, the more humility they display. Sometimes one will say, "I have sinned, be not angry with me, only tell me what I must do." I speak of those who are in the state of their natural simplicity, for those who have been made slaves or deal with the Spaniards are greatly changed. What I told above of how the common people mistreated the new rulers to try their patience, well illustrates their great humility and long-suffering.

Having treated the ruler-elect in the manner described above, they led him to a room of the temple where he remained for a year, and sometimes two, performing penance. During the day he sat on the ground. At night they gave him a sleeping mat, and at certain hours of the night he went to burn incense before the idols. The first four days he slept not at all save a little while during the daytime, seated. There were guards with him who pricked him in the legs and arms with maguey thorns if he fell asleep, saying, "Awake, you must not sleep but watch, and you must look after your vassals. You are taking charge not to sleep but to guard. So do you keep your eyes open and be vigilant to look after your own."

When he had finished his penance, his kinfolk and servants gathered the great quantity of provisions needed for the feast that was to be held. They made a list of the lords, principales, friends, and allies who must be invited. They set out in some large rooms the presents that were to be given to each guest. When all was ready, they fixed the day for the feast, reckoning from the day of the ruler's birth, to make sure the festival should not fall on an even-numbered day, for such a thing they regarded as unlucky.[11] This count involved a complicated calculation.

The day being fixed, they sent invitations to the neighboring lords and to the new ruler's friends and kinsmen. The messenger who went to summon each guest returned in advance of his coming to prepare his quarters and all else that he might need.

If some lord was ill or could not come because he was detained, he sent in his place one of his chief vassals, and with him came many other principales. They brought with them the ruler's chair and set it in its place, for each ruler had a place appointed for him according to his importance. This chair was vacant, and next to it sat the man who came in place of the absent lord. Before this chair they placed all the lord's presents and food, and performed before it all the ceremonies and reverences that they would have made had he been present.

In the morning of the day of the feast, all the assembled lords escorted the new ruler to the temple. He was accompanied by a multitude of people who sang, danced, and rejoiced. At the temple they invested him with the title of ruler. After the ceremonies they served food to the guests and gave them many presents. This involved them in very great expense, for they gave to many people, not only to the lords but to their servants, relatives, and allies; they also gave many alms to the poor and needy.

We see, then, that though they lacked knowledge of the true God, these rulers suffered hardships and fasted and displayed patience and long-suffering to come into their dignities; and they gave thanks to their idols and gave alms and performed other good works, though without merit because they lacked faith. As Lactantius[12] says, speaking of the gentiles in Book IV, Chapter 9, though there was some trace of charitable works among them and they practiced this virtue, their works were like bodies without heads because they had no knowledge of the true God, Who is the head and the principal element, without Whom all virtues are like members without life.

In the New Kingdom of Granada I was told that the ruler

of Sogamoso,[13] before succeeding to that estate, did penance
for seven years in the temple, shut away from men and sun
and light, seeing only those who served him; the Indians did
this to test his capacity for endurance. This ruler came to see
me from his town, which was more than 30 leagues away;
he came with great pomp. Whenever he came to a town,
the first thing he asked was whether there were any poor
people there, Spaniards or Indians, for that land is very cold.
He was not a Christian because of neglect by those whose
obligation it was to instruct him. This was also true of his
vassals and the other people of that country. But during my
stay there, friars began to come there and to teach Christian
doctrine.

Another ruler (I believe he was the lord of Chía) first had
to serve in a lower capacity that he might show himself fit
to rise to a higher estate. In Cabo de la Vela I was told that
the rulers of that coast also had certain days of fasting, called
coyma, which they respected absolutely. They were not
Christians either. I happened to be there at the time of that
fast and saw how rigorously they kept it.

Once, when I was making a tour of inspection in Guatemala, a learned religious of goodly life (who is now bishop)[14]
told me that the people of that land, of whose religious instruction he had charge, used to offer certain prayers and
have certain fasts in the time of their heathendom, that they
were accustomed to rising many times a night to pray, and
that the most devout and aged natives slept with their legs
crossed that sleep might not interfere with their rites. Thus,
when their legs grew tired, they awoke and could return to
their prayers. I refrain from mentioning other things that I
could tell about this subject, to return to my main theme.

When some inferior lord or some principal came to visit
the ruler or to console him on some misfortune that had be-
fallen him, the visitor made a speech. Although not very

systematic, this discourse contains some good advice. When pronounced in their idiom, it sounds much better than in a foreign translation. The religious[15] who translated it told me he had not changed a letter of its substance. It goes as follows[16]:

My Lord: May it be well with you when you stand on the side and left hand of God. In the lordship and dominion that you hold you are His helper and stand in His place, and you must consider very seriously what you do. You are His eye and ear and feet and hands, that you may look and hear and seek the good of all. God placed in your heart the words that issue from your mouth that you may tell your people what they must do.

Before you is the mirror of sky and earth in which you may see, as in a picture, that which is finite and that which is infinite.

You must remember your forefathers, that you may imitate those of goodly life. God has given you feet and hands and wings beneath which your people may find shelter. The Lord who created you honored you by giving you authority to reign over your realm; consider that you are the instrument of His justice to punish the wicked and help the weak. God helps and preserves all; before Him the wicked man fears, the innocent man is happy.

You shall not want for labor, but consider that nothing is accomplished without labor. You will have no repose in sleeping or eating; you will know anxiety as you reflect on the past, seeking to foresee the future. Lord: Cares and fears crowd upon you when you consider the past and the present and the future, so that you may not take pleasure in your food, nor in your drink, nor in your sleeping. Your heart will be afflicted in striving to preserve and augment your realm. Take courage, then, and do not grow faint, for you are the father and mother of all.

You are a great tree of shelter and protection for all; you have people who will aid you, who are your feet and hands. They gather in your shadow to breathe the air of consolation. Your hands console them, but your justice punishes the wicked. You have the necessary instruments to purify and make perfect all, to cause the people to grow daily in good manners. To each you offer a pattern of life. You honor each according to his merits, and as his merits increase you increase the honors. You are an example and model for all, so that you will leave your fame in this mortal world as if in a painting.

You must honor and take counsel with aged men, for thus you will know how to order what is just and avoid injustice. God did you a great favor in putting you in your place. Look to His honor and service; take courage and do not falter, for that high lord who gave you so heavy a burden will aid you and give you a crown of glory if you do not allow yourself to be defeated by evil. You can win much merit in the task that God assigned you if you do no evil.

The dead do not see our faults, they cannot come to advise you; do nothing that may give the living a bad example. Consider that your forebears knew hardship and care in ruling over their realm and did not sleep free of care; they strove to increase their realm and leave a memory of themselves. The order of things that they left was not established in a single day. They took care to console the poor and afflicted, the people of small means. They honored the aged because they found good counsel in them. They willingly assisted the needy. Since they left you honors and burdens, lift up your heart, be not dispirited, but be such as you ought to be, valiant and courageous, and never do a mean thing. I do not want to give you more pain with my words.

Reply of the Ruler

My friend: Be welcome, your words have made me happy, and you have done God a service. Ah! That I were worthy of these many good words and precious counsels that have issued from your bowels! Your counsels are surely worthy of being cherished and kept in the heart. I must not scorn the labor and the love with

which you have warned and consoled me. If I be such as I should
be, I must take your words to heart. Where also may I hear such
words and advice? My friend, you have certainly done your duty
before God and His kingdom and His people in telling me this. I
thank you greatly. Rest and take your ease, my friend.

A lady who visited the ruler's wife would speak to her as
follows:

My Lady: May it be well with you all the years of life that
God is pleased to grant you. You must serve in His name, and
you must acknowledge the mercies you have received from His
hand. You must be zealous and tireless in His service, putting into
it all your thoughts, all your breath. Trust in God, and falter not.
Who better than you can assume the burdens that God has placed
upon you? What would your vassals and the poor do without
you? All commend you to God, that you may shelter them beneath your great wings, as the bird does its young, and like the
bird's young they huddle about you that you may shelter and
counsel them.

Take care, my Lady, that you forget not the least of them, for
you are the haven and shelter and consolation of all. My Lady,
give gladly some comfort to your people; cause them no sadness
nor do them any evil thing, but rear them little by little as children are reared. Do not strangle them in your sleep with the arm
of neglect. Be not stingy or niggardly, but open wide the lap of
charity; open wide the wings of pity beneath which your children, who are your vassals, may find comfort and consolation.
Thus they will increase, and your crown will be increased, and
you will be obeyed without question as the mother and mistress
of all.

If you do this, you will deserve to be loved and served by all.
Be not sparing with them either in works or in sweet and consol-
ing words, and they will gladly do what you command. From
time to time they will seek out their mother and mistress to show

her what they have done; and when God is pleased to take you out of this life, all will weep when they recall the love you showed them and the good works they received from you. Little by little, you are drawing closer to death, my Lady, so consider well what I have said.

If you do what I tell you, my Lady, you will leave a good memory and example of yourself even in distant lands, and you will remain in the hearts of all. If you are not grateful to God for the mercy He has done you in giving you honor and high estate, yours will be the guilt, the offense, and the perdition. If you are grateful, He will reward you. I shall trouble you no further with importunate words.

Reply of the Ruler's Wife

My sister: I thank you very much for your good advice. To God's love I owe this great favor. Who am I? I received your counsel, but the favor was done, not to me, but to God and His people. Who am I to be puffed up with pride? Am I not a vessel prone to corruption? I shall not forget your love and the words and tears with which you encouraged me. Ah! That I were worthy of taking and acting on your maternal advice! I am most grateful to you. Rest and take your ease, my sister.

Spaniards who know these people will not be surprised to find that they are capable of such excellent reasoning and advice.

Once, when I was making a tour of inspection in Guatemala, traveling through mountainous country over dreadfully rough roads, messengers daily came to ask me when I would visit the towns of their lords, who lived far away; the lords who lived nearby came to visit me. These chiefs spoke so warmly to me, thanking me for the hardships I endured for their sake in that rugged land, that it made me very happy to hear them and lightened the great hardships I had in fact to bear on that tour. These chiefs said that they knew I had come for the sake of their wives and children and themselves, that they were all grateful to me and sent their greetings. Those who lived nearby brought their children, even the infants.

Spaniards unjustly charge these people with lack of intelligence and ingratitude. When they do give evidence of such traits, it is because they are stupefied with fear because of the cruelties that have been committed against them. That is why we Spaniards find it difficult to believe the good things we hear of them. Take an Indian, however primitive, who has not been corrupted. He may never before have seen or talked with a Spaniard, yet when he meets one, he will give him all the Spaniard asks for, and will do all he can to please him. And they are so intelligent that they can present their plea or petition to the very viceroy or the entire Audiencia, without flutter or nervousness, and all so well phrased that one might think they had lived all their lives in the press of affairs and amid very well-informed people.

I know that this and some other things I shall tell of are not altogether to the point. But I pray Your Majesty to pardon me, for all I do is with the intent of serving Your Majesty, that it may be understood how unjustified are those who defame these people. Moreover, I do not know whether I shall ever have another opportunity to say this. Withal, I do not say all that could be said, and what I have to tell is not overmuch.

The supreme lords the Indians called *tlatoques*, from the verb *tlatoa*, which means to speak, because they, as supreme lords, had civil and criminal jurisdiction, and the government and command of all their provinces and people whose lords they were. They had subject to themselves two other kinds of lords.

If, at the death of a ruler, the son, grandson, or whoever was to succeed was still a youth, it was customary for some old kinsman to govern in his place according to the rule whereby the closest relative who was qualified was chosen to act as regent. If there was no suitable relative, they chose some other principal, who was elected for this purpose and confirmed by another ruler. For Texcoco and Tacuba the confirmation was made by the ruler of Mexico, and for Mexico, by the rulers of Texcoco and Tacuba. The regent was, as it were, a tutor or guardian for the youthful new ruler. On the regent's death (for he held power during life) the successor named by the deceased ruler took office. This arrangement prevailed not only in regard to the supreme lord but in regard to the inferior lords of provinces in which they were supreme. Some maintain that if the guardian or assistant was a relative, he lost his post when the young ruler came of age, but that the latter continued to consult the former guardian in all the work of government. They also say that if the regent was not a relative, his power expired when the lord came of age. I found this was the case in a large town near Guatemala City. The age of majority for the ruler was thirty and over.

From the above it is evident that, aside from the ceremonies, almost all they did in the matter of succession and election of their rulers conformed to Natural Law, and in some degree to the Divine Law, and even to Civil and Canon Law, although they were ignorant of this. I could cite other things to show that these people are not so devoid of intelligence as some people assert. The same conclusion flows from many other things to be told of in this book and in my treatise on tributes.[17] As occasion offers, I shall single out and call attention to these things.

Lords of the second kind were called *tectecutzin* or *teules*. They were of many sorts and were named after their dignities and pre-eminencies, which, being very long and not to the point, I omit. They were like the *comendadores* of Spain, who hold encomiendas, some being of greater value and income than others.

It may be of interest to note that in naming dignities and offices, and also towns, mountains, forests, and the like, the Indians assigned names that indicated the quality or property of each place, its fertility or infertility, or the things in which it abounded. Thus they gave Michoacán its name because it was a land of many fish, and Tehuantepec was so named because it was a land of vipers, and so on.

The lords who were called tectecutzin, or teules, in the plural, held office for life, because the rulers promoted them to these dignities for their exploits in war or in the service of the state or the supreme lords. The rulers rewarded these lords with these dignities, just as Your Majesty grants an encomienda for life. Some of these dignities were high, others of an inferior kind.

The houses of these lords were named *teccalli*, which means the palace of such a lord (from *teccutli*, "lord," and *calli*, "house"). This teccutli or lord had command and dominion over certain people attached to that teccalli, and some had command over more people than others.

The benefits these lords received were these: Their people gave them personal service in their households and brought them fuel and water, the assignment of tasks being made by the lord. Their people also worked certain fields for the lords, the size of the fields depending upon the number of people. Because of this they were exempt from service to the ruler and from working his fields, and their only other obligation to the ruler was to serve in time of war, from which none was excused. In addition, the ruler furnished them with wages, meals, and lodgings, for they served as gentlemen in waiting in his palace.

These lords were responsible for the working of the fields, both for themselves and for their people, and they had overseers who saw to this. The lords also had the duty of looking after the people in their charge, of defending and protecting them. Thus these lords were appointed and intended to serve the general as well as their private good.

When one of these lords died, the ruler granted his dignity to one who merited it by his services, and a son did not succeed his father unless the ruler promoted him to this dignity. The rulers always inclined, however, to give preference to sons over others, if they deserved it. Otherwise they remained *pilles*, which means principales or hidalgos.

Lords of the third kind are called *calpullec*, or *chinancallec*, in the plural. This word means heads or elders of very ancient ancestry, and comes from *calpulli*, or *chinancalli* (both mean the same). A calpulli or chinancalli is a barrio of known people or an ancient lineage which holds its lands and boundaries from a time of great antiquity. These lands belong to the said kindred, barrio, or lineage, and they call such lands calpulli,[18] meaning the lands of that barrio or lineage.[19]

There are many such calpullec[20] or lineages or barrios in each province. The barrios assigned for life to lords of the second class also had their heads or calpulli. The lands these barrios possess they obtained in the distribution made when these people first came to this land. At that time each lineage or group obtained its shares or lots of land with their bounds, which were assigned to them and their descendants. These lands, which they call calpulli, they still possess today. They do not hold them individually but communally. Individuals cannot alienate their lots, but can enjoy their use for life and leave them to their sons and heirs.

Calpulli is the singular, calpullec the plural form of the word. Some of these calpullec or barrios or lineages are larger than others, and some possess more land than others, depending on the manner in which the ancient conquerors and settlers apportioned the lands among the various lineages. If a certain family dies out, the lands remain in the common ownership of the calpulli, and the head or chief elder assigns them to some other member of the same barrio who has need of them.

Thus the Indians never give these lands to a person who is not a member of the calpulli or barrio, just as the Israelites were not permitted to alienate their tribal lands and possessions. This, by the way, is one reason why some are disposed to believe that the natives of these regions descend from the people of Israel, since many of their ceremonies, practices, and customs conform with those of that people. Thus it is said that the language of Michoacán, which once was a great kingdom, has many Hebrew words; and this and almost all other Indian languages resemble Hebrew in their pronunciation. Men who have traveled in the provinces of Peru and other parts of the Indies make the same point about the rites and ceremonies of those regions. The calpullec of New Spain are what the Israelites called "tribes."

A barrio or calpulli might rent land to another barrio in order to meet the public and communal needs of the renting calpulli. Only for this reason, and no other, could land be rented. If it can be helped, the Indians never allow people of one calpulli to work the lands of another, that there may be no mixing of the two groups and that none may leave his lineage.

One reason why the Indians rented these lands, instead of allowing another calpulli to have them for nothing, was that sometimes the land they gave had already been cultivated. The rent was small or simply a part of the harvest, depending on the terms of the agreement. Members of one calpulli would rent from another because the land was better than that which they had or received from their calpulli or because their calpulli had no more land to distribute, or because they could work both their own and the rented fields.

If a member of one calpulli or barrio went to live in another, he lost the lands that had been assigned to him for cultivation. This is a most ancient custom among them, and one that is never broken or contravened in any way. The vacated fields remain the common property of the calpulli; and the chief elder distributes them among landless members of the barrio.

If some land is left vacant or becomes uncultivated in a calpulli, the Indians take great care lest the member of another calpulli encroach upon it. They engage in great litigation over this, each calpulli hotly defending its lands.

If a member of a calpulli has no land, the chief elder, in consultation with the other elders, gives him land in accordance with his needs, condition, and capacity to work it, and he can pass on this land to his heirs. The chief elder does nothing without consulting the other elders of the calpulli or barrio.

If a member of a calpulli held land and cultivated it, no one could intrude on this land, nor could the chief elder take it away and give it to someone else. If the land was not good, he could leave it and look for other land that was better and apply to the chief elder for such land. If this land was vacant and could be given without prejudice to another, it was given to him in the manner aforesaid.

A person who held land from his calpulli and did not work it for two years running through his own fault and negligence, or without such just cause, such as the condition of being a minor, an orphan, very old, or too ill to work, received warning that he must work it the next year or lose it to another. And so it was done.

Inasmuch as this land is the communal property of the calpullec or barrios, there has been much impropriety in allotting it to Spaniards. Let some Spaniard observe or learn that some of this land is not being cultivated, and he will apply to the governor for it. As a rule the individual who is appointed to look into the matter has little interest in the Indians' welfare. If by some chance a good Christian is appointed, the petitioner usually finds ways and means of having him replaced by another more satisfactory to himself, especially if there is some possibility of collusion or bribery, which is ever present. As a result, the examiner invariably submits the opinion that the land can be given to the petitioner without prejudice to another, because it is lying idle. It does no good for the people of the barrio or calpulli to contradict him, to offer proofs that the land has been cultivated, and to affirm that the land is being held in reserve for landless members or those who marry. The officials reply that it is all a clever ruse. Incorrect information of this kind was given to Your Majesty by some persons who seem to have had a personal interest in the question, as appears from a section of a letter that Your

Majesty sent to the Audiencia of Mexico City in September 1556.

To give a field or other land to a Spaniard is to cause great injury to the Indians. The Spaniards have taken their lands, pushed back their boundaries, and put them to an endless labor of guarding their fields against the Spaniards' cattle, yet those cattle continue to eat and destroy the Indians' crops. Sometimes an official will give away Indian land that is under cultivation or sowed, claiming that cultivation is a mere ruse designed to keep the land out of Spanish hands. That is why some Indian towns already are so diminished and encircled by Spanish farms that the natives have no space in which to plant. Elsewhere their fields are surrounded by cattle ranches from which they receive great injury, for their small plantings are destroyed or eaten by the cattle, which wander about without restraint. In vain do the Indians keep watch day and night over their fields. As a result they suffer need and hunger throughout the year. There are still other impediments to their sowing and enjoying the fruits of what they sow, as will presently be told.

Failure to comprehend that the calpullec or barrios hold their lands in common has been the cause of the Indians' having been left without enough land for their needs. This is especially true of towns that are situated near the Spanish towns or that have good land. Great mischief has been done by taking the land from the Indians. Great harm has also been done by herds belonging to the encomenderos, who always keep their cattle in the towns they hold in encomienda.

The commoners of these barrios or calpullec always have a head, and cannot conceive of being without such a head or elder. He must be one of them and not of another calpulli, nor a foreigner, for they would not suffer such a thing. He must be a principal, and capable of defending and protecting them. They choose him from among themselves and hold him for their lord; he is like the *pariente mayor* in Biscay or the Montaña.[21] He does not hold office by right of succession, for on the death of an elder they choose another, an old man whom they regard as best qualified because he is the wisest, most honorable, and ablest of all. If the deceased elder left an eligible son, they elect him, always choosing a relative of the deceased if suitable for the post.

This principal is responsible for guarding and defending the calpulli lands. He has pictures on which are shown all the parcels, and the boundaries, and where and with whose fields the lots meet, and who cultivates what field, and what land each one has. The paintings also show which lands are vacant, and which have been given to Spaniards, and by and to whom and when they were given. The Indians continually alter these pictures according to the changes worked by time, and they understand perfectly what these pictures show. It is also the business of the elder to give land to one who needs it; or, if his family has outgrown his parcel of land, to give him more. The elder is also responsible for protecting the people of the calpulli and for representing them before the Spanish judge and governors. The members of the calpulli also meet in the principal's house to deliberate concerning the group's needs and the payment of tribute, and to plan their festivals. This is very expensive for the elder, for to keep his guests happy and peaceful he must provide them with food and drink at these meetings, which are held frequently throughout the year.

I shall tell of the revenue that these lords receive, and how they defray the cost of entertaining the commoners, in my reply to the fourth article of the royal cedula.

One must understand the concord and unity that once prevailed in these calpulli if one would treat them justly and put an end to the confusion that now prevails in almost all of them. Today they are so divided that they can never return to the peace and order they once enjoyed. Because Spanish officials have made no effort to understand this communal system, they have adjudged to many Indians as private property lands which they held from their calpulli, simply because these persons could prove that they and their forebears had possessed and worked such land. These Indians have been cajoled into doing this by Spaniards and mulattoes and mestizos who exploit and profit by their folly. In vain do the principales contradict what these Indians say and explain with loud remonstrance that the land belongs to the calpulli. They are not heard, and this is a great injury to the other members of the calpulli, for the individuals to whom the land is adjudged as private property sell and alienate it to the prejudice of the calpulli.

Lords of the fourth class were such by virtue not of dominion or command, but of lineage. These lords were called *pipiltzin*, which is a general term denoting nobles, or as we would say in Castile, caballeros. This category included all the sons of the supreme lords or rulers, who were called *tlacopipiltzin* ("sons of rulers"), and all their grandsons and great-grandsons, whom they called *pipiltzintl*. This class included other persons called *tecquiuac*, who were hidalgos, sons of nobles holding important charges. All these and their successors were free of tribute because they were hidalgos and warriors. A certain number of them were always in attendance in the ruler's palace as ambassadors to various regions, and were reassigned by his order; they also served as his ministers and executors of justice. In addition to being free from tribute they had many other privileges, and the ruler provided them with wages and board. Now, however, they are reduced to tribute-payers, and are abased, miserable, and poor.

The second part of this article asks about the power and jurisdiction that these caciques and lords exercised in the time of their heathendom. I reply that the supreme lords had civil

and criminal jurisdiction, and appointed governors and officials
and ministers for the administration and execution of justice.
My replies to the questions that follow, being the third and
fourth parts of this article, will throw more light on the matter.

In order to reply to the third part of this article, which asks
what power these lords exercise at present, I must first explain their mode of government before and immediately after
the land was conquered by the Spaniards. For a better understanding of this, it should be noted that the Mexican kings
and their allies, the kings of Texcoco and Tacuba, left the
natural lords[22] of these provinces in command of all the land
they conquered and acquired. This was true of the lesser as
well as the supreme lords. They also allowed all the commoners to keep their land and property, and permitted them to
retain their customs and practices and mode of government.
The kings of Mexico, Texcoco, and Tacuba reserved for
themselves certain lands which were cultivated for them by
all the commoners. On these lands were grown the things that
each region yielded. The conquered people did this by way
of tribute and in acknowledgment of vassalship. The commoners brought the produce to the majordomos whom the

native ruler appointed for the collection of tribute, and these majordomos in turn took it to the persons sent thither for the purpose by the ruler of Mexico, or Texcoco, or Tacuba. Each person thus paid tribute to the ruler whose subject he had become and to whom he owed the duty of obedience and service in war. This was the general rule in all the provinces subject to the Confederacy. The former rulers preserved all their former authority and governmental power, with civil and criminal jurisdiction.

In the provinces not subject to the Confederacy, such as Michoacán, Metztitlán, Tlaxcala, Tepeaca, Cholula, Huexotcingo, and Yopitzinco, Acapulco, Acatepec, and others, government was in the hands of native rulers. The people brought them tribute consisting of the things they grew. The common and general mode of paying tribute consisted in the payment in kind of the things that were grown or made in the land, each man paying in the products of his craft or trade. The whole of what each man gave was small, representing little value and less labor. But since the number of people was very great, a large quantity of tribute was collected.

When New Spain was conquered by the Spaniards, this mode of government of the natives was retained and continued for some years. Moctezuma alone lost his kingdom and dominion, which were vested in the royal Crown of Castile. Some of his towns were given in encomienda to Spaniards. All the other lords of provinces, both those who were subject to him and those who were independent, including the rulers of Texcoco and Tacuba, possessed, ruled, and governed their lands, but they did this as representatives of Your Majesty or of encomenderos. These lords did not have as much land or as many vassals as they had once had, but the people brought them tribute of produce and other things as before the Conquest, and they were obeyed, feared, and respected. The towns that they retained also brought them tribute to give to Your Majesty and the encomenderos. Each ruler appointed persons to collect this tribute; and Your Majesty's officials in the Crown towns and the encomenderos in their towns received the tribute from the ruler.

Thus the ancient dignity and authority of the rulers were preserved, and they were well obeyed by their subjects, who served them in their ancient way by giving them tribute and service. Even today, in both Crown and encomienda towns, the Spaniards make the lords responsible for the collection of tribute. The Spaniards even harass the lords about this, although they are ruined and abased and are no longer obeyed by their subjects.

At that time the alcalde's rod of justice was unknown, and there were no *gobernadores* or alguaciles, those agents of abuse and ruination of the lords. One cause of their downfall has been the arbitrary action of the encomenderos, who stripped the lords of their authority if they would not do the Spaniards' will in regard to tribute and personal service. In the lord's place they would set up some macehual who would do all that was demanded of him. The example of the encomenderos was followed by the *calpisques*, persons appointed by the encomenderos to compel the people in their towns to give personal service daily, and to rent out their service to others, to send people to the mines, to compel payment of tribute, and to harass the lords and all the commoners in every way they could think of. These calpisques also removed and set up lords at their will and pleasure.

The result of having appointed all the alcaldes, *regidores*, alguaciles, and fiscales, of whom there are now a great many, is that many of them rob the common people, and do so brazenly, with no one to say them nay. The *escribano de gobernación* draws in a pile of money at the beginning of every year, for all these officials run to the governor for confirmation of their posts. Some or most of them fall ill or even die by the wayside, for they come from different climates and great distances (some journey 100 leagues and more). In this business they fritter away what little money they have or assess the people of their towns to defray the cost. It is most necessary that a stop be put to this going away for confirmation of office and that these Indian officials simply be chosen in their own towns. It would be still better, however, to do away with the alcaldes and alguaciles for the present, because they are good for nothing but to rob and harass the commoners, and make idlers instead of tribute-payers of them. Besides, today there are everywhere Spanish *alcaldes mayores, corregidores, tenientes,* and alguaciles who have civil and military jurisdiction over the Indians and Spaniards of their towns, but it would be very prudent to keep them out of the Indian towns, as will be explained below.

When the natural lords governed, then, they kept their people in peace and subjection. These lords sent for the tribute their subjects were to give, and took care that the communal fields and those of individuals were cultivated, and saw to it that each town provided the people needed for personal service to the Spaniards. They took into account the capacity of each town to do or give what was expected of it, they gave each man his due, and to them everyone applied for everything. That is the reason why today the lords are still troubled with such matters. All the towns were peaceful then, without intrigues and lawsuits. The lords possessed their remaining lands, tenants, lessees, and patrimonies in peace; they received their tribute according to ancient custom, as the lords they were, and in the manner they used to receive it through inheritance from their forebears or other just cause before they gave obedience to Your Majesty.

The land being well governed, then, and most conveniently for both the lords and their subjects, certain religious began urging with saintly zeal a certain course of action upon the

caciques and lords who came to confess to them, to discuss
with them matters of Christian doctrine or conscience, and
to give account of their rule and tributes. They urged these
lords to reduce the tribute they collected from their subjects
because the latter were also paying tribute to Your Majesty
and to his encomenderos in his royal name to compensate
them for providing the Indians with religious instruction and
priests, with ministers of justice, and with an Audiencia to favor and protect them. The lords agreed to do what these
servants of God advised them, for they were ever obedient to
the friars and held them in great respect. What they agreed
upon was put down in writing, and the lords signed it, that
there might be a record of their undertaking. This arrangement appeared very good to certain lawyers and other learned
persons, and they gave it their approval. The viceroy who
governed New Spain at that time also thought so well of it
that he determined to make a similar agreement with the
other lords of the land, and began to take steps to this end.

Yet this move, which was inspired by saintly zeal to help
the *macehuales* (who are the commoners and peasants), has
been the cause of their present turbulence and of the total
ruin and abasement of the natural lords. For subjects and vassals had a pretext for complaining of their lords, saying that
they did not do what they had agreed and had been ordered
to do. Moreover, Spaniards, mestizos, and mulattoes now began to appear among the Indians and incite them against their
lords, fishing in troubled waters. As a result, lords and commoners alike have been ruined spiritually and temporally,
while the men who threw them into turmoil prosper on their
misery.

Under the old system of government, then, the whole land
was at peace. Spaniards and Indians alike were content, and
more tribute was paid, and with less hardship, because government was in the hands of the natural lords. This state of

things continued until some of their subjects began to persecute the lords in the manner aforesaid. These ambitious, cunning troublemakers were egged on by Spaniards, mestizos,
and mulattoes who know the native language and go among
the Indians in order to rob them. Learning that the officials
who had jurisdiction over them would attend to their complaints if they were paid for it, the Indians sought to rob and
ruin their natural lords. In this manner began the plague of
lawsuits that they bring against each other in their towns,
subjects against lords throughout New Spain, towns against
towns, and provincial towns against provincial capitals. This
has given rise to much expense, the death of great numbers
along the roads, comings and goings to hear suits; and all the
while the Indians do not know what they are litigating about,
what they want, or why they carry their cases to the Audiencia. They succeed only in throwing away their money and
their lives, being egged on by men whose only interest is in
squandering the Indians' estates.

Lords and principales, and many commoners, together with
their wives and children, who always go with them to carry
provisions, have lost their lives. Many lords and principales
and macehuales have been sentenced to labor in the mines and
on public works, where they are left to die, lost and forgotten
by their wives and children.

Great turmoil in the provinces and towns and very great
confusion in everything have resulted from this. Lords and
commoners alike have been impoverished and ruined; all have
suffered great spiritual and temporal decline.

No harmony remains among the Indians of New Spain because the commoners have lost all feeling of shame as concerns their lords and principales, because they have risen up
against their lords and lost the respect they once had for them.
Withal, it is most necessary for the spiritual and temporal welfare of these people that they be well governed; and the

lords used to make them do what was needful and proper for both. For the common people are like children, and having lost their fear and sense of shame, they lose all the good that was implanted in them. Only those whom they fear and respect will they obey and only for them will they do what they must do. That is why the lords and principales are so necessary, for they alone understand and know how to deal with the Indian commoners.

This state of affairs has led to other evil consequences, easily divined from what was said above, and all because there is so little understanding of these people, of their character and condition. As for the outsiders who pretend affection for and interest in these people, their only real interest is in fomenting the present disorder and confusion.

Had these people not been allowed to engage in their senseless lawsuits, they would not have ruined each other, the deaths of many would have been avoided, and they would not find themselves in their present sorry state. Far better had it been to make them go to their caciques and lords, who know the truth of what each man claims, than to listen to troublemakers who were incited by others. This would have avoided many offenses to Our Lord: false swearing, hatreds, enmities, ruin of towns and provinces, and great wickedness on the part of those who urge them on in order to rob them, all leading to confusion so great that a solution now appears hopeless.

All this could have been avoided had there been observance of what Your Majesty provides in one of the New Laws, namely, that common law proceedings should not be allowed in suits between or with Indians, that such cases should not be drawn out but should be summarily determined, and that their customs should be observed when they are not clearly unjust. In addition, attorneys, lawyers, and solicitors should not be allowed to take part in the proceedings, for the facts in such cases are easily ascertained if they are not confused and muddied by lawyers and others of that breed. In dealing with Indians, it is easy to learn where the truth lies, for the lords and principales will state the truth with all candor. The very parties to a suit will speak the truth if they are not induced to act to the contrary by outsiders among them, by lawyers, or by others of that kind. Even if some do not tell the truth, there always are present many others who know and are willing to tell the facts of the case.

When these commoners rose up against their lords, they justified their ambition to destroy them and usurp their places by displaying a seeming zeal to aid the common people, for they stirred up the multitude by declaring their aim was to defend the commoners and free them from their lords. To this end they called upon the commoners to disobey their lords. Thus factions arose among the Indians, and since the lords had no means of defending themselves, they were quickly overthrown. The rebels and their corrupters always begin by making the vassals rise against their lords and stop giving the service and tribute they formerly gave. Thereby the lords are reduced to great poverty, abasement, and misery; they become stupefied, as it were, not daring to speak, not knowing what to say or to whom to complain or how to complain.

All men are against them, for all have been poisoned with false information to the effect that the lords rob and harass their subjects. As for the encomenderos, they care little, for they do not lose their tribute; indeed, the encomendero's tribute is paid better than before that he may keep silent and side with the rebels who hold the commoners in the hollow of their hands. In a single moment, then, the rebels tear down and ruin their lords, for all their wealth and sustenance consists in the service their vassals give them, and if this be withheld for even one day, the lords lack food and all the other necessities of life. Meantime their enemies, who are numerous, and who rob the people for themselves and for the benefit of their hangers-on who incite and assist them, never lack for anything, because they receive and enjoy what formerly was given to the lords, on top of all they can steal. In this way they go on ruining and annihilating the lords.

Another cause of the ruin of the lords has been the practice of naming them gobernadores of the provinces and towns of which they are the natural lords. Now their numerous rivals among their own people, aided by Spanish and mestizo allies, commenced suits against the lords, charging them with misgovernment, and were able to prove whatever served their ends. As a result the Audiencia deprived the lords of their offices, which meant the end of their authority, and appointed their subjects and rivals to these offices, thus making the lords subjects of subjects. These evils continue, and all is topsy-turvy, with the lords ruined and abased and commoners raised to high estate.

Many of the lords, seeing the power and swift rise of the rebels, followed their example and rose up with a part of their towns, allowing the rebels to do what they pleased in the others. Here lords and commoners alike rob and connive to be appointed governors, alcaldes, and regidores to help them in their robbery. These lords cater to the wishes of the multitude and the rebels and the Spaniards and mestizos who egg them on, and all steal and live by the sweat of the poor macehuales. And since all is turned topsy-turvy, these wretches soon achieve all their ends.

As a result the land has lost the splendor and majesty and good government it once enjoyed under its lords, without benefit of alcaldes, regidores, alguaciles, or gobernadores; for the lords were well obeyed and all did what was ordered and each did his duty. To this end the lords appointed persons who maintained order, causing less affliction than the Indians now suffer from all the ministers and rods of justice; the provinces and towns were united and peaceful, the lords were obeyed and esteemed. Now all has come to ruin because the lords are ruined and abased, and their authority, dominion, and system of government done away with.

Some Spaniards assert that the lords rob their subjects, and say that that is why certain persons have incited the macehuales against them and why the lords' dominion, vassals, tribute, tenants, and mayeques have been taken from them. (These mayeques are people who live on the lords' lands, and some have risen up and seized the land for themselves, while others give the lords only what they please, the lords meanwhile not daring to say a word for fear that these people will sue them and rise up against them.) There is no truth, however, in the unqualified statement that the lords rob their subjects. This is true only of the lords who have joined with the rebels to be able to live as they do, and of the commoners who have risen up and made themselves lords in the ways described above. These last are public and most harmful robbers, for they have usurped what is not theirs through inheritance. And because they fear that some day others will revolt against them and lay them low as they did their natural lords, they steal all they can as long as they remain in power; for when they fall, they will return to what they were at first. This conduct is the mark of the tyrant. And these people, who are improperly called caciques, lords, and principales, being naught but intruders, have caused the Spaniards to say that the lords are robbers.

The natural lords cherish and support their vassals, for they love them as their own, as their inheritance from their forebears. They fear to lose them and strive not to offend them lest they rise up against them, as have other vassals against their lords. Therefore the natural lords seek to ease their vassals' burdens, treat them like their own children, defend and protect them. Of such lords but a very few remain.

The lords who act in a contrary manner are the ones who have taken the way of the rebels, who do the will of agitators who steal and eat at the expense of poor folk who know not how to resist, do not understand what is in their interest, or believe those who say they are acting in their interest. The commoners have suffered great injury, yet never seek revenge or reprisal, and they do what they do because they are blinded by the desire of being without lords who correct them and compel them to live virtuously.

It was necessary for me to speak at such length about the lords and principales, indicating the difference among them, with their names and mode of succession, in order to comply with Your Majesty's order. Besides, when Your Majesty wrote to the Audiencias of those lands for information on the topics cited in the royal cedula, it was generally believed that the inquiry was being made for the purpose of ordering the reinstatement of the Indian lords in their dominion. If this were to be done (and it is proper and necessary that it should be done), it were useful to have set down here in such detail the dignities, lords, lordships, and their mode of succession. It were also well to know how they have been ruined and destroyed, and which lords ought to be restored to their former estate, and which should not be restored. This can easily be determined on the basis of the information given above.

It remains for me to reply to the question (the fourth part of this article) concerning the benefits in government and way of life that the Indians derived from the rule of their lords. Although the answer is already clear from what was said above, I shall tell more particularly what these benefits were. To do this satisfactorily I must trace the history of the subject from the time of the heathendom of these people to the present. This will enable me to add some detail to my replies to the second and third part of this article.

The benefits that the subjects derived from the rule of their lords were very great; they would be as great today if the same order existed. The lords looked after everything and saw that the Indians lived a proper life. The confusion and troubles of the present time were unknown. The lords saw that the commoners paid their tribute, that they cultivated their fields and worked at their crafts, that they assembled to be assigned to service for the Spaniards. As a result the misdeeds and troubles that now abound were avoided. The lords also saw that the Indians attended classes in religious instruction and sermons, and they put down their vices and drunkenness.

Now all is changed, chaos prevails, and some of the lords carry on as scandalously as the commoners. Formerly, if a lord misbehaved, he took care that the commoners did not see it, lest he give a bad example.

To make my meaning plainer, I shall describe their system of government and justice as it functioned before the land was conquered by the Spaniards and for some years thereafter. I set down what I heard from some religious of advanced age who personally witnessed the things I tell of.

There were three principal lords in New Spain, to whom almost all the important provinces and towns of the land were subject. They were the rulers of Mexico, Texcoco, and Tlacopan, or Tacuba; and better order and justice prevailed in their dominions than in all the other states. There were judges who functioned in the manner of an Audiencia in each of their cities. Since there was little or no difference in their laws and administration of justice, it will suffice to describe the order that existed in one kingdom. I shall tell in particular of the arrangements in the realm of Texcoco.

In Texcoco there was a ruler named Nezahualcoyotl [23] who reigned forty-two years; he was a man of good judgment who ordained many laws for the government and preservation of his extensive kingdom. He was succeeded by a son named Nezahualpilli [24] who reigned forty-four years and ordained additional laws, for he knew that time worked changes and that new problems required new solutions. Father and son ruled so well and maintained such good order in the land that the rulers of Mexico and Tlacopan regarded the kings of Texcoco as their fathers, both because of their close kinship with those kings and because of their esteem for them. Accordingly the rulers of Mexico and Tlacopan governed their states with the same system and laws that Nezahualcoyotl and Nezahualpilli had established; they even sent many cases to Texcoco to be tried in its courts. In matters of war, however, Mexico always had ascendancy, and only there were such affairs discussed and settled.

These three rulers had many provinces subject to them, and each province was represented in the city of its ruler, Mexico, Texcoco, or Tlacopan, by two judges; they were men of good judgment, especially chosen for the purpose, and some were relatives of the ruler. Their salaries consisted in produce from fields set aside for them by the ruler; these fields were cultivated for them and provided support for them and their families. On this land lived Indians who cultivated and took care of the fields, keeping part of the produce for themselves. These Indians also gave the judges service and fuel and water for their houses; this took the place of the tribute commoners had to give the ruler. When a judge died, such land passed to his successor in office, for the fields together with the people who lived on them and cultivated them were applied to this purpose.

In the rulers' houses were certain rooms and halls raised seven or eight steps from the ground, like mezzanines; here the numerous judges held court. The judge of each province, town, and barrio had his own place, and to this place came the subjects of each. Here, too, were heard and decided cases involving connubial disputes and divorce.

When a divorce case was heard—which was rare—the judges attempted to reconcile the parties. They harshly scolded the guilty party, and they asked the pair to recall the good will with which they had entered on marriage; they urged them not to bring shame on their parents and relatives who had promoted the marriage; the judges also reminded them that people would point the finger of blame at them, for it would be known that they had been married. Many other things the judges said in order to reconcile them.

The friars who have lived in that land a long time declare that after the Indians came under Spanish rule they lost the good order and harmony they once had, that lawsuits and divorces have grown much more frequent, and that disorder and confusion reign everywhere.

Once I asked an Indian principal of Mexico City why the Indians now were so prone to litigation and evil ways, and he said to me: "Because you don't understand us, and we don't understand you and don't know what you want. You have deprived us of our good order and system of government; that is why there is such great confusion and disorder. The Indians have thrown themselves into litigation because you egged them on to it, and they follow your lead. But they never get what they want, for you are the law and the judges and the parties to the suit, and decide matters as you please.

Indians who live apart from you and have no dealings with you do not litigate but live in peace. When we were pagans, there were very few lawsuits, men told the truth, and cases were decided very quickly. There was no difficulty in determining which party had justice on its side, and today's delays and snares were unknown."

Another Indian, hearing that a Spanish *visitador* was on his way to that land, said: "It's not for our good; judges and *visitadores* daily come to us, we don't know why. Heaven's justice alone is good."

Another said that earthly justice was like a scrawl, and that Heaven's justice alone was straight and good.

Another Indian, scolded by a Spaniard who called him thief, liar, and other offensive names, said: "You have set us the example." Aged Indians say that with the entrance of the Spaniards all was turned upside down, that the Indians have lost their ancient justice and harmony, and that liars, perjurers, and adulterers are no longer punished as they once were because the principales have lost the power or freedom to chastise delinquents. This, say these Indians, is the reason why there are so many lies, disorders, and sinful women. They say many other things, which it would take me too long to tell.

The Indian judges of whom I spoke would seat themselves at daybreak on their mat dais, and immediately begin to hear pleas. The judges' meals were brought to them at an early hour from the royal palace. After eating, they rested for a while, then returned to hear the remaining suitors, staying until two hours before sundown. Appeals from these judges were heard by twelve superior judges, who passed sentence in consultation with the ruler.

Every twelve days[25] the ruler held a council or conference with all the judges to discuss difficult cases or important criminal cases. Every case that the ruler had to consider was first carefully examined and the facts ascertained. Witnesses

VALLEY OF MEXICO

SCALE ⊢———⊣ MILES

told the truth not only from respect for the oath they swore but from fear of the judges, who were very skillful in getting at the facts and displayed much wisdom in their questioning and cross-examination. They punished very severely one who did not tell the truth.

The judges received no fee, large or small, and accepted no gift from any person, great or humble, rich or poor. They showed great rectitude in their judgments; the same was true of all the other ministers of justice.

If it was discovered that a judge had accepted a gift, or drank to excess, or was negligent in something, the other judges reprimanded him sharply among themselves, if it was only a small matter. If he did not mend his ways, at the third offense they ordered his hair to be cropped and stripped him of his office, to his great shame, for the Indians regarded this as a great ignominy. If the offense was a serious one, the ruler deprived the judge of his office forthwith. A judge once favored a principal in a suit and gave an untruthful account of the matter to the ruler of Texcoco. The king[26] ordered the judge hanged and judgment reversed in favor of the commoner; and so it was done.

The judges had at their sides scribes who were very skillful painters. These painters indicated in native characters who were the parties to suit, what it concerned, and the various claims, witnesses, and the finding or sentence. The only delay or appeal allowed was an appeal to the ruler in consultation with the appeal judges. A suit could not continue longer than eighty days, the period within which the general conference (to be explained presently) must be held. Once a decision was handed down, none dared reopen the case. It was not like the situation at present, when suits drag on endlessly, each new judge beginning the case anew, especially when each judge hears it by himself, apart from the other members of the Audiencia.

What is certain is that Indians who have preserved their natural simplicity and do not have dealings with Spaniards or mestizos (who incite the Indians to litigate) are very shy of lawsuits. I observed this very clearly during a tour of inspection I once made in Guatemala. Some Indians came to ask me for the return of land that some other Indians had taken from them. I summoned these Indians, and one of them said, "It's true, I entered his land because he was not working it." I explained that the owner wanted it back, and the Indian replied, "All right, give it to him." Another Indian said, "When I entered his land, it was waste, and now I have planted it with cacao trees" (or some other trees); "let us divide it between us." And the owner said that that was agreeable to him, and that I should give them a paper to record the deal. Not another word had to be written, and they kept that agreement as if it were a sacred law. This sort of thing happened to me many times a day.

I observed other things that revealed the great simplicity and goodness of the Indians. These people will not lie unless they are led astray. This is true of an Indian who commits some offense. If you take his confession at once after the deed, he will tell the truth very plainly. But let someone get into the jail and speak to him before he confesses, and you will never get the truth out of him, for he will stick to the version in which he has been coached.

To the twelve appellate judges mentioned above were attached twelve persons who were chief constables, as it were, authorized to seize principales, and they went to other towns to make arrests as ordered by the ruler or the judges. Other persons served as summoners and messengers, and they carried out their errands with the greatest diligence, by night or day, in rain, snow, or hail, without the slightest delay.

There were ordinary judges in the provinces and towns who had jurisdiction in cases of lesser importance. They could arrest offenders and could examine and do preliminary work on complex cases, leaving final decisions to the general councils that were held together with the ruler every four months (their month had twenty days). To this council people came from all the land to appear before the ruler, and here the difficult and criminal cases were decided. This council sat for ten or twelve days. In addition to deciding cases, the council conferred about all matters touching the whole kingdom, in the manner of a Cortes.

The Indians had their laws, and death was the penalty for many offenses. At one time they used to stone adulterers to death, but this penalty was later changed to death by strangling or some other means. They diligently sought to learn if any had committed sodomy and punished this offense by death, for they held it a grave sin and one seen only among beasts. Intercourse with animals was unknown among them.

They executed the penalty of the law strictly, making exception of none, and they did not even spare their own children. A ruler of Texcoco[27] ordered his son put to death because he had relations with one of the ruler's wives, and the woman was also slain in conformity with the law, which imposed the death penalty on both parties. For the same reason another king of Texcoco[28] ordered four of his sons put to death, one after another, and the four wives together with them. In Tlaxcala a great lord of many towns and vassals, brother of that Maxiscatzin[29] who was very valorous and second of the four lords of Tlaxcala and captain general of the whole province, committed adultery. The lords of Tlaxcala, Maxiscatzin among them, met in council and decided that the adulterer should die for his offense, for none might break the law with impunity; and so the sentence was executed on him and the woman.

One who entered a place where young maidens were reared in seclusion incurred the penalty of death, and the girl who admitted a man suffered the same fate. A son of a great lord scaled a wall and entered the house wherein the daughters of the king of Texcoco were reared and spoke to one of them. He stood as he did this, and nothing more happened. The ruler learned of it, but the young man was warned and hid so that he could not be taken. But the ruler ordered that the maiden, his own beloved daughter, be strangled. Many prayed him to pardon her, but he would not relent, saying that he must not break the law in anyone's behalf, for thereby he would set a bad example to other lords and dishonor himself. He added that he would be regarded as unjust if he enforced the law against his vassals but not against his own children, and that it was not right that so evil a deed should go unpunished.

This same ruler, named Nezahualpilli, had a married daughter of his put to death because she committed adultery, and the adulterer with her. The sentence was carried out, although the husband was willing to pardon her, for, said the king, men would say that the husband had pardoned his wife out of deference to the king and not of his own free will. The maidens and women of the palace were ordered to attend these punishments, and the reason for the punishment was explained to them in order to dissuade them from such offenses. However, younger girls were not summoned lest they be moved to reflect on the vice that had been committed. Death was the penalty for creating a scandal, especially in the markets or other public places. Death was also the penalty for pandering, and was enforced with great strictness.

They had public prisons for offenders.

No one could drink wine[30] without permission from the lords or judges, and its use was allowed only to the sick and to persons more than fifty years of age. The Indians said that aged persons needed the wine because their blood was turning cold, but they could drink only three small cups at a meal.

One must drink a great deal of this wine in order to get drunk. There was general permission at weddings and festivals for all persons over thirty to drink two cups. Men who transported wood and heavy stones had the same license because it was such hard labor. A woman who gave birth to a child could drink the first few days after the birth, but not thereafter. Many persons would not drink at all, in sickness or health. Lords, principales, and warriors considered it shameful to drink, and regarded one who got drunk as infamous. The penalty for drunkenness for both men and women consisted in cropping the offender's hair publicly, in the market place, after which his house was razed. The Indians said that one who got drunk and lost his senses did not deserve to have a house in the town and to be counted among its citizens. He was also removed from all public offices and was disqualified to hold office in the future.

I have cited these penalties because some learned friars had scruples about punishing Indians for drunkenness and so consulted some other religious, in Spain, on the matter. These religious opined that since Spaniards were not punished for drunkenness it was not right to punish Indians for the same offense, especially if it carried no penalty in the time of their heathendom. But from what was said above it is clear that this offense was punished very severely.

Spaniards, including some religious (but not those who have lived a long time in that land and made a deep study of Indian customs), make the great mistake of saying that in the time of their heathendom the Indians enjoyed much license in the matter of drinking. They say and believe this because after the Spaniards conquered the land the Indians took to drinking wine without restraint. Aged Indians declare that their people grew bold in this and other ways because the authority and power of the native judges to punish them came to an end. Spanish judges, they say, are not so zealous in inquiring into and punishing their offenses. Little by little the authority and activity of the Indian justices declined until it was completely dissolved, and therewith ended the good order and way of life the Indians once enjoyed.

Much responsibility for the present excesses in drinking on the part of the Indians falls on those Spaniards and mestizos, men and women, who for love of an easy life have devoted themselves to making the native wine. These people lure the Indians into their homes and keep them there until they have gotten them drunk, for the Indians will pay whatever is asked for the wine. [After getting them drunk they take the Indians' clothes and money and throw the drunken ones in the street. Later, if questioned by the natives, they claim these possessions were taken in the street, and the Indians dare not complain lest they be punished for drunkenness.[31]] The profits of this business are great, for the cost of making the wine is small and they sell it at what price they please. However numerous, excommunications and other penalties for selling wine to the Indians have not put a stop to this traffic.

The Indians also had laws forbidding marriage in certain cases. They considered it unseemly and impermissible for a marriage proposal to come from the woman's side; the initiative must always come from the man's side. Certain old women, who were held in honor, acted as matchmakers. The parents or relations never accepted the first overture, though they might be perfectly willing. Instead they politely rejected the invitation, but did not dismiss the matchmakers and entertained them as guests. After agreement had been reached and the marriage had taken place, the couple retired to a room to do penance and fast for four days before cohabiting. In some places they fasted and remained in seclusion for twenty days.

The Indians regarded the keeping of concubines as scandalous, but tolerated it as a lesser evil if the man and the woman were single, for the penalty for adultery was death. If a man wanted a girl for a concubine, he applied to her parents, but not in the same way as for a marriage proposal. In the former case he asked for the girl, saying he wanted to have a son by her. Accordingly, when the first son was born, the girl's parents asked the youth to marry her or else set her free, for he now had a son. He then either married her or returned her to her parents, in which case they did not cohabit again.

The Indians also had laws relating to wars. They regarded the killing of a merchant or a royal messenger as legitimate cause for war. When a ruler wished to discuss war, he convened all the elders and warriors and gave them to understand that he proposed to wage war on such-and-such a province. He explained his reason, and if it was one of the causes cited above, all said that he was right and the cause just. But if it was a trivial cause, twice or thrice they advised against war, saying there was no reason or cause for it, and sometimes the ruler accepted their advice. But if he summoned them again and again, and insisted on war, they yielded to his importunities out of the respect they bore him, saying they would do his will, for they had told him their opinion and disclaimed responsibility in the matter.

If war was decided on, they sent certain shields and blankets to the people on whom they proposed to make war, to let them know of it. Having received the message and declaration of war, the people of that province assembled to deliberate on what they should do. If they determined that they could defend themselves, they prepared for war; but if they thought themselves too weak to resist, they collected gold ornaments, featherwork, and other presents and went out on the road with these gifts to yield to the invader.

Towns that surrendered peacefully gave tribute as friends and responded to calls for aid in the wars of their conquerors.

Towns that surrendered after defeat in war had to pay greater tribute.

If a principal who had been taken prisoner by the enemy made his escape and returned to his people, they immediately ordered that he be put to death. They said that since he had not been man enough to resist and die in battle he should have died a prisoner, for this was more honorable than to return home as a fugitive.

They also had laws concerning the making of slaves, and others that regulated buying and selling. The charging of interest was unknown among them. Loans were made on the basis of a pledge to return the thing lent or the deposit of security.[32] They practiced many mechanical arts with great skill and harmony.

Lords, principales, and commoners alike showed much vigilance and zeal in rearing, instructing, and punishing their children. Mothers generally (and this was true even of the wives of lords) nursed their children if they were able. If not, they sought a wet nurse,[33] and to test her milk they put a few drops on a fingernail; if it was too thick to run, they considered it good. The mother or wet nurse did not change her diet when she began to suckle a child; some ate meat, others healthful fruit. A child was suckled for four years. Nursing mothers felt such tenderness for their sucklings that they refrained as much as possible from having intercourse with their husbands in order to avoid becoming pregnant. If a woman was widowed and left with a suckling child, she would on no account marry again until the child was weaned; to do the contrary was regarded as very disloyal. Children of rulers were reared on a uniform diet, and great care was taken with their eating.[34]

When a ruler's son reached the age of five, he was sent to the temple to serve there and to be instructed in what pertained to the service of the gods. The priests brought him up with much care and diligence, and he must be first in everything. A ruler's son who was not very diligent in temple service was punished severely. He remained in this service until he married or was of age to go to war.

A ruler's daughter was reared with much discipline and propriety, with great solicitude and care on the part of her mother, nurse, and elder brothers. When she reached the age of four, they impressed on her the need for being very discreet in speech and conduct, in appearance and bearing. Many daughters of rulers never left home until the day of their wedding, but some few were sent to the temple because their mothers had promised it to the gods in childbirth or some illness. A ruler's daughter went about in the company of many elderly women, and she walked so modestly that she never raised her eyes from the ground; if she was careless in this, her duennas immediately made signs to her. She never spoke in the temple, save to say the prayers she had been taught; she must not speak while eating, but must keep absolute silence. The rule that a man, even a brother, must not speak to an unmarried woman was observed as strictly as if it were law.

The palaces of the rulers were large buildings. Because of the dampness the rooms were raised an estado or more off the ground, forming entresols of a kind. Each palace possessed vegetable and flower gardens, and the women's apartments were by themselves. The maidens could not go out to the gardens without guards. If they took a single step out the door, they were harshly punished, especially if they had reached the age of ten or twelve. Maidens who raised their eyes from the ground or looked behind them were also punished cruelly; the same was done to girls who were careless or lazy. They were taught how to speak to the ruler's wives and to other persons, and were punished if they showed themselves negligent in this. They were constantly admonished to heed the good counsel they received.

When they reached the age of five, their nurses began teaching them to embroider, sew, and weave, and never permitted them to be idle. They had definite hours when they could divert themselves in the presence of their mothers, nurses, and guards. A maiden (even a child) who stopped work without permission was punished. Nurses who neglected the training or punishment of their charges were imprisoned. The nurses had to be as if deaf, blind, and mute with regard to all that went on in the palace.

The nurses made the ruler's daughters work from morning until late in the day, lest idleness make them dull; they made them keep themselves clean and wash themselves often with great modesty. If someone accused a maiden of being derelict in something, she could clear herself by swearing it was not so, saying, "Does not our Lord God see me?" and naming their chief idol. Therewith she was acquitted, for none dared swear falsely, fearing that the god by whom they swore would punish them with some grave infirmity.

When a ruler wished to see his daughters, they came as if in procession, a matron coming before as guide, and attended by many people. They never came without the father's permission. Entering the chamber, they stood before their father, who ordered them to sit; then the guide spoke and greeted the ruler in the name of all his daughters. Meanwhile they sat very silently and modestly, even the smallest child. The guide gave the father the presents of roses and other flowers, and fruit, they had brought him, the embroidery they had woven for him, and cotton mantles which they use for clothing and which were very finely made.

The father spoke to his daughters, advising them to be good and heed the counsel of their mothers and teachers, to show much respect and obedience for them, and to work carefully. The maidens made no other reply than to approach him one by one and make a low obeisance, after which they departed. None laughed in his presence, but all acted very so-berly and modestly, and so they left, very pleased with what their father had told them.

The other principales and the common people also gave much attention to rearing and admonishing their children. They kept them from the ways of vice, made them serve the idols they regarded as gods, and took them along to the tem-ples. They also saw to it that their children pursued the em-ployment for which they showed ability or inclination. As a rule, however, a son followed the occupation of his father. Fathers punished their sons cruelly if they proved mischievous. If a son absented himself from the parental home, he was brought back two, three, or more times; but if he proved in-corrigible, his parents gave him up as wicked. The majority of such boys ended up by becoming slaves.

Fathers warned their sons severely against lying, and a fa-ther punished a son who committed this offense by pricking his lip with a maguey spine. As a result, boys grew up accus-tomed to telling the truth. Aged Indians, asked why their peo-ple lie so much nowadays, reply that it is because falsehood goes unpunished. They say another cause is that the Spaniards are so haughty and cruel that the Indians are afraid to say anything that will displease them, and therefore say "yes" to everything, no matter how incredible. Besides, the Indians neither trust nor understand the Spaniards; as a result, if a Spaniard asks an Indian some question, the latter is always wary, and rarely replies directly or openly. The Indians say they learned this trait from the Spaniards.

There were many young men among them. Sons of rulers and the sons of some principales were trained in the temples. The others were brought up in Houses of Youth maintained by the barrios.[35] Each house was headed by an elder who as-sembled the boys and had charge of their instruction. The youths brought fuel to the temples, repaired them, and did the same for the house in which they stayed. They also cultivated fields set apart for the support of their house.

Their teachers saw to it that they fasted at the appointed times, punished severely all their offenses, and kept them from idleness. There were definite hours when the teachers admonished and reproved the youths and showed them where they had gone astray. Boys who showed special aptitude went to war, and the others went along to watch and learn from them how to fight. So well trained were they that a boy would never give excuses for not doing what he was ordered to do, but quickly did it without any delay.

When the young men were of age to marry, which was at the age of twenty or slightly over, they requested permission of their elder. One who married without seeking such permission was regarded as an ingrate and poorly bred. This consent was in addition to that which he secured of his parents. Marriage without parental permission was very rare, for it was considered an infamous thing.

If a youth was poor, he was aided by his house at the time of marriage with produce from its storehouse. If he was the son of a rich man, on his departure from the house his father gave presents to the house and to the captain who had taken care of him.

During the time the boys were in such a house, they occasionally received permission to go for a few days to help their fathers, if they were farmers; and they brought back to the center some of the crop they had harvested. They received a Spartan training, for they ate but a little hard bread, and they slept with little covering and half exposed to the night air in rooms and quarters open like porches. The Indians used to say that since warfare was so continuous it was proper that the youths be inured to hardships.

If a youth did not marry after having passed the age for marriage, he was dismissed from the house, especially in Tlaxcala. However, almost none refused to marry when admonished to do so.

When a youth departed from the house in which he had been brought up, the elder made a long speech in which he told the youth to be very diligent in serving the gods and to remember what he had learned there, to work hard to support his wife and household, not to neglect the rearing of his children, and to be brave in war. If he did these things, the gods would aid him. He should respect his parents, honor the aged, and follow their advice.

When a youth married, he was inscribed in the register of the married men, who also had their group leaders and captains; for all were assigned to a group, for tribute payment and other purposes, with great system and regularity. Although the land was thickly populated, there was a record of every person, great and small, and each carried out the orders of his superior without fail.

Parents not only reared their children with much discipline and care but also gave them much good advice. Indian principales have preserved these counsels in their picture writings. A religious[36] of very long residence in that country, and well acquainted with the Indians, translated these speeches from their language. He says that he had some principales write down the substance of the speeches in the Indian language, and they did this without his being present. They took the text from their picture writings, which they understand very well; and he did not change a word, save to divide the material into paragraphs and sentences for a better understanding of the meaning. He asked them to take out the names of their gods, substituting the name of the true God and of Our Lord. I give these speeches here verbatim to show that the Indians are not so dull-witted as some would make them out to be. I pray Your Majesty to pardon me if he feels this material is not pertinent to the things about which Your Majesty wishes to be informed. I have done all with the intent of serving Your Majesty, in the belief that Your Majesty will be served by knowing these things, for they are true and verified by servants of God. The speeches follow:

Oh my very precious son, born and reared in the world through God, on whom we your parents and relatives set eye at birth: You have emerged like a chick from its shell, and as the chick prepares for flight so you prepare yourself for labor. We do not know how long God will wish us to enjoy you. Commend yourself to God, oh son, for he created you and is your father who loves you more than I. Send up your sighs to Him day and night, and place your thoughts in Him. Serve Him with love, and He will reward you and free you from all danger. Have much reverence for God and His things, and pray devoutly before Him and prepare yourself for the festivals. One who offends God will die a bad death, and his will be the fault.

Revere and greet your elders; console the poor and the afflicted with good works and words.

Honor and love, serve and obey, your parents, for the son who does not do this will not succeed.

Love and honor all, and you will live in peace.

Follow not the madmen who honor neither father nor mother; they are like animals, for they will neither take nor hear advice.

Take care, son, that you do not mock the old, the sick, the maimed, or one who has sinned. Do not insult or abhor them, but abase yourself before God and fear lest the same befall you.

Give poison to none, for you will offend God in His creature to your own shame and harm, and you yourself will die therefor.

Be honest and well behaved, son, and do not annoy others or go where you are not invited, lest you make trouble and be regarded as ill bred.

Do not hurt another, and be not an adulterer, or lewd, for this is a wicked vice that destroys those who indulge in it and gives offense to God.

Do not set a bad example, or speak indiscreetly, or interrupt the speech of another. If someone does not speak well or coherently, see that you do not the same; if it is not your business to speak, be silent. If you are asked something, reply soberly and without affectation or flattery or prejudice to others, and your speech will be well regarded.

Son, do not give yourself to idle gossip or jesting or lies. Cause not discord where peace prevails, for such things bring ruin and shame to him who causes it.

Be not a gadabout, stroll not through the streets, and do not stay overlong in the market place or the bath, lest the demon gain mastery over you and swallow you up.

Be not too fine in dress, for this is a sign of little sense.

Wherever you go, walk with peaceful air, and do not make wry faces or improper gestures, else you will be regarded as giddy, and such things are bonds of the devil.

Do not seize another by the hand or by his clothing, for this is a mark of a giddy nature.

Watch well where you are going, and if you meet others, do not walk in front of them.

If you are entrusted with some charge that may be designed to test you, decline it politely, and do not accept though it advantage another, and men will think you sober and prudent.

Do not enter or leave before your elders, and do not cross in front of them. Always give them precedence, and do not speak before them or in any way infringe on their seniority save when others set you some task, for otherwise you will be thought to be ill bred.

Be not forward in eating or drinking. Be civil to others, for humility helps to attain the gift of God and one's elders.

When you eat, give part of your food to a needy person who comes to you, and you will win grace thereby.

If you are eating with others, lower your head and do not eat ravenously and noisily, for men will think you giddy. And do not finish eating before the others who dine with you, lest you give offense.

If you are given something, no matter how small, do not reject it or show annoyance, and do not think you deserve more, for you will lose favor before God and men.

Commend yourself wholly to God, for all good comes from His hand, and you do not know when you will die.

I seek that which will advantage you. Suffer and hope. If you would marry, tell us first, for you are our son, and must not marry without first informing your parents.

Be not a gambler or thief, for the one comes from the other, and is a great offense; thereby you will avoid seeing yourself defamed in the squares and market places.

Follow the good, my son, for as you sow so will you reap; and live by your labor. Thus will you live happy and with praise, and your kindred will love you.

Life in this world is filled with hardships; it is not easy to satisfy one's needs. With hardships have I reared you. Never shall I abandon you, and I have never done anything to cause you shame.

Do not gossip if you would live in peace, for gossip is a cause of offense and quarrels. Keep to yourself, son, what you overhear; let it be heard from another and not from you. But if you are asked to tell what you overheard and cannot decline, tell the truth without adding anything, good or bad.

Keep secret what took place before you. Be not talkative, for this is a serious fault; and if you tell a lie, it will not go unpunished. Be silent, for chattering brings no gain.

If someone sends you with a message to another, and that one complains or gossips to you, or speaks evil of the man who sent you, do not return annoyed and do not let the answer be known to him who sent you. If he asks how you fared, reply with mild and peaceable words, keeping silent about the evil things you heard, lest you set them by the ears so that they come to wound or kill each other. Then will you say sorrowfully, "Ah, that I had not said it!" But men will not absolve you and will hold you for a troublemaker.

Have nothing to do with another man's wife. Live cleanly, for you have but one life to live in this world, and life is short and filled with hardships, and all comes to an end.

Offend no man, and take away no man's honor. May God grant you merits, for it is for God to give to each what He pleases. Take what He gives you, son, and thank Him. If it be much, do not be proud or puffed up, but humble yourself and your merits will be greater and others will have no occasion to murmur. Do not take what belongs to another, for you will offend God.

When someone is speaking to you, keep your feet and hands still, and do not move them about, or look here and there, or get up and sit down; for if you do, you will appear giddy and ill bred.

If you live with another, be careful to serve him diligently and seek to please him. Thus will you get what you need, and it will go well with you with whomsoever you live. But if you do the contrary, you will be sent away.

Son, if you do not heed your father's advice, you will come to a bad end, and the fault will be yours.

Be not proud of what God gives you, and do not scorn others, for you will offend the Lord who honored you.

If you prove to be such as you should be, men will regard you as a model to use in comparing and punishing others. In giving you these counsels, son, I comply with my duty as a father who loves you; take care that you do not reject my advice, for it will bring you good.

Reply of the Son

My father: You have done great good to me, your son. Haply, I shall make some use of the words that issue from your bowels, the bowels of a father who loves me. You say that you have now complied with your duty and that I shall have no excuse if I do not heed your advice. You will not be blamed, my father; mine will be the guilt, for you have given me good advice; but consider that I am still a youth who does not understand what is best for him. Since I am your flesh and blood, you must not cease to advise me; do not be satisfied with this one time. I trust that you will give me other paternal advice with the same loving spirit; and do not abandon me if I do not immediately act upon it. With these brief words, my father, I reply to your good counsel. God will repay you the good you did me.

Such were the homilies that principales and merchants addressed to their sons. Peasants and commoners advised their sons as follows:

My son: May it be well with you all the time you live on earth, daily awaiting sickness or punishment from the hand of God. Hardship by day and by night is the lot of His people.

Do not sleep overlong or neglect the service of him with whom you live, lest you lose his favor.

You are endowed with all that you need in your occupation. Flee not the labor to which God has assigned you, for you did not merit more; so be content with your estate.

By serving another in some occupation you aid your people and the Lord, and you will gain what you require to rear your children.

Do what pertains to your office. Labor, sow and plant your trees, and live by the sweat of your brow. Do not cast off your burden, or grow faint, or be lazy; for if you are negligent and lazy, you will not be able to support yourself or your wife and children. Diligence and good service refresh the body and delight the soul.

See that your wife is diligent in all that pertains to your work and household.

Advise your children what they must do, and let both of you, as parents, give your children good counsel that they may live without offense to God or yourselves.

Son, fear not the labor in which you pass your days; for with it you gain your food and the means of rearing your children.

Again I tell you, son, to take care of your wife and household. Labor so that you can console your relations and people who come to your house, receiving them with a portion of your poverty. And they will know the kindness that is in you, and thank you for it, and do the same for you.

Love and show charity; be not proud, and do no harm to others; be well bred and civil. And you will be loved and well regarded.

Do not hurt or offend another. Do your duty, and be not puffed up on that account; for you will anger God and will not escape punishment.

If you do not travel the road of honesty, how can God fail to strip you of what He gave you, to your abasement and injury?

Obey your elders, flee the idle, and follow in the way of the industrious; else you will live in need and pain.

Do not grumble or answer rudely your parents or those who counsel you to labor; for you will cause them pain.

If you be rude, you will get along with none and will be able to live with none. All will reject you, and you will destroy yourself and your wife and children; for you will find no place to receive you and will lack the means to live, and yours will be the fault.

If you are ordered to do something, listen attentively and reply civilly. If you can, do it; if not, tell the truth, do not lie. For if you cannot do it, they will assign it to another, and then they will not hold you responsible.

Be not an idler or loafer; live quietly and do not wander from place to place, so that you may leave a house for your wife and children when you die. Thus you will leave the world consoled; for you will have left them a place to live, and this is enough. Son, heed my advice.

Reply of the Son

My father: I thank you very much for the advice you have given me with loving words. Great will be my fault if I do not heed such good advice. What am I but a poor macehual who lives in a poor house, a servant, a poor peasant? God has done me great mercy in remembering me so that you, my father, might give me such good counsel; where else may I hear such goodly speech; the precious words of your heart are beyond price or comparison. Ah that I were worthy of heeding them well! Such counsel is not to be abandoned or forgotten. I have been much consoled by it, and you have done your duty, the duty of a loving father.

Mothers did not neglect to admonish and advise their daughters. When a ruler married off a daughter, her mother addressed a very long homily to her before she left the house. She told her daughter that she should love and serve her husband, that he might love her in turn, and said:

My daughter: Consider that you are about to go with your husband, that you are now leaving us. You know it is customary for a wife to follow her husband and live with him in his house. Now that you are married and must go with your husband, see that you live in such manner that you set an example to other wives. Consider that you are a ruler's daughter and a ruler's wife, and that you must live virtuously. Take great care to serve God and to make offerings to him in the fashion of rulers' wives. Be diligent also in serving and pleasing your husband, that God may treat you well and give you sons who will succeed to the realm. If your husband goes to another town, when you learn that he has returned come out of your chamber with your women to receive him; greet him with much love and modesty. Then your husband will love you greatly, and we your parents shall also love you when we hear of your good manners and breeding and of the love you and your husband bear each other; we shall be very pleased to hear this. But if you do what does not befit a lady of your quality, you will bring us great pain and shame.

Having said these and other things, the mother said, "Go then, daughter, with your mothers[37] who have reared you; they will serve you and take care of you. Go, then, daughter, and do nothing evil or shameful."

Mothers charged their daughters above all with the service of God and the guard of their virtue, and with service and love for their husbands. It seems to me that their advice conforms with what the parents of Sarah, the inlaws of Tobias, told their daughter.

Mothers who were not rulers' wives also gave advice to their daughters, saying:

My daughter: I bore you and have taught you good breeding and good order, and your father has honored you. If you are not what you should be, you may not live with good and virtuous women; nor will any man take you for wife.

Hardship and suffering are our lot in this world, and our powers daily waste away. We must serve God, that He may aid us and give us health; we must live with diligence and care to obtain our needs.

See to it, then, beloved daughter, that you are not careless or lazy. Be cleanly and diligent, and look after the house and keep all in order as it should be, each thing in its place. Thus will you learn what you must do in your house when you marry.

Wherever you go, go with great modesty. Do not hurry or laugh as you walk, and do not glance about, either at those coming toward you or at any other, but go your way; and thus will you gain honor and good name.

See that you are well behaved and speak soberly; reply civilly to any who question you.

Perform your household duties, weave and embroider; and so you will be well beloved and will merit the food and clothing you receive. In this labor you will find comfort and will thank God that he fitted you for it.

Give yourself not to sleeping, to the bed, to laziness. Do not be used to sitting in the fresh cool shade; for this teaches sloth and vice, and with such a habit one does not live well or decorously. Women who give themselves over to it are not loved.

Whether seated or standing, walking or working, my daughter, always think good thoughts and work well; and do what you must do to serve God and your parents.

If you are called, do not wait to be called a second time, but go promptly to do what you are ordered to do, to avoid giving offense or making it necessary to punish you for your sloth and disobedience. Listen well to what you are ordered to do, and do not give a rude reply. If you cannot do what is asked of you, make your excuses civilly, but do not lie or deceive anyone; for God sees you.

If another is called and she does not promptly respond, do you go diligently and hear and do what that one had to do; and thus will you be loved.

If someone offers you good counsel, take it; do not reject it, lest that person grow angry with you and hold you in scorn.

Walk modestly and quietly, not in such a way that men will think you giddy.

Be charitable; do not scorn or hate others; and be not avaricious.

Do not assign a bad sense to the words of others; do not envy the good that God was pleased to do to others.

Do not cause others hardship or suffering; for thereby you will bring the same on yourself.

Do not do evil; and do not follow the promptings of your heart; for thereby you will make yourself evil and will ensnare yourself to your own hurt.

Do not keep company with women who lie, or are lazy, or gad about, nor with low women, lest you harm yourself. Attend to your housework, and do not frivolously leave your house. Do not frequent the market place, or the public squares or baths; for this is very bad and leads to perdition and harm. And one who follows evil courses find it difficult to give them up; for evil inspires evil desires.

If a man speaks to you, do not believe him and do not look at him; be quiet and pay no attention to him. If he follows you, do not reply to him, lest your speech trouble his heart; and if you take no heed of him, he will stop following you.

Do not enter a stranger's house without cause, lest he bring some charge against you.

If you enter the house of relatives, show respect to them and be not lazy; do what you see is fitting for you to do, and do not simply look at the women who are working.

When your parents give you a husband, do not be disrespectful to him; listen to him and obey him, and do cheerfully what you are told. Do not turn your face from him; and if he did you some hurt, do not keep recalling it. And if he supports himself by your industry, do not on that account scorn him, or be peevish or ungracious; for you will offend God, and your husband will be angry with you. Tell him meekly what you think should be done. Do not insult him or say offensive words to him in front of strangers or even to him alone; for you will harm yourself thereby, and yours will be the fault.

If someone visits your husband, thank him for coming, and do him some service. If your husband is disabled, you must show him how he is to live; and you must take care of the household, and secure persons to work your fields and store the harvest; and you must not be negligent in anything.

Do not waste your estate, but aid your husband; and you will obtain what you need for yourselves and your children.

My daughter, if you do what I have told you, all will love and esteem you. I have complied with my duty as a mother. If you take my advice, you will live happily; if you do not, the fault will be yours, and the future will show you the results of not heeding this advice. It shall never be said that I failed to advise you as a mother.

Reply of the Daughter

My mother: You have done me great good. It were a great misfortune if I did not heed your advice. What would become of me if you did not give me such good counsel? With suffering you reared me; even now you have not forgotten me, for you give me such counsel. How shall I repay you? God grant that I be worthy of heeding even a part of your advice! If I be such as I should be, my mother, you shall have part of God's reward to me, and God will repay you for the care that you have taken of me.

Catholic Royal Majesty: Such was the mode of government of these people in the time of their paganry; such was their administration of justice and management of their commonwealths; and such was the discipline and correction with which they reared their children.

To be sure, they had some unjust and wicked laws, some cruel, tyrannical, and most mistaken laws; for they were like blind men in that they lacked the evangelical law. But the same is and has been true of other infidels. But through the mercy of God all that has ceased since they received the gentle law of Jesus Christ, our Lord and Redeemer, and great is the fruit that has sprung therefrom. It would be greater still had there not arisen obstacles to their progress.

It may appear that aside from what I myself learned I have relied solely on the findings of religious (who, to be sure, are persons of much credit who saw with their own eyes some of the things described above). I shall therefore cite what Hernando Cortés wrote His Majesty the Emperor, our lord, who is in glory, soon after Cortés entered that land. Speaking of Tlaxcala, he writes as follows:

"Finally they yielded themselves as subjects and vassals of Your Majesty, offering their persons and property for your royal service. This they did, and have done until today, and will always do, as I believe and Your Majesty will hereafter see."

Further on, Cortés writes:

"In response to their pleas, I came to the city [Tlaxcala], which was about 6 leagues from my quarters and camp. This city is so large and wonderful that although much of what I might say I shall omit, the little that I shall say is almost incredible. For it is larger and much stronger than Granada, the buildings are just as fine, and it contains a great many more people than Granada did when it was taken, and is much better supplied with provisions, such as bread, birds, game, and river fish, and good vegetables, and other things to eat.

"There is a market in this city, in which, every day, above thirty thousand people sell and buy, not to mention many other small markets in different parts of the city. This market contains everything in which they trade, not only provisions but also clothing and shoes. There are jewelry shops, for gold,

TVMVLO IMPERIAL
de la gran ciudad de Mexico.

EN MEXICO.
Por Antomo de Eſpinoſa
1560.

and silver, and precious stones, and other finery of featherwork, as well arranged as any to be found in any of the
squares or market places of the world; there is much earthenware and crockery of many kinds, equal to the best in Spain.
They also sell a great deal of wood and charcoal, and herbs,
both edible and medicinal. There are houses like barber's
shops, where men are shaved and have their heads washed;
and there are baths, too. In fine, there prevail good order and
polity among them, for they are a rational and intelligent
people, and superior to the best that Africa can show.[38]

"This province contains many extensive and beautiful valleys, well tilled and sowed; not a foot is left uncultivated. The
province is 90 leagues in circumference; and its form of government, as far as I can judge, resembles that of Venice, or
Genoa, or Pisa, because there is no one supreme ruler. There
are many lords all living in this city; the common people are
peasants and vassals of the nobility. Each peasant has his own
land, but some have more than others. In waging wars, which
are continuous among them, they all gather together; and thus
assembled, they decide and plan them.

"I believe that they must have some system of justice for
punishing the guilty, because one of the natives of this province stole some gold from a Spaniard, and I told this to Maxiscatzin, the greatest lord among them. They made inquiry
and pursued the thief to a city which is near there, called
Cholula, whence they brought him prisoner, and delivered
him to me with the gold, telling me that I might punish him.
I thanked them for the diligence they had shown in the matter, but told them that inasmuch as I was in their country,
they should punish him as was their custom, since I did not
wish to meddle with the punishment of their people. They
thanked me for this, and took him with a public crier, who
proclaimed his offense, leading him through the great market

place, where they put him at the foot of a building like a theater[39] which stands in the middle of that market square. The public crier now ascended the platform and in a loud voice again proclaimed the man's guilt. All having looked upon him, they beat him on the head with sticks until they killed him. We have seen in their prisons many others who, we were told, were held there for thefts and other offenses they had committed."

Speaking in the same letter of Moctezuma, who was the greatest lord of that whole land, of his service, of the many strange things that he gave the Spaniards, and of the great city of Mexico, Cortés writes as follows:

"These things, aside from their intrinsic value, were so marvelous in point of novelty and strangeness as to be beyond price, nor can it be that any prince ever heard of in the world could possess so many and such rare things. Though what I say may sound fabulous to Your Majesty, it is true that of all the things created on land, as well as in the sea, of which Moctezuma had ever heard, he had very exact likenesses made of gold, silver, jewels, and featherwork, so perfectly that they seemed almost real. He gave me a large number of these for Your Highness, besides others he ordered to be made in gold, for which I furnished him the designs, such as images, crucifixes, small jewels and necklaces, and many other things of ours which I made them copy. The royal fifth of the silver that I received came to 100 and some odd marks,[40] which I made the natives cast in large and small plates, bowls, cups, and spoons, which they executed as perfectly as they could from our descriptions.

"Besides these things, Moctezuma presented me with a large quantity of articles of cloth, which, though fashioned of cotton and not silk, could not be equaled by anything else in the world for texture, richness of colors, and workmanship. They included many marvelous garments for men and women, hangings for beds, incomparably finer than any made of silk, and material like tapestry that could be used to adorn drawing rooms and churches. There were also coverlets and quilts of featherwork and cotton, in various colors, also very marvelous, and many other things so curious and numerous I do not know how to describe them to Your Majesty. He also gave me a dozen blowguns of the kind he used for hunting, so well made that I know not how to portray them, for they were decorated with beautifully colored paintings depicting many different kinds of birds, animals, flowers, and various other objects, and the mouthpieces, the ends, and the middle of the tubes were finely wrought gold, several inches deep. He also gave me a pouch of gold thread, and told me he would give me pellets, also of gold, to be kept in it. Moreover, he gave me some turquoises set in gold, and many other, almost innumerable things.

"Much time and many very expert chroniclers would I require to give an account to Your Royal Excellency of the greatness and the strange and wondrous things of this great city of Tenochtitlán, of all the dominions and splendor of Moctezuma its sovereign, of the rites and customs of these people, and of the order prevailing in the government, not only of this city but of others belonging to this lord. I shall never be able to describe the hundredth part of what there is to relate, but, as far as I am able, I shall tell of some of the things I have seen. I know very well that what I shall say, although imperfectly told, will appear so wonderful that it will hardly seem credible, for even we, who see the things I describe with our own eyes, are unable to comprehend their reality. Your Majesty may be assured that if there is anything wanting in my relation, it consists rather in falling short than in overdrawing, not only in this but in all other matters of which I shall give an account to Your Highness; but it seems to me only just toward my Prince and Sovereign to tell him very clearly the truth, without interpolating matters which diminish or exaggerate it."

After having spoken of the site of the city of Mexico and of other matters, Cortés writes as follows:

"This great city of Tenochtitlán is built on the salt lake, and the distance from the mainland to the city is 2 leagues,[41] whatever the direction from which you approach it. It is entered by four artificial causeways, each two lance-lengths in width. The city is as large as Seville or Córdoba. Its streets (I speak of the principal ones) are very broad and straight; some of these, and all the lesser streets, are half dry land and half water, on which the people go about in canoes. All the streets have openings at regular intervals, to let the water flow from one to the other, and at all these openings, some of which are very broad, there are bridges, very large, strong, and well constructed, so that, over many, ten horsemen can ride abreast. . . .

"The city has many squares where they are always holding markets, and carrying on trade. One of these squares is twice as large as that of Salamanca, and is surrounded by arcades where there are daily more than sixty thousand souls buying and selling, and where are found all the kinds of commodities produced in these lands, including foodstuffs, jewels of gold and silver, lead, brass, copper, tin,[42] stone, bones, shells, and feathers. Stones are sold, cut and uncut, also adobe bricks, tile, wood, both in the rough and manufactured in various ways. There is a street for game where they sell all kinds of birds, such as chickens,[43] partridges, quails, wild ducks, flycatchers, widgeons, turtledoves, pigeons, reed birds, parrots, owls, eaglets, owlets, falcons, sparrow hawks, and kestrels, and they sell the skins of some of these birds of prey with their feathers, heads, beaks, and claws. They also sell rabbits, hares, venison, and small dogs which they castrate and rear for the table.

"There is a street set apart for the sale of herbs, where can be found every sort of root and medicinal herb that grows in the country. There are houses like apothecary shops, where they sell medicines compounded in the form of liquids, ointments, and plasters. There are places like our barber's shops, where they wash and shave heads. There are houses where one can buy and drink. There are porters like the *ganapanes* of Castile, who carry burdens. There are much wood and charcoal, braziers of earthenware, mats of different kinds of beds, and others, much thinner, used as cushions, and for carpeting halls and bedrooms. There are all sorts of vegetables, and especially onions, leeks, garlic, common cress, water cress, borage, sorrel, edible thistles, and artichokes. There are many kinds of fruits, among others cherries and plums, like the Spanish ones. They sell bees' honey and wax, and honey made from maize stalks, which is as sweet and syrupy as that of sugar, also honey of a plant called maguey in the other islands,[44] which is better than must; from these same plants they make sugar and wine, which they also sell.

"They also sell skeins of different kinds of spun cotton, in all colors, so that the place looks like one of the silk markets of Granada, but much larger. They also sell as many painter's colors as in Spain and of hues as excellent as they can be. They sell tanned deerskins with hair and without, both white and of different colors; and much earthenware, most of it exceedingly good, many sorts of pots, large and small, pitchers, tiles, an infinite variety of vessels, all of very remarkable clay, and most of them glazed [45] and painted. They sell maize, both in the kernel and made into bread, which is very superior in its quality and flavor to that of the other islands and the mainland of South America; they sell bird pies and fish pastries, also much fish, fresh and salted, stewed and raw; eggs of hens and geese and other birds, in great quantity, and tortillas made of eggs.

"Finally, they sell in the city markets all other things that are found in the whole country; and because there are so many and so many kinds, besides those I have mentioned, that I do not remember them or do not even know their names, I do not mention them.

"Each kind of merchandise is sold in its proper street, and they do not mix their merchandise; thus they preserve excellent order. Everything is sold by count and measure, but so far we have not seen anything sold by weight.

"There is in this square a very large building, like a Court of Justice, where there are always ten or twelve persons sitting as judges, and delivering their decisions upon all cases which arise in the markets. There are other persons in the same square who go about continually among the people, observing what is sold, and the measures used in selling, and they have been seen to smash some measures which were false.

"This great city contains many mosques,[46] or houses for idols, very beautiful edifices situated in its different parishes or wards. The principal ones are served by priests of their cult who live all the time in these temples. For these priests they provide very good lodgings set apart from the shrines in which they keep their idols. All these priests dress in black, and never cut or comb their hair from the time they enter the religious order until they leave it; and the sons of all the principal families, both of chiefs and of noble citizens, are in these religious orders and habits from the age of seven or eight years till they are taken away to be married. This happens more frequently with the first-born, who inherit the property, than with the others. They have no dealings with women, nor are women allowed to enter the religious houses; they abstain from eating certain dishes, and more at certain times of the year than at others.

"Among these mosques, there is one, the chief of them all, whose greatness and details no human tongue can describe, because it is so large that within its enclosure, which is surrounded by a high wall, a town of five hundred houses could easily be built. Around the interior of this enclosure stand very handsome buildings, filled with large halls and galleries, where the priests have their quarters. There are as many as forty towers, very tall and well built, the largest with fifty steps leading to the top; the tallest one is higher than the tower of the Cathedral of Seville. They are so well built, both in masonry and timber, that they could not be better made or constructed anywhere; for the interior of the shrines, where they keep their idols, is of carved and decorated stonework, and of timber carved in relief and painted over with monsters and other shapes. All these towers are places of burial for the lords, and each shrine is dedicated to the idol to which the lord gave particular devotion. Within this great mosque, there are three halls wherein stand the principal idols, of wondrous size and height, and much decorated with carved figures, of both stone and wood. . . .

"There are many fine large houses in this city, and the reason for this is that all the nobles of the land, vassals of Moctezuma, have houses in the city and reside in them for a part of the year; moreover, there are many rich citizens, who likewise own very fine houses. These people have not only large and fine rooms but also very beautiful flower gardens of different kinds, in the upper as well as in the lower stories.

"Along one of the causeways leading to the city, there are two cement aqueducts, each two paces broad, and an estado high, through one of which a volume of very good fresh water, as big around as a man's body, flows into the heart of the city and supplies all with sufficient water for drinking and other purposes. The other aqueduct, which is empty, is used when they wish to clean the pipe, and remains in use until the cleaning is finished. Since the water has to pass over the bridges spanning the gaps through which the salt water flows, it is carried over in conduits as thick as an ox and of the same length as the bridge, and thus all the city is supplied. Canoemen peddle the water through all the streets, and the way they take it from the aqueduct is this: The canoes stop under the bridges where the conduits cross, and there are men who are paid to fill them from above. At all the entrances to the city, and wherever the canoes are unloaded, which is where the greatest quantity of provisions enters the city, there are guards, in huts, to collect a specified duty on everything that comes in. Up till now I have not been able to learn whether this goes to the sovereign or to the city, but I believe it is to the sovereign, for in other market places of other provinces we have seen them levying this toll for the ruler. The markets and public places of this city are daily filled with laborers and masters of all trades, waiting to be hired.

"The people of this city are finer and more ceremonious in their dress and ways than those of other provinces and cities, for since the sovereign, Moctezuma, has always resided there, and all the nobles, his vassals, frequent the city, better manners and more ceremony prevailed. But to avoid being prolix in describing the things of the city (though I would fain continue), I shall only say that the mode of life of its people was almost the same as in Spain, with just as much harmony and order; and considering that these people were barbarians, so cut off from the knowledge of God, and of other civilized peoples, it is wonderful what they have attained in every respect." [47]

Cortés relates many other things about the other cities, their temples and buildings, and the service of Moctezuma. He says that when Moctezuma went out, a lord always went be-

fore him bearing three long, thin rods (Cortés believes this
was done to give notice of Moctezuma's approach); and
when he descended from his litter, he took one of these rods
and carried it before him. Cortés goes on to say that the ceremonies of his court were so numerous and diverse that it
would require more space than he had to relate them, and a
better memory than his own to retain them, for he does not
believe that any of the Sultans or other infidel lords of whom
we have information had such ceremonies in his service. He
tells many other notable things about Moctezuma's dominion,
grandeur, and government, and about the other lords. He also
tells of the crafts the Indians had and of those they have
learned from the Spaniards.

There are among the Indians many singers and musicians
who play flutes, flageolets, sackbuts, trumpets, and violins.
These Indians know how to read and write, and very skillfully compose books of plain song and songs with organ ac-
companiment, with very beautiful large letters at the beginning, and they bind these books. Many of them know Latin.

The Indians generally know all they need to know to earn their living; they know how to perform both rural tasks and those of the town. An Indian does not have to look for someone to build his house for him, nor does he have to search for materials, for everywhere he finds the wherewithal to cut, tie, sew, and strike a light. Almost all, including the boys, know the names of all the birds, animals, trees, and herbs, knowing as many as a thousand varieties of the latter and what they are good for; they also know many edible roots. All know how to work stone, build a house, twine a cord, and where to find the materials they need. They know all the other crafts that do not demand much art or complicated tools. If night overtakes them in the country, immediately, with a good will, they begin making huts or cabins, especially when they are accompanying lords or Spaniards.[48]

A religious,[49] one of the first twelve friars to come to that land, tells these and other things in a book that he wrote concerning the manners of those people and their conversion to Christianity.

Since they received the law of Jesus Christ, Our Lord and Redeemer, they have shown themselves zealous in what concerns the Faith, and have a great inclination for it. The religious I spoke of has a chapter on this subject in his book. Since this book remains in manuscript, I shall give a part of it here, but not word for word, for I omit the authorities cited therein. This is what the book says:[50]

"Some Spaniards wonder at and find very difficult to believe the change that has come over the Indians. In particular, those Spaniards who do not leave their towns, and so do not see the Indians, declare that their show of piety and penitence must be false. These Spaniards may indeed wonder that the Indians have been converted by the word of Christ, and that they come from afar to be baptized, make confession, get married, and hear the word of God, in whose power it is to work such change and make sons of confession and salvation from these stones. Very notable is the faith of these neophytes, and it is such as I never beheld in Christendom. These people never saw the casting out of demons, nor did they see Him Who healed the lame, gave hearing to the deaf, sight to the blind, and Who revived the dead, *sed in auditu auris obedierunt fidei.* What was preached and told to them was very little, like St. Philip's loaves, which would afford but a few crumbs to each of the multitude that ate of them. But God multiplied the word of the preacher and enlarged it in the souls and minds of the Indians, so that the fruit is much greater than the seed that was planted.

"These Indians are free of almost all the impediments to salvation that hinder the Spaniards, for they are content with very little. Their food is very poor, and so is their dress. Some sleep on a mat, but most of them do not even have that. They do not care to acquire wealth, and they do not wear themselves out striving for estates and dignities. They are content with their poor blankets, and on waking, they are fully dressed and prepared to pray. If they wish to flagellate themselves, they find no hindrance or impediment in their way.[51] They are incredibly patient and long suffering, and meek as sheep. I do not once remember having seen one of them nurse a grudge. They, the humble and scorned, live only to serve and work. Great is their patience and endurance in time of sickness. They sleep on the ground, with an old mat for a bed, at best, with a stone or a piece of wood for a pillow. Their houses are very small, some being of thatch. The saints sought such a life, and we read about it for our instruction and wonder thereat. Now we may read about it in the book of life and see it with our own eyes, and what we see is more than what we have read and learned, indeed, more than we could believe.

"If an Indian woman is in childbirth labor, the midwife

comes quickly, for they are like the women of Israel and can give birth without the attendance of a midwife. If it is her first child, the woman is attended by a relative or a neighbor, for they do not have to go far for help. The mother suckles and looks after her newborn child, or even twins, without any of the attentions and comforts that we extend to a woman just delivered of a child. The first thing they do for their children is to wash them in cold water. Because of such rearing, and because they wear very little clothing from childhood, the children grow up healthy and strong, cheerful, able, and teachable, so that one can make whatever one wishes of them.

"Now that they have come to knowledge of God they find few impediments to the Faith and to following the law and life of Jesus Christ. I have seen some Spaniards filled with remorse when they reflected on the life of these people, so peaceful and so well adapted for salvation, and then considered their own, so stormy and filled with impediments to the service of God.

"When a child was born, the relatives who came to see it greeted the child with these words, 'You have come to suffer; suffer and endure.' The parents gave a bow and arrow to a male child because warfare was so frequent among them. To a female they gave a spindle and a distaff for making cloth. In this way they indicated to their children from the first that they must work and live by the sweat of their brows." The author tells of many other notable things on this theme.

The religious[52] who translated the speeches that were made to the lords and the counsel that parents gave their children, also translated many years ago a speech that an Indian principal made to the natives of Texcoco just after the work of conversion began among them. It reads as follows:

Take care, you who are here and hear the preaching of the true God, that you heed what comes from Him and is given to you, for His house has been opened and its secret revealed unto you. Through their preaching the Fathers now spread and diffuse among you the good they brought us. Consider that a Father is like a great spreading leafy tree under whose boughs we find shade and air, consolation and instruction. Consider this well whoever you be, lord or vassal, rich or poor, and do not hold a Father in scorn.

And you, oh wretched one, whoever you are, take comfort from this preaching as you seek your fortune or worldly good, when seated, walking, or journeying, when afflicted, tearful, or sad.

Remember this, you who are a woman, as you sit at your spinning or other labor, as you nurse your children, and do not reject the good that is offered you, do not reject the advice of one who tells you of God, placing his words in your heart as if he were placing precious jewels about your neck.

You who are a peasant, think upon God as you go ascending or descending with your staff and burden, covered with sweat, exhausted, filled with anguish, longing for journey's end that you may find repose. This teaching of God must bring you strength and consolation. But if you do not accept it, you will anger God, and He will send you sickness or death. Do you think you can turn yourself into a robust tree, a strong stone? Do you think you can hide yourself from God in some hole or mountain or cave? Consider that He grows wrathful and punishes one who offends him. We are mud, and like mud, will He destroy us if it be His will. Hear and accept what is for your good. Whither will you flee, unhappy one?

These things of God will console you in your labor. Look to it that you walk and live in the way of God; place yourself under His hand and protection, for He alone knows when He will set His feet on you and bring you to your end. We are not strong, but very weak and mortal.

Behold the Heavens where are the glory and wealth of Our

Lord Jesus Christ, Who gives to those who believe and serve and love Him. Hear and heed the teaching of God, and do not forget it; place it and feel it in your heart that you may live well and be saved. Consider that if you do not receive the things of God, He will show you His prison and the torment of the damned and the demons of hell and will cast you among them. Then will you say: "Truly, it is just as the Father described it to me. Ah, that I had taken his advice! Ah, poor me!"

Consider that God is showing and giving you what your parents never saw. Be glad and joyful thereat, and give thanks to Him; humble yourself and say to your heart: You did not know or feel before what God now tells and gives you. Commend yourself to Him from the heart, and take care that you do not grow proud no matter how much you may know or learn of the things of God.

God is like a very pretty, lovely bird under whose wings all find shelter and protection. He is a father who calls and governs us all in this world. Consider that God does not lightly give rewards and distribute His gifts; faith and services and good works are needed to merit them. By His grace is your soul purified and made clean that you may live in His service for as long as it pleases Him that you shall live in His temple and enjoy it. Since He has enlightened your heart and freed you from the infinite follies of paganism, and since He has done us such great favor by giving us the Faith and its teachings, do not cease to thank Him.

Let all rejoice at the mercy of God, Who will pardon a sinner, however great a sinner he be, who believes and comes to Him: surely we shall find mercy at His hands. Weep and repent of your faults, and do not say: "Is He perchance a cleaner or pardoner of sins?" [53] Do not think such thoughts, but firmly believe that the true God alone can pardon us; humble yourself and bend your knees before Him, for all fear and tremble before Him.

Dispose yourselves to believe and be Christians, you who are yet unbaptized, for you do not know when you will die; perchance God will show you His mercy and favor in giving you the holy baptism. If you receive baptism as you ought to do, He will cleanse you and cleanse away your sins, and you must guard against offending Him. But if you should fall into sin and cause God pain, you must hasten to confession and you will be pardoned, for this the Fathers preach to us. God comforts and grants favors to those who keep His commandments, and He frees them from demons.

Let us rejoice, then, at God's great mercy in having cleansed and purified us in the holy baptism and in having enlightened us and brought us out of so many evils, blindnesses, and errors. Let us thank Him profusely, for we have heard and learned His holy doctrine, so openly given, for the Father conceals nothing and tells all that God entrusted to His apostles and disciples. Now the Father teaches us of the Sacraments and other divine matters, which all should hear, for by these means Our Lord purifies and cleanses sinners and pardons them and frees them from hell. Let us all accept, then, this holy doctrine which is preached to us; let us receive it and give thanks to Our Lord, and let us remember Our Lady, the Holy Virgin Mary, devoutly supplicating her to pray for us to her blessed son Jesus Christ, that through her intercession He may ever give us grace to live well and die in the Holy Catholic faith which we have received.

If they knew so much of the law of Jesus Christ so many years ago, what must they know now, when there are among them some good Latinists and well-educated men. To be sure, they have their share of vicious, wicked people, but it is the same with the Spaniards, who are the sons, nephews, and kin of Christians, and born, raised, and drilled in Christian doctrine. All the friars affirm that there is a great Christian spirit among the natives who retain their natural simplicity and have no dealings with Spaniards or the crafty sort of Indians.

The religious know and say this because they are always among them, laboring to instruct and confess them, to teach them the law of Jesus Christ, and to implant good manners in them. But the average man does not know this, nor does the prejudiced person who sticks to his prejudices through thick and thin, affirming what he knows only by hearsay.

One who knows the ancient system of government and justice of those people, how they enforced their laws and reared their children in the time of their heathendom, and how they live now that they are Christians, will understand how little justification have those who deny them any intelligence and will allow them no human trait other than the shape of men. A statement of this kind appears in a Spanish version of the Epistles of St. Jerome, in such a way that one cannot tell if it was really said by the glorious saint or by the person who translated the Epistles from Latin into Spanish. The statement is actually the translator's and not that of the Sacred Doctor. So common an error is this, however, that almost all fall into it without ever reflecting on whether what they say about the Indians is true or not. Don Hernando Cortés makes this error in his letter to the Emperor, our lord, from which I quoted above. Cortés has high praise for the Indian mode of government and way of life. Speaking of the people of Tlaxcala, he says that "there prevail good order and polity among them, for they are a rational and intelligent people, and superior to the best that Africa can show." Farther on, speaking of the Mexicans, he says, "The people of this city are finer and more ceremonious in their dress and ways than those of other provinces and cities, for since the sovereign, Moctezuma, has always resided there, and all the nobles, his vassals, frequent the city, better manners and more ceremony prevailed. . . . The mode of life of its people was almost the same as in Spain, with just as much harmony and order. . . ." But he immediately goes on to say, "Considering that these people were barbarians, so cut off from the knowledge of God, and of other civilized peoples, it is wonderful what they have attained in every respect."

Now, if Cortés finds "wonderful" what they had attained in every respect, wherein does he find them lacking in reason, and why does he call them "barbarians"? He has told so much about their good government and orderly ways, and he says over and over again that neither he nor his comrades who were with him could tell or grasp or explain in their fullness all the things of that land, or the grandeur of its ruler, and his service and government, and that no matter what he might say, it would still be but a small part of the whole. He says many other things in praise of what he saw, and rightly so, for the religious mentioned above says the same things in his book. Both men have much to tell about the other rulers as well.

But having said all this, Cortés concludes by calling the Indians a barbarian and uncivilized people, immediately after finding admirable the good order they display in all their affairs. This is certainly due to a very common fallacy, an error into which fall not only the common sort but even men of quality and learning who have not found out the truth for themselves but do not wish to appear ignorant of what has been written about these people. That is what has happened to some people who have written about the Indians in Latin or Spanish, and who cite in support of their statements other writers who saw or observed no more than they themselves.

This fallacy may also arise from the fact that we are accustomed to calling infidels "barbarians," which conforms with what the royal prophet says in Psalm 114, "in exitu Israel de Aegypto, domus Jacob de populo barbaro," [54] where he calls the Egyptians barbarians because they were idolaters. Yet in other respects the Egyptians were a very sage people.

Thus the Sacred Scripture, seeking to extol the wisdom of Solomon, says: "et proecedebat sapientia Salomonis sapientiam omnium orientalium et Aegyptiorum;" [55] and many sages among the ancient philosophers, even the Greeks, went to study with them. Aristotle, in the first book of his *Metaphysics*, states that the science called mathematics was discovered in Egypt; Plato, in his *Timaeus*, says that the Egyptians knew the courses of the stars from a time of great antiquity. These philosophers say that the Egyptians enjoyed great fame for wisdom before the Greeks, as is mentioned in a gloss to the fifth book of Seneca's *Divine Providence;* Cicero makes the same point in the beginning of the first book of *De divinatione*. Pythagoras and Plato, desirous of increasing their knowledge, went to Egypt to study; Lactantius tells of this in Book 4, Chapter 2,[56] and St. Jerome in the Epistle to Paulina that begins: "Frater Ambrosius."

Martial called the Egyptians barbarians in the first of his epigrams because their language, customs, and idolatry differed from those of the Romans. The Romans and Greeks called peoples of different speech "barbarians" for the same reason. Yet there were certainly other pagan peoples of great good order in government and ruled by many just laws. In the Civil Law there are many laws which illustrate this meaning of the word barbarian, "ut in titulo de eunuchis, et in titulo quae res exportari non debeant L.," and Cardinal Adrian, in *Elegantis linguae romanae*, says, "barbarum quod externum, alienum, peregrinum." [57] Gisbertus Longlius offers the same definition of the word in his annotation of Plautus's comedy *Asinaria, The Comedy of Asses*. Glossing the meaning of a phrase, Plautus uses in his prologue, he writes: "Maccus vortit barbare; at si, inquit, significatione hujus dictionis penitus introspiciat, barbari nihil aliud erit quam romanoe graecis siquidem non modo scythoe, sed etiam latini barbari censebantur atque hinc est cur Plautus alibi Naevium barbarum poetam

appellat." [58] For the same reason the Egyptian Mercurius Trismegistus called "barbarians" those nations which did not
practice the ceremonies of Egypt, as appears from Chapter 9
of his dialogue *De voluntate divina,* where he says that the
religion of Egypt was destroyed because "inhabitavit Egyptum
scytees aut indus aut aliquid talis, id est vicinia barbara." [59] St.
Paul used the word in this same sense of people who speak
different languages when he wrote to the men of Corinth:
"Therefore if I know not the meaning of the voice, I shall
be unto him that speaketh a barbarian, and he that speaketh
shall be a barbarian unto me." The Holy Doctors, writing
of the infidels, also call them barbarians; and the Holy Mother
Church, in the prayer that is said for the Emperor on Holy
Friday, declares: "Oremus: pro christianissimo Imperatore
nostro, ut Deus noster subditas illi faciat omnes barbaras nationes, etc.[60] Here by "barbaras nationes" is meant "infidels."

Again, perhaps the Spaniards call the Indians barbarous on
account of their great simplicity, for they are by nature free
of duplicity and cunning. In this they are like the people of
Sayago[61] and all other folk who live in villages and mountains
and remote areas where they do not meet cunning persons.
Because of this great innocence of the Indians, those who
trade with them can cheat them very easily. They sell the Indians things that they have no use for, and do not even know
the use of, at excessive prices. In exchange these traders receive cacao beans, cotton, or blankets, on which they realize
big profits. To these simple trusting people they sell horns
made in Paris, strings of beads, hawk's bells, and other baubles,
receiving in exchange very valuable objects, including gold
and silver, where they are found.

But we could also call the Spaniards barbarians in this
sense, for at the present day, even in the best-governed cities,
little toy swords and horses, and brass whistles, and little wire
snakes, and castanets with bells, are sold in the streets. Many

foreigners come with this stuff from their lands; they also bring merry-andrews, puppets, tumblers, acrobats, and dancing dogs. Gypsies go about telling fortunes and playing the child's game of stick and strap called *correhuela*. With these and other childish tricks these jugglers gain much money. Others pretend to be blind and harangue people in the public squares; many of the common sort gather round to hear them, after which the beggars do a thriving trade selling verses they have had printed. In Italy crowds gather to listen to charlatans who declare they have unknown new oils that will cure every sickness, sore, and wound, even oil of peter, and these charlatans have not hands enough to give out all the nostrums they sell there.

If this can happen among such enlightened folk as ourselves, in such well-ordered commonwealths, why should we wonder at the innocence of the Indians? Nor is there any reason for calling them barbarians, for there is no doubt that they are a very able people who have learned very easily and quickly all the mechanical arts known to the Spaniards who live in New Spain. Indeed, some Indians learned these arts in a few days simply from looking on at Spaniards. For the rest, I have said there are among them good Latinists and musicians. Let those who call them barbarians consider that by the same token they could call "barbarians" the Spaniards and other peoples famed for great ability and intelligence.

From what has been told above we may also judge whether these Indians, who observed their laws so strictly as to impose the most rigorous penalties on their own sons, were at all inferior to the famous Romans and other ancient peoples in justice and government, or less ingenious in justifying their wars. Whoever considers the question maturely must conclude that they were the equals of the ancients in all respects, or fell but little short of the ancients in their achievements. But just as Alexander envied Achilles in that Achilles had a

Homer to sing his feats, so the Indians could envy the ancients for having many excellent historians to celebrate their exploits. As Sallust observes, and as St. Jerome remarks in his life of St. Hilarion, the lives of the virtuous have only the fame and influence that is in the power of writers of genius to grant them. The picture writings in which the Indians recorded their history are either badly damaged or lost, and the only persons who have seriously attempted to study them are a small number of religious. I could say much more on this subject, but I fear it will be thought I have written not only enough but too much.

Turning to the question of the advantages the Indians derived from the rule of their lords in what concerns their government and way of life, I shall make plain those advantages, and also show the harm done by removing the lords and abolishing their rule, by telling what has happened since the passing of that system of government.

The Indians who have replaced the natural lords in office are naught but a pack of thieves, for they are quite content to have the people bear their sufferings in silence. The new officials do not wish or seek the reform of abuses, for they are very well off under the present system.

The Indian official who is supposed to summon his people to religious instruction will excuse those who bribe him or stand him to a drink, for the Indians are much more indifferent than they formerly were to such instruction. Besides, the religious are not the kind of men they used to be and so lack the authority and credit they once enjoyed among the natives. This is a major reason for the widespread confusion and disorder.

The Indian officials commit great outrages under cover of punishing the offenses of their people. These officials have grown up in the Spanish towns and keep company with Spaniards, so that they are completely changed from what they once were and have quite lost the natural simplicity of their people. As a result they lend themselves to every wickedness and can do their evil work all the better because of the great simplicity of the other Indian commoners. Throughout the land, those Indians who hold the office of *regidor,* alcalde or alguacil, *escribano,* fiscal, are generally persons who were reared with Spaniards or grew up in their service, or had been their slaves, or had had frequent dealings with them. Such Indians are very cunning and shameless.

The Indian alguaciles go about sniffing at Indians whom they meet in the streets or on the causeways to the city, whither such Indians are bound to sell some things or on other business. They will arrest an Indian and falsely charge him with being drunk, with resisting an officer and breaking his staff of office (the alguacil actually broke it himself), adding that the Indian tore the alguacil's cloak and pummeled him. If the Indian has some money, he gives it to his accusers so they will let him go; if he is penniless, they lead him off to jail, though the charge is almost always a false one. There the Indian sits three or four days, or even longer, until Saturday, when the oidor comes to make his visit; the Indian must pay the jailer's fees for all that time. Finally he is sentenced to forced labor, for all the alguaciles (who are numerous) agree as one man that he was drunk, and the escribano and the keeper of the jail (who are all Indians) join in the chorus. As a result, the Indian loses his crops, cannot attend to his tasks, loses what he brought to sell, and he and his wife and children all suffer unjustly.

If the Indian insists on denying his guilt and defending himself against the aggression of the alguaciles, the latter testify that the Indian broke an alguacil's wand of justice and tore the alguacil's cloak and shirt—all of which the alguacil himself did.

The oidor who visits the jail must be paid for his services. So the alguaciles trump up another charge and claim that the Indian beat one of them half to death, and the Indian must pay for the cure and the injury done. In order to get more money out of the Indian the alguacil sits at home pretending he is at death's door from the blows the Indian gave him. In truth it is the poor prisoner who was beaten and cuffed and cudgeled, and it is his clothing that was torn. But he dares not speak, nor does he know what to say, for all are against him. So the alguaciles have the formal accusation drawn up to their liking, and the oidor bases his decision upon it.

While the poor prisoner languishes in jail, the oidor orders the doctors to examine the alguacil. Since they are all in collusion to squeeze money out of the Indian, the doctors report that the alguacil is very ill. If the oidor should send some Spaniard to examine the alguacil a second time, the alguacil puts on a grand show to prove that he is indeed very ill. He smears himself with certain unguents that give him a very sickly appearance, and his relatives crowd all around at the visit and set up a chorus of weeping (for each gets his cut of the spoils). I have already said that the Indians who fill these offices of justice and live among the Spaniards are disposed to do every kind of evil, for their ancient natural simplicity has given way to a very great cunning and wickedness. The people in the remote country districts, on the other hand, are all of a notable innocence.

During all this time, while two, three, and more visits are being made to the alguacil in expectation that he will say he is better, the poor Indian is languishing in jail. The alguacil gains by this delay, for the longer this business takes, the more money the Indian will have to give him. In the end, in addition to the loss the prisoner and his family have suffered through his long confinement, the law skins him completely, and to obtain payment he is put out to forced labor. He is punished the more severely on account of the resistance he is alleged to have made.

If an Indian manages to tear himself away from the alguaciles who try to seize him, he leaves his cloak in their possession; however, he is happy to lose it if thereby he avoids going to prison and running the risk of being put out to forced labor and being subjected to the other abuses mentioned above. The alguacil remains in possession of the *manta* (which is a garment the Indians wear in place of a cloak); and if it is a good one, the alguacil is satisfied, for that is what he is after, but if it is threadbare the alguaciles chase hotly after the Indian and will not let him get away. Later his flight is used as evidence of resistance to arrest, and to convict him of having been drunk.

The Indian officials charged with seeing that the Indians work their parcels of land will fine one who could not work his land through no fault of his own, either because he had to labor on public works or because he became ill from the forced labor to which he had been assigned. Others who have worked their fields are told that they did not do so, or did it poorly, and are forced to bribe the official or pay him a fine. It sometimes happens that Indians lose their crops or even their lands because they are put out to forced labor, or for other reasons. Most frequent of all, however, is the practice of fining the Indians.

The Indian officials charged with rounding up men for the weekly *repartimiento* or draft of Indians for service in the households and estates of the Spaniards also steal all they can. They go from house to house and compel the Indians to pay a bribe if they would escape being led off to the repartimiento. Sometimes an Indian will pay an official twice the sum he would earn if he went to serve. Some who served the previous week are forced to go, simply because they cannot pay a bribe. It avails these Indians naught to complain that they have already served their week. The sole interest of the Spaniards is to have the labor they require for their estates and other enterprises. The official who distributes the Indians cares even less, for he too is guided by self-interest; an employer gives him a *cuartillo* for each Indian that he leads away.

It would be much better if the repartimiento were abolished and if each Indian town sent every day or week a certain number of Indians (according to the town's population) to hire themselves out to Spanish employers. Many Indians do this now, but few Spaniards will hire such men, for they can get them through the repartimiento at half the cost. As a result, only those Spaniards who cannot get repartimiento Indians will hire the free laborers.

If the repartimientos were abolished, the Spaniards would go to the public squares and other places where the free laborers wait to be hired, and there would be an end to the injuries and losses that the Indians suffer from being taken away to the repartimiento. For at present they often lose their crops because the time for harvesting them passes while they are away, so that in one day they lose everything; and on top of this they are fined for not cultivating their fields, though the fault is not theirs. Not only Indian officials but some alcaldes mayores and corregidores do this on the pretext of zeal for the public welfare, but they keep the fines for themselves; they cause the Indians to be seized and fine them costs and jailer's fees.

Whereas if the Indians came voluntarily or were sent by their caciques to hire themselves out to employers for a wage agreed on between the parties, each would come at a time when he was not needed at home; for some finish their cultivation earlier than others. Moreover, the cacique would see to it that those Indians who had least to do at home were sent, with due regard for the season of the year and its tasks. Thus there would never be a shortage of paid laborers, for some Indians are so poor that their plantings are very small, and they finish their farm work quickly. The caciques would not send merchants or artisans, for they gain more in a day by their trade and crafts than an employer could give them in a week, and that without leaving their homes and families.

I could write much more on this subject, for there is no end to the miseries these wretched folk suffer, but what I have said suffices to give an understanding of their hardships and sufferings and of what needs to be done to remedy their condition, which is the purpose of Your Majesty's inquiry.

I must now turn back to the fourth article of the cedula, for it seems proper to discuss the questions raised in this article before the others. If I should tell some things here that I have already told before, it is from necessity. Plato justifies such repetition, declaring that it is proper to say something two or three times over if it is done to clarify one's meaning. There is all the more reason for such repetition inasmuch as different articles of the cedula inquire concerning the same things.

The fourth article reads as follows:

ARTICLE 4

Item: You will inform yourselves on what kinds of persons paid tribute, if they were peasants alone, whom they call macehuales, or if merchants and other sorts of people also paid it; and if there were among them any classes of men who were free of tribute.

This article contains two questions: first, what kinds of people paid tribute; second, whether some were free of tribute.

As to the first question, from what I have been able to learn four kinds of people, comprising all the commoners, paid tribute.

Tribute-payers of one kind were called *teccallec;* these people were attached to certain principales, and were subject to the inferior lords called *tectecuhzin,* of whom I said that they did not hold office through right of succession. Instead the supreme ruler assigned that title and office to one who had distinguished himself in war or in the service of the state or of the ruler. The teccallec paid these inferior lords the tribute that was ordinarily paid to the supreme ruler. I have already related all this in replying to the first question in Article 9, when I described the different kinds of lords.

Tribute-payers of the second kind were called calpullec or chinancallec,[62] which means recognized barrios, or ancient and recognized lineages, that live apart from others. These calpullec were numerous, and included almost all who paid tribute to the supreme ruler. They cultivated a parcel of land for the maintenance of their head or principal, and also gave him household service according to the number of people in the barrio. They did this to compensate him for the care he took of them, and on account of the great expense to which he was put by the meetings held every year in his house for the general welfare. They did this not by command of the supreme ruler, nor as an obligation of any kind, but as a most ancient custom of these people. This tribute was in addition to the tribute paid to the supreme ruler.

Tribute-payers of a third kind were the merchants. They belonged to recognized lineages, and no man could be a merchant save by inheritance or by permission of the ruler. The merchants had certain liberties, for it was said they were necessary for the commonwealth. Merchants paid tribute in the things they dealt in, and artisans gave tribute in what they made. None of these rendered personal service or labored on public works save in time of need. Nor did they have to work on the *milpas* or maize fields that were cultivated for the ruler, because they satisfied their obligations by paying their tribute. Among them there always was a principal who spoke for all in their dealings with the ruler or his governors. These governors also dealt with the calpullec and with the teccallec, for all the different kinds of people were found in each barrio.

The tribute given to the supreme ruler was for the support of the commonwealth and for their wars, which were frequent. The supreme ruler (who was obeyed by other lords who were also called supreme in their lands) secured his share of the tribute, and from this he paid the governors and ministers of justice, gave wages and board to many principales according to their quality, and supported the captains of war. All these people commonly ate in the supreme ruler's palace, where each had his seat and station assigned to him according to his dignity or quality and the office he held in the ruler's palace or in war or government. The ruler could not dispose of the tribute as he pleased, for the people and the principales would be displeased if he took what was not his share, since all the rest was destined for other purposes. Since there were so many people, much tribute was collected, and there was enough for all needs.

Tribute-payers of a fourth kind were called *tlalmaitec* or mayeques. They were peasants who lived on the lands of others. The first two kinds of tribute-payers held lands individually or in common in their barrio or calpulli. The mayeques, however, held no land of their own, but lived on that of others. This came about because in the beginning, when the first conquerors of the land divided it up, the ancestors of these mayeques received no part of it. The same thing happened when the Christians conquered the land, some acquiring land and Indians, while others obtained neither land nor Indians.

These mayeques could not leave the land to which they were attached, nor were they ever known to attempt such a thing. The sons and heirs of the lords of such lands succeeded to them; and the land passed together with the mayeques who lived on it, and with the same obligation of service and rent that the mayeques, their forerunners, had had to pay for their use of the land. The rent consisted in payment of a part of the mayeque's harvest to the lord, or in working a piece of land for the lord, and varied according to the number of mayeques and their agreement with the lord. The same was true of the service, which consisted in the provision of fuel, water, and domestic service.

These mayeques paid no tribute to the supreme ruler, but only to the lord of the land. They did not join in working the communal lands used to provide tribute to the supreme ruler, because instead of this they paid tribute to the lord of the land they cultivated. They considered and called this land their own, because they had the useful dominion thereof, and the owners the direct dominion. This system was of immemorial antiquity and had the consent of the supreme rulers. The mayeques served the supreme ruler only in time of war, for then no one was excused, and the supreme ruler also had civil and criminal jurisdiction over them.

When a lord was dying and left sons, he could divide his patrimonial estates and leave to each son such mayeques and land as he pleased, because his were not entailed estates.

The first two kinds of tribute-payers, the teccallec and calpullec, comprising all the commoners, and the merchants and artisans who lived among them and belonged to these barrios and calpullec, were made tribute-payers of Your Majesty and of individual encomenderos at the time of the Conquest. The lords and some other owners of patrimonial estates were allowed to retain the mayeques who lived on their lands, but since that time they have all lost their mayeques.

There were certain designated lands called *tlatocamilli*, which means lands of the lordship. A lord could not dispose of such land, for it belonged to the lordship and passed with it; but he could rent it to whomever he pleased. The rent received from such lands was large because they were extensive and very good. All the rent received from such land was consumed and spent in the lord's house, for this was the general custom of the lords. To the lord's house came all travelers, and the poor, and principales, and many others. On account of their hospitality these lords were honored, obeyed, and well served; and to comply with their obligations they expended their patrimonial tribute when the tribute from the tlatocamilli did not suffice.

The second question in this article asks if any natives were free of tribute.

What I have been able to ascertain is that the peasantry paid tribute in kind and in personal service, whereas the merchants and artisans paid tribute in kind, but gave no personal service, save in time of war. The *tecutles* and the pilles paid no tribute of any kind. They constituted, as it were, a class of hidalgos and caballeros. They served in war, held public office as governors and ministers of justice, and attended the supreme ruler in his palace, some serving as guards and squires who accompanied him everywhere and others as the ruler's messengers and agents. Still others had charge of leading the peasantry to the tribute fields or other communal labor, or of supervising their festivals or the service they gave the ruler. Accordingly, the people were divided into barrios, to each of which a principal was assigned. Other principales did not have charge of people, but only attended the ruler. To all these persons the ruler gave wages and board; he also gave to each, according to his office and quality, some peasants to provide him with fuel, water, and domestic service, and to work his fields for him.

The peasants who did this work were not assigned for life, but were replaced by others at intervals. Nor did they have to labor on the *milpa* or tribute field of the supreme ruler or render him personal service while engaged in such work, for they complied with their obligation by serving one of these principales instead. The rule, then, was that a peasant always served some one lord or principal (save in time of war), and that he never paid tribute to two lords at a time. And his tribute consisted in personal service, or in working a milpa or field either for the supreme ruler or for another lord in the ruler's place and by his order.

Persons under paternal authority and orphans were also free of tribute. Then as now (when there no longer exists the good order they once had in rearing their children), orphans went to live with a relative and served him for their food, and they continued to serve until they married. There was not then, nor is there now, any question of payment for this. Orphans, widows, and lame or disabled persons did not pay tribute though they owned land until (in the case of orphans) they were old enough to work it or (in the case of widows and lame or disabled persons) found someone to work it for them or assist in its cultivation. Nor was the land taken away from such persons and given to others, for it was not their fault that they could not work it. Other classes that were free of tribute were beggars, the hidalgos or principales, mentioned above, and the mayeques belonging to lords or other individuals. The mayeques were exempt because the tribute they gave such persons was in place of the tribute they owed the universal or supreme ruler.

Those who served the temples or were assigned to the cult of their idols paid no other tribute of any kind.

Now I turn back to the opening of Your Majesty's cedula and comment on its first article, which reads as follows:

ARTICLE 1

To the president and oidores of the royal Audiencia de los
Confines: Because we wish to be informed of the things
stated above, I order that immediately upon receiving this
Cedula, you the president and one of the oidores of that
Audiencia shall inform yourselves from ancient Indians,
having first administered the oath to them, what tribute the
Indian towns and their inhabitants paid, in the days of their
heathendom, to their principal lord or the lord who had
universal dominion, or to other lords before him, and what
were the kinds, quantity, and value of the tribute, and what
would be its worth each year expressed in gold pesos.

This article contains three questions: First, what tribute did
the natives pay their lords. Second, what were the quantity
and value of this tribute. Third, what was its yearly value expressed in gold pesos.

There was good order and harmony as concerns the kinds
of tribute paid by the subjects, for each province or town
gave tribute according to its climate, people, and lands. Each
town or province paid tribute in the things that were grown
there, so the people did not have to leave their natural sur-

roundings to seek tribute. Never did the people of the *tierra caliente* have to go the *tierra fría,* or vice versa.

Tribute was most commonly paid in maize, peppers, beans, and cotton. Each town had fields set aside for this purpose. On this land the rulers kept slaves who guarded and worked the fields with the aid of the townspeople. The people of neighboring towns also gave aid if they had no tribute land of their own, but if they had such land, they worked it and did not go elsewhere. Tribute was also given by providing water, fuel, and domestic service for the ruler's house. Artisans paid tribute in the products of their craft. Tribute was never apportioned by heads. Instead the ruler assigned to each town and craft what it must give, and each town and craft in turn apportioned its tribute among its members and brought it at the appointed times. It was like the *encabezamiento* that is made in Castile.

Thus the peasants worked the tribute fields and harvested and stored the crops; the artisans gave tribute from the things they made; and the merchants gave of their merchandise— clothing, feathers, jewels, stones—each giving of the commodities in which he dealt. The merchants' tribute was the most valuable of all, for they were rich and prosperous people.

The Indians had fields planted to cotton for tribute in those areas where cotton was grown. Some towns, which did not grow it themselves, gave cotton as tribute because they had subject to them places where it was cultivated. The ruler in turn handed this cotton over to other towns which did not grow cotton but worked it into a very good cloth. This excellent cloth was made by the people of the tierra fría, who are better workers than those of the tierra caliente. Thus some towns gave cotton, and others turned it into cloth. Maize, chili peppers, and beans were planted and given as tribute in those places where they grew; fish, fruit, and game were given as tribute in other places.

Where gold was found, a small quantity of gold dust was given as tribute; the Indians gathered it in the rivers without much toil. The ruler took great care that some subjects should not be burdened more heavily than others. Each subject gave a little, but there were so many people that large amounts of tribute were collected. In fine, the tribute the people gave cost them little labor and did not impose great hardships.

What I have said above answers the second question, which asks what were the quantity and value of the tribute. Although each man gave only a little, yet the whole came to a great deal because there were so many people. At that time all their products had a very low value among them. They did not use money in trade. They carried on their commerce by bartering certain things for others, a most ancient and worthy mode of trading, much used among nations and the most conformable to nature.

The rulers exacted greater tribute from those towns which they had conquered in war and which had rebelled against them.

The lesser lords made gifts to the supreme ruler at certain festivals held every year; they did this in acknowledgment of their subjection and vassalage.

The merchants, who were rich and prosperous, and cherished by the rulers, had the custom of making gifts to the supreme ruler at these festivals. These gifts, which were in addition to the tribute the merchants paid, were made not as an obligation but as voluntary donations. The presents were collected from all, each giving what he pleased, and the leading man among them gave them to the ruler. All that they gave went into a common fund that the ruler expended for the enjoyment of all on these festivals.

When a festival had ended, the supreme ruler gave to the

lesser lords, his vassals, and to the lords of neighboring towns who attended these festivals, rich cloaks and other presents, according to the quality of each lord. Thus these lords departed content and well rewarded for what they had brought.

All these supreme and lesser lords, and other private citizens, had their own patrimonial estates on which lived their mayeques or tlalmaitec. The tribute given by these mayeques belonged to their lord, and he could dispose of them and of the rents he secured from his patrimonial estates as he pleased, for they were his exclusive property.

To sum up, then, two classes of tribute-payers are those called teccallec and calpullec, comprising almost all the commoners, who now pay tribute to Your Majesty and to encomenderos. The merchants and artisans, composing a third class of tribute-payers, also pay tribute to Your Majesty and to encomenderos.

Tribute-payers of the fourth class are the mayeques or tlalmaitec, who pay tribute to and serve the lords of the lands they cultivate in those places where the lords have not been deprived of their mayeques. There are few if any such lords left.

The third question asks the value of the tribute, expressed in gold pesos. This question is difficult to answer. Each tribute-payer gave but a little, and that little had a low value for the Indians, but today it is worth a great deal. What I can state with certainty is that one Indian pays more tribute today than did six Indians of that time, and one town pays more in gold pesos today than did six towns of the kind that paid tribute in gold. Because gold was not extracted with the same toil as today, it was not valued so highly. As best I can estimate, what each tribute-payer gave came to the value of 3 or 4 reales at the most, including the domestic service he gave. All was so well apportioned and with such good order that each man's portion of labor was small, and his turn of domestic service came one or two times a year at most. Those who had two turns of service were persons who lived near the lord's house, for it was taken into account that such persons did not spend as much time coming and going as those who lived far away.

ARTICLE 2

You will also inform yourselves what tribute they paid to the principales, their caciques, and the quantity and value thereof, in addition to what they gave their universal ruler to whom these caciques were subject; and you will inform yourselves of the yearly value of such tribute.

This article contains two questions. First, what was the tribute they paid the lesser lords, and what was its value. Second, what was the yearly value of this tribute.

I say in reply to the first question that the vassals of the natural and supreme rulers of provinces subject to Mexico and its allies, Texcoco and Tacuba, paid tribute to their rulers in the same way that they paid it to the universal ruler, for the rulers of conquered provinces continued to receive tribute as before. These rulers applied their tribute in the same way as did the rulers of Mexico and its allies. The people of these provinces paid tribute to the lesser lords in the same way as was done in Mexico, and the lords bore the same names. All these lords, the lesser lords as well as the supreme rulers, had their own patrimonial estates and mayeques. There were also specified lands that belonged to a particular lordship.

It is impossible to determine the value of this tribute. I shall only say that the whole did not come to very much. The most common and general type of tribute was produce.

It is likewise impossible to answer the question concerning the yearly value of this tribute, because of the difficulty of comparing the value of commodities at that time with their value at present.

ARTICLE 3

In addition to the information that you secure from witnesses, you will cause to be brought before you any paintings, tablets, or other records of that time that may substantiate what is said, and you will cause the religious to search and ask for such records among the Indians. You will also secure information about all these matters from such religious and all other persons who have some knowledge of them.

I have done all I could to verify the accuracy of all that I have written.

ARTICLE 5

You will also inform yourselves of the times during the year when they paid their tribute, and of the order they observed in the apportionment, collection, and payment of the same.

This article contains two parts or questions: First, at what times during the year was the tribute paid. Second, what order they did observe in the apportionment, collection, and payment of tribute.

In reply to the first question, I say that the tribute crops were gathered at harvest time and stored in houses and bins that each town had designated for that purpose. The Indians took the produce from these storehouses as needed and used it for the purposes I have described. An exception to this system was the practice in the district of Mexico, where the tribute was brought to the city in order to feed its people, for they lived in the middle of a lake and so had no land on which to grow food.[63]

In the matter of the tribute paid by artisans and merchants, the customs varied from place to place. In some places they paid tribute every twenty days, in others every eighty days, counting in months of twenty days each. In effect, each man had to pay tribute once, twice, or three times a year. The tribute was apportioned among the various towns and crafts, and the nature of the tribute and the distance to be traveled from each town were taken into account. Accordingly not all men paid every twenty or eighty days, for their turns came at different times. Thus there were tribute-payers all year round, and the houses of the lords lacked for nothing. It was the same with the tribute of fruit, fish, game, pottery, and other things for the table and service of the lords; each tribute-payer gave his tribute in two, three, or more payments, as was convenient.

The second question asks about the order the Indians observed in the assignment of tribute. The ruler, taking into account the number and bent of the people in each town, indicated to each town the amount of land it must cultivate and what should be grown on this land. As I have said, the most common form of tribute was produce of the kind that was grown locally. To the merchants and artisans they also indicated what they should give, taking into account the production of each town or province or the things they dealt in. They did the same with the people who had to give domestic service and with those who had to provide for the needs of war. In every case these people took into account the number and capacity of the inhabitants and the character of the land. There was never any question of moving people from one town to another, or even from one barrio to another. Indeed, they observed as strictly as if it were law (though not through the use of force) the rule that where a man's father and ancestors had lived, there must he live and end his days. This rule was almost never broken. As a result there was no uncertainty, change, or confusion in the matter of tribute.

The supreme rulers, both the universal ruler and their subjects, appointed majordomos from among those pilles of whom I spoke to see to it that the Indians labored on the communal fields and worked their own fields and performed the other obligations I have told of. These majordomos collected tribute from the ruler's vassals and from the provinces subject to him. Where there were other inferior lords, however, such majordomos were unnecessary, for these lords did what the majordomos had to do. In either case, they brought the tribute to the supreme ruler or to the person he had appointed for that purpose.

In time of pestilence or crop failure, these inferior lords, or the majordomos, reported the occurrence to the supreme and universal lord, but only if they were certain of it, for otherwise they would never dare mention it to him. He would then order that the tribute should not be collected that year from the towns so afflicted. If the crop failure and shortage were very great, he would also order that aid be given for the support of such towns, and seeds for the next year's sowing, for it was the ruler's object to relieve his vassals as much as possible.

Personal service (provision of water, fuel, and domestic service) was assigned or apportioned for each day among the ruler's towns and their barrios in such a way that each individual had to go only twice a year at most, and, as I said before, those who went twice were those who lived nearby. Such individuals also paid a somewhat lighter tribute than others. Sometimes a whole town would bring the portion of fuel that was its share at one time, especially if the people lived a fair distance away from the ruler's residence. However, most household work was done by slaves, of whom the lords had a great number.

ARTICLE 6

You will also inform yourselves whether the tribute the Indians paid was in proportion to the value of the land they cultivated, or in proportion to the value of their estates, or whether the tribute was personal and assigned by heads.

There were different customs in respect to the matters with which this article deals, but there was a common pattern throughout the region now called New Spain, including Mexico, Tlaxcala, Huexotcingo, Cholula, down to Oaxaca, and many other provinces. Michoacán had different customs from those of Mexico and its neighbors, because in Michoacán all, principales and peasants alike, held land of their own, while other common land was worked for the universal ruler, for the inferior lords, and for the temples.

The Indians did not pay tribute in proportion to the value of their land or estates, for they paid tribute in produce and other commodities. All tribute, save that paid by artisans, merchants, fishermen, hunters, and those who gave fruit and pottery, was produced by communal labor.

The mayeques paid rent and service to the lord of the land on which they lived.

Tenants paid rent to the owner of the land that they worked according to the terms of the agreement made between them. These tenants differed from the mayeques in that they rented the land for one, two, or more years and gave no service to the owner of the land, because they gave personal service to the universal or supreme ruler like the others, and they joined in the communal labor on the tribute fields cultivated for the ruler.

Tribute was never assigned by heads; indeed, the Indians did not even know of such a thing. That is why the counts of the Indians, which the Spaniards have been making in recent years,[64] with a view to apportioning the tribute among them by heads, has caused so much unrest among them.

In some places lands were set aside to be rented, and the rent was used to supply the needs of the state. These lands could not be alienated, and all who cultivated them, whether lord or commoner, even the supreme ruler himself, had to pay a stipulated rent. These lands were called tribute lands.

ARTICLE 7

Item: You will inform yourselves who owned the lands and farms that the Indians possessed, and whether the tribute-payers were serfs and paid tribute as such to the lord of the land, or whether they paid tribute in virtue of the universal or particular dominion of the rulers.

The reply to these questions may be deduced from what I have already said, and there is no need to repeat it. In summary, I shall only say that almost all the Indians had their own land which they held individually or communally, like the *teccaleques* and *calpulleques* of whom I spoke. Those persons who did not hold land from their community or barrio, or preferred not to, rented it from some lord or other private party, or from some other barrio.

The mayeques were serfs and paid tribute as such to the lord of the land that they occupied and worked. They had no such obligation to the supreme universal ruler, and paid him no tribute, but in time of war or need they were obliged to serve him in virtue of his universal dominion and the jurisdiction he had over them.

The other tribute-payers paid tribute in the manner I have described, and gave personal service and served in time of war in virtue of the supreme ruler's universal dominion and jurisdiction.

ARTICLE 8

You will also inform yourselves what tribute the Indians now pay their caciques and principales, its kind and quantity, and whether the Indians pay their caciques and principales the same tribute that they paid them in the time of their heathendom, and in the same way, or whether there has been some change in this.

The reply to this question may be gathered from my reply to the third part of Article 9, which I put first. The long and short of it is that all the lords, supreme rulers and inferior lords, caciques and principales, are so poor that they do not have enough to eat, and have been dispossessed of their lordship, land, tenants, and mayeques. One of the causes of their ruin is that they have been deprived of the title of lord and made governors. Let one overstep his authority in the slightest, or be charged with such offense by his rivals, and the Spaniards strip him of his government, which in effect deprives him of his status of lord. Indeed, some Spanish officials seek precisely this, declaring that it befits Your Majesty's service and the good of the land that these lords should not be; and they set a commoner, a macehual, in the lord's place.

On a tour of inspection I once made, some lords appeared before me to tender resignation of their lordship and government, and I could not persuade them to withdraw their resignation and continue serving in office. When I asked them why they were resigning, they replied they did so from fear of being sued by the macehuales, and from a desire to be free of responsibility for tribute collection, and because travelers and others importuned them for food and mistreated them because they could not provide it. They added that Your Majesty's officers and the encomenderos badger them about the tribute and even order their arrest because the tribute has not been collected.

The Indians do not bring to any lord or cacique today the tribute they used to bring. Indeed, all the lords have been dispossessed and have themselves been made tribute-payers. To accomplish this, and to deprive the lords of their mayeques, the Spanish officials declare that Your Majesty has made known his wish that all should pay him tribute. If anyone claims the contrary, say these officials, let him appeal. Forthwith they despoil the lord of his rights and compel him to pay tribute for himself and his mayeques to Your Majesty or his encomendero. Since the lords do not know how to appeal, nor to whom an appeal should be directed, or before whom it should be made, and since they do not have the money needed for litigation, they lose their liberty, and their mayeques and lands as well. For the mayeques rise up against their lords and seize their land, declaring that it belonged to their forebears and now belongs to them. Since the Spanish officials do not understand how this land was held, the mayeques have their way. Thus the lords are ruined and cowed, for they dare not speak and know not what to say.

ARTICLE 10

You will inform yourselves if the Christian Spaniards, when they conquered that land, imposed new tributes on the Indians in addition to those they paid in the time of their paganry, and how they used the Indians. You will also inform yourselves whether the Spaniards were careful not to require other tribute or service of the Indians than what they used to give their universal ruler, and whether the requirement that the Indian towns give food to their Spanish encomenderos was a new imposition and how this was done.

The actions of the Spaniards at first were so outrageous and senseless (and still are in some places) that if I had to tell all that pertains to this article it would make a very long story. To make it as short as possible I shall comment with all brevity, considering that I could write endlessly about the matters with which this article deals. For a better understanding of these matters I shall have to refer to events and conditions both past and present.

This article contains two questions: First, were new tributes imposed on the Indians when the land was conquered. Second, how did the Spaniards use the Indians.

In reply to the first question, I say that as soon as the land was won, Captain Hernando Cortés summoned the lords and caciques to Coyoacán, which is an important Indian town, two leagues from Mexico City, that Cortés took for himself along with some other important towns of this region. Those who could went to Coyoacán; and when they were assembled, Cortés told them that they were no longer to take their tribute to the ruler of Mexico or to the rulers of Texcoco or Tlacopan, as they used to do, but that they were to give it to the Emperor, delivering it in his name to Cortés himself and the other Spaniards who were there. The Indians were not to cultivate the tribute land as they used to do; and each town of any consequence was to be independent of every other. The lords and caciques who were present, having fresh in their minds the treatment they and their people had received from the Spaniards, accepted what Cortés told them. One can imagine how freely they gave their consent!

Cortes distributed the land among his Spaniards and to himself without stipulating how, or when, or how much was to be paid in tribute, so that each Spaniard arranged with the lord and principales of the town commended to him what they must give him every eighty days. Some, but very few, went to the Captain for confirmation of their agreement. Since their appetite and greed were their only measure and rule, they demanded all they could in tribute, personal services, and slaves, never caring whether the Indians were able to comply. One can judge from this whether care was taken that the Indians pay no greater tribute than they had been accustomed to pay their lords. The Spaniards compelled them to give whatever they asked, and inflicted unheard-of cruelties and tortures upon them. Because of this, and because of the plagues that have afflicted them, of which more later, so many people have died that there is not one third the number there used to be.

The second question asks how the Spaniards used the Indians. I could say much about this, but I shall discuss the matter as briefly as possible. I have said that because of the sufferings and cruelties the Spaniards inflicted on the Indians, and because of the plagues that have vexed them, there is not one third the number there used to be. Now, many Spaniards, including some oidores, assert that the Indians labored harder in the days when they were heathen than they do now, yet they did not die out. Therefore, say these Spaniards, it cannot be that their present labors are the cause of their dying out. They go on to say that if the Indians do have any arduous work nowadays, it consists in building monasteries and churches, in cultivating the fields of their caciques and communities, and in their public works.

I shall therefore describe the work they did before the coming of the Spaniards, and how they performed this work. Then I shall tell how they have worked since giving allegiance to Your Majesty, that the cause of the great and continuing destruction of these people may be understood. I shall show that there is no comparison between the tribute labor they perform today and the work they did in their commonwealths, and that there is no reason to believe that freeing them from communal labor would relieve their plight. To begin with, no Indian would be a party to doing away with this labor, which is a most ancient custom among them. Second, their communal labor was and is performed very differently from the labor they do on Spanish public works and for private Spaniards. From this it will become clear how the Spaniards have used the Indians.

In the old days they performed their communal labor in their own towns. Their labor was lighter, and they were well treated. They did not have to leave their homes and families, and they ate food they were accustomed to eat and at the usual hours. They did their work together and with much merriment, for they are people who do little work alone, but together they accomplish something. Six peons will not get as much done as one Spaniard, for since they do not get much food they have little stamina and do not do as much work.

The building of the temples and the houses of the lords and public works was always a common undertaking, and many people worked together with much merriment. They left their houses after the morning chill had passed, and after they had eaten what sufficed them, according to their habits and means. Each worked a little and did what he could, and no one hurried or mistreated him for it. They stopped work early, before the chill of the afternoon, both winter and summer, for they all went about naked or with so few clothes it was like wearing none. At the slightest rainfall they took cover, because they tremble with cold when the first drops fall. Thus they went about their work, cheerfully and harmoniously.

They returned to their houses, which, being very small, were cozy and took the place of clothing. Their wives had a fire ready and laid out food; and they took pleasure in the company of their wives and children. There was never any question of payment for this communal labor. In this same way, with much rejoicing and merriment and without undue exertion, they built the churches and monasteries of their towns. These are not as sumptuous as some have said, but accord with what is necessary and proper, with moderation in everything.

It is said that the Indians are being worked to death cultivating fields for their caciques and principales, and enriching these lords, but those who say this are very mistaken. For the Indians did this when they were pagans, and they still do it in the same manner, working all together for two or three hours and then returning to their homes. They go out late, when the sun is high, and return very early. They work so near their town that they can return home daily at the hour of their choosing. It is the same with their fields, because they farm near and around the town. They go out to work on full stomachs, having eaten according to their custom. They are with their wives and children, their neighbors and kin. If a wind rises, or if it rains or turns cold, as frequently happens after midday, they return to their houses; and when the storm passes, they go back if it is not too late and work a while. The men help one another, and the women and children, even small ones, also work for short periods. When they go home, they find a fire made so that they can warm themselves, and food and drink is ready for them. Their houses are cozy and sheltered. All this is necessary for them, because they go about naked, the most they ever wear being a dirty wretched cloth to cover their genitals and, sometimes, a very sorry shirt.

Others say that drunkenness is the cause of their dying out, because many do die of it, and they kill one another when they are drunk. But this conclusion too is erroneous, for the same condition exists in other places where the people are not dying out. To be sure, it is necessary to try to prevent drunkenness, for it is the cause of extremely grave sins and crimes, and great excesses; and what I say is not intended to excuse them, but to make clear that this is not the reason they are dying out.

Neither drunkenness nor their well-organized communal labor is killing them off. The cause is their labor on Spanish public works and their personal service to the Spaniards, which they fulfill in a manner contrary to their own ways and tempo of work. To make this clear, I shall relate some things that have been and are being done to the Indians.

What I have said concerning their ancient mode of laboring on public works applies to the Indies in general, for I saw it in operation with my own eyes in all the regions through which I have traveled. I know it is the same in those regions which I have not visited, for so I was told by very trustworthy persons who were there and observed it.

As for the labor system established by the Spaniards, whose operation in New Spain I shall describe, this system too is the same throughout the Indies, so that one might think all the provinces were following one common directive. This system has destroyed the Indians everywhere, and will finish them off completely if timely relief is not provided. True, a stop has been put to this oppression in some places, but it continues elsewhere, for the Spanish judges either are blind to it or wink at it, and some actually approve of it and even coerce the Indians to do the Spaniards' bidding.

What has destroyed and continues to destroy the Indians is their forced labor in the construction of large stone masonry buildings in the Spaniards' towns. For this they are forced to leave their native climates, to come from tierra fría to tierra caliente, and vice versa, 20, 30, 40, and more leagues away. Their whole tempo of life, the time and mode of work, of eating and sleeping, are disrupted. They are forced to work many days and weeks, from dawn until after dusk, without any rest.

Once I saw, after the hour of vespers, a great number of Indians hauling a long heavy beam to a construction site owned by a very prominent man. When they stopped to rest, a Negro overseer went down the line with a leather strap in hand, whipping them all from first to last to hurry them on and keep them from resting; he did this not to gain time for some other work, for the day was over, but simply to keep up the universal evil habit of mistreating the Indians. Since the Negro struck with force and they were naked, with only their genitals covered, the lashes must have caused them cruel pain; but not one spoke or turned his head, for they are ever long-suffering and submissive. It is a routine thing to drive them, to work them without letting them pause for breath, and to harass them in every possible way. At the time of this incident I had already resigned from the office of oidor, with Your Majesty's permission, on account of my disabilities.

A religious,[65] a great servant of Our Lord, and one of the first twelve friars to come to New Spain, in a work of his lists ten plagues that have decimated and yet continue to lay low these miserable folk, and he compares these plagues to those that befell Egypt. He was a man of great goodness and virtue who would say naught but the truth. Speaking of the construction of buildings, he says:

"The seventh plague was the building of the great city of Mexico. In this work, during the first years, more people were employed than in the building of the temple of Jerusalem in the time of Solomon. So great was the number of Indians engaged in actual construction, in bringing food for the workers, and in providing food and service from their towns for the Spaniards, that a man could scarcely make his way through some streets and over the causeways, broad as they are. In the work of construction some were crushed by beams, others fell from heights, and others were caught beneath buildings that were being torn down in one place in order to erect others elsewhere. The Indians not only had to do the work but had to get the materials and pay the masons, carpenters, and stonecutters. What was more, they must bring their own food or go hungry. They carried all the materials on their backs and dragged the beams and big stones along with ropes, and since they are not very strong, four hundred men were used to convey a stone or beam that should have required one hundred men. It is their custom, when they transport such things, for the gangs of Indian laborers to sing and shout to lighten their labor; and their songs and shouts never ceased by night or day because of the great haste and fervor with which they built the city during the first two or three years."

Further on, the same author writes:

"It took no little pride and arrogance to erect these buildings, for to build them it was necessary to demolish the Indian towns and houses. The Indians had to tear down many structures and even their own homes, and bring materials from afar to Mexico for the construction of this proud city." [66]

They have been destroyed by the great and excessive tribute they have had to pay, for in their great fear of the Spaniards they have given all they had. Since the tribute was excessive and continually demanded, to make payment they sold their land at a low price, and their children as slaves. When they had nothing left with which to pay, many died for this in prison; if they managed to get out, they emerged in such sorry state that they died in a few days. Others died from being tortured to tell where there was gold or where they had hidden it. They have been treated bestially and unreasonably in all respects.

Their numbers have also been diminished by their enslavement for work in the mines and in the personal service of the Spaniards. In the first years there was such haste to make slaves that they poured into Mexico City from all directions, and throughout the Indies they were taken in flocks like sheep to be branded. The Spaniards pressed the Indian lords to bring in all the slaves, and such was the Indians' fear that to satisfy the Spaniards they brought their own vassals and even their own children when they had no others to offer. Much the same thing happens today in the provision of Indians for the Spaniards' service, and in the enslavement of Indians on the pretext that they had risen in rebellion, contrary to Your Majesty's orders.

They have been reduced by the thousands by their toil in the gold and silver mines; and on the journey to the mines 80 or 100 leagues away they were loaded with heavy burdens to which they were not accustomed. They died in the mines or along the road, of hunger and cold or extreme heat, and from carrying enormous loads of implements for the mines or other extremely heavy things; for the Spaniards, not satisfied with taking them so far away to work, must load them down on the way. Although the Indians brought some food from home, the amount was scanty, for they had no more; and it ran out on their arrival at the mines or on the return journey home. Countless numbers died, and many fled to the woods, abandoning their homes, wives, and children, and thus the towns on the way to the mines or around them became depopulated. The Spaniards still compel the Indians to go to the mines on the pretext that they are being sent to construct buildings there and are going voluntarily; these Spaniards claim that Your Majesty does not prohibit such labor, but only forbids work in the mines. In actual fact the Indians never go voluntarily, for they are forced to go under the repartimiento system by order of the Audiencia, contrary to Your Majesty's orders.

They have also been exhausted by the long journeys they have had to make, a thousand carriers at a time, sometimes more, sometimes less, carrying backbreaking loads of merchandise for days on end. The Spaniards made them go from the tierra caliente to the tierra fría, and vice versa, a change to which they are unaccustomed and which is fatal to them. The Spaniards also loaded them down with their household furnishings, beds, chairs, tables, and all the other appointments for their household and kitchen service. Thus weighted down, women and boys as well as children, they trudged over field and mountain, and returned to their homes half dead, or died on the way. In addition to all these burdens they had to carry the provisions on their backs. The Spanish encomenderos still compel the Indians to serve as carriers on the journeys these encomenderos make with their entire households to and from their towns. Most of the townspeople are occupied almost all year long in such labor and in serving the encomendero during the time he stays in their town.

The Indians have also been laid low by the labor of making sheep, cattle, and pig farms, of fencing these farms, of putting up farm buildings, and by their labor on roads, bridges, watercourses, stone walls, and sugar mills. For this labor, in which they were occupied for many days and weeks, they were taken away from their homes, their accustomed tempo of work and mode of life were disrupted; and on top of everything else they had to supply the materials for these projects at their own cost and bring them on their own backs without receiving any pay or even food. Now they are paid, but so little that they cannot buy enough to eat, for they are still used for such labor with permission from the Audiencias.

They have been exhausted by their journeys to carry tribute every year to the Spaniards' towns. They came a great distance and from a different climate, and brought with them but a little poor food. When they arrived, worn out and famished, they were made to fetch water and wood, sweep the house and stables, and take out the rubbish and manure. They were kept at such labor two, three, or more days without being given food, so that they were forced to eat the food they had brought from home, if anything was left, and so had nothing for the journey home. This is still being done.

They have been destroyed by the household service they have had to give to the Spaniards. They still give this service in some places, or are hired out to the mines. Those whose turn it was to serve a week and provide the Spaniards with food and fuel sometimes had to start out two weeks beforehand; thus in order to serve one week they must spend four weeks in coming and going. The roads were filled with Indian men and women, exhausted, dying of hunger, weary and afflicted; and the roads were strewn with the bodies of men, women, and even their little ones, for they used them to carry food—something these people had never before done.

Yet another multitude has been killed off and continues to

be killed off by being taken as carriers on conquests and expeditions, and still others to serve the soldiers. They were taken from their homes by force and separated from their women and children and kin, and few if any returned, for they perished in the conquests or along the roads, or died on their return home.

In the New Kingdom of Granada I heard many Spaniards say that one could not lose one's way between that country and the province of Popayán because it was marked with the bones of dead men. On that road there are certain birds that, when an Indian falls, pick out his eyes and kill and eat him; it is well known that these birds appear whenever the Spaniards make an incursion or discover a mine. Indian women bearing loads have been known to kill the infants at their breasts, saying they could not carry both and did not want their children to suffer the hardships they suffered.

In Guatemala I heard a prosecutor for the Audiencia say that when he was a soldier on some incursion or conquest, he saw another soldier drop his dagger in the marsh they were crossing, where it sank. An Indian woman bearing a load and an infant at her breast happened to pass, and since it was growing dark he took the child from her and set it in the marsh where the dagger had fallen. The next day he returned to look for his dagger, saying he had left the child as a marker.

Needless to say, they were taken in collar chains, and mistreated along the way; and when an Indian, man or woman, was worn out from the burden he was carrying, the Spaniards cut off his head so as not to have to stop to unchain him, and his load was distributed among the rest.

Yet another multitude perished in the seaports building ships for the Marqués [Cortés] to send to California and the Spice Islands.[67] By the thousands they were made to carry provisions, materials, and rigging on very long journeys of 40, 50, and more leagues. They trudged through forests and mountains and over wretched roads, crossing rivers and marshes far from their native lands, without food, clothing, or shelter. Wherever they went the alcaldes mayores and corregidores, and their lieutenants and alguaciles, worked them unmercifully, and fined them, and took their food and whatever else they pleased. These officials also took part of the supplies the Indians had gathered for the ships, so the Indians' work was never done. For when they had brought what was required of them, a Spanish judge would take what he pleased for his own trafficking, and order them to gather more for the ships.

Then there was the dike that was built in Mexico City,[68] and the fencing of a large part of the Valley of Toluca to protect the Spaniards' cattle, from which the Indians suffered incalculable damage. The dike, several Spaniards told me, was of no use whatever. All the people of the land were summoned, and they came from 30 and 40 leagues away. It was built at the Indians' expense, although it meant nothing to them even if it had been of use. It is always thus, for it is not enough that they give their labor and provide their own food; they must also bring and pay for all the materials for these public works. It was an incalculable waste of people as well as of their pitifully small means. They provided the earth, the stone, the stakes; thus they contributed both the labor and the materials though they received no benefit from this dike, whose cost has been estimated at 300,000 ducats.

It is said the number of laborers and masons occupied in this work was well over two million. Since the causeway is very long, the work took about four months, and each day a very great number of people were engaged in it. They worked hard all day in the water, mud, and cold, having no shelter by day or night. As a result, at the end of the week they returned home exhausted and fell ill from their ordeal. Countless numbers died.

I hardly need mention the people who were summoned to

divert the water each time the fountain burst in Chapultepec, the source of the water brought to Mexico City. They were made to work day and night, holiday or not, in the water and the cold, and without pay though the work was for the benefit of the Spaniards alone. It did not take many days, but the labor was great.

These are the things that have worn down the people of this land. They have resulted in disrupting their way of life, their routine of work, diet, and shelter, and in taking them from their towns and homes, their wives and children, their repose and harmony. I believe that their excessive labor, their exposure to hunger, cold, heat, and wind, their sleeping on the ground in the open, in the cold and the night dew, are the cause of their plague or *cámaras*. There is no cure or relief for the disease, and they die on the fourth or fifth day. Death brings an end to their suffering, from which they are never free as long as they are alive.

I could mention other things that are causing the extinction of these wretched people, but the great increase in the number of farms owned by Spaniards is in itself a sufficient cause. Ten, fifteen, and twenty years ago there were fewer farms, and there were many more Indians. The Indians were forced to work on them and suffered hardships therefrom, but since they were many and the farms few, it was not so noticeable. Now the Spanish farms are many and large and the Indians very few, and they must clear, cultivate, and weed as well as harvest and store the crops, so that all this labor now falls on the few that remain. There are ten times more Spaniards and Spanish farms and estates and ranches than there were, while there is barely one third as many Indians. And these few are continually being attacked by plagues, of which many die, whereas the work is continually increasing. Seeking escape from their oppression, many flee to the woods and mountains, leaving their fields, towns, and homes, and wander from place to place in search of a spot where they may find rest. But wherever they go they find hard work, want, and misfortune.

The Audiencias continually instruct the provincial capitals to send repartimientos of Indians for labor in the Spanish towns and their districts. On construction sites, farms, and cattle ranches, the Spaniards pay each Indian 2½ or 3 reales a week. Some Indians come a distance of 20, 25, and more leagues, depending upon the provincial capital to which they are subject and the distance from that capital to the place where they must go to be assigned to employers. Consequently, to arrive on Monday they must leave their homes on Wednesday or Thursday of the week before. The Spaniards dismiss most of their Indians on Sunday, after Mass; those who worked very well, in the employer's opinion, they let go Saturday evening. As a result, the Indians do not reach their homes until the following Wednesday or Thursday. But many never see their homes again; they die on the road from the hardships and excessive labor they have had to endure almost without food, for the food they bring from home does not last them for so many days. Moreover, they have had to work without their poor mantles, for when they enter the employer's house or other place of work, he takes their mantles from them on the grounds that he must keep them as security that his Indians will not run away. In fine, in order to serve a week for 2½ or 3 reales, the Indians must spend two weeks or longer away from home.

Since the Spanish construction projects, farms, ranches, and herds are so numerous and large, the Audiencias outdo themselves dispatching orders to the corregidores and alcaldes mayores to provide Indian laborers for the Spaniards. These officials fully understand the injury this is causing and know that the Indians are dying out, but their only concern is to aid the Spaniards. It avails the principales naught to complain and cry out that they cannot provide all the people that are demanded of them; indeed, they are arrested, fined, and mistreated for their pains.

The religious warn of the consequence of what is taking place, but no one believes them. The invariable reply is: Let the order be carried out, let the Indians go and help the Spaniards. On account of this intolerable abuse the Indians are dying like flies; they die without confession and without religious instruction, for there is no time for such things. The fewer the Indians, the more burdens the Spaniards load on those who remain. Because of this and the ill treatment they receive, the Indians return home with their health shattered. Thus disease preys on them all year long, nay, all their lives, for its causes never cease.

When they go to the construction projects or other places of labor, they bring from home certain maize cakes or tortillas that are supposed to last them for the time they are gone. On the third or fourth day the tortillas begin to get moldy or sour; they grow bitter or rotten and get as dry as boards. This is the food the Indians must eat or die. And even of this food they do not have enough, some because of their poverty and others because they have no one to prepare their tortillas for them. They go to the farms and other places of work, where they are made to toil from dawn to dusk, in the raw cold of morning and afternoon, in wind and storm, without other food than those rotten or dried-out tortillas, and even of this they have not enough. They sleep on the ground in the open air, naked, without shelter. Even if they wished to buy food with their pitiful wages they could not, for they are not paid until they are laid off. At the season when the grain is stored, the employers make them carry the wheat or corn on their backs, each man carrying a fanega, after they have worked all day. After this, they must fetch water, sweep the house, take out the trash, and clean the stables. And when their work is done, they find the employer has docked their pay on some pretext or other. Let the Indian argue with the employer about this, and he will keep the Indian's mantle as well. Sometimes an enemy will break the jar in which an Indian carries water to his master's house, in order to make him spill the water on the way, and the employer docks the Indian's wages for this.

So the Indian returns home worn out from his toil, minus his pay and his mantle, not to speak of the food that he had brought with him. He returns home famished, unhappy, distraught, and shattered in health. For these reasons pestilence always rages among the Indians. Arriving home, he gorges himself because of his great hunger, and this excess together with the poor physical condition in which he returns help to bring on the cámaras or some other disease that quickly takes him off. The Indians will all die out very quickly if they do not obtain relief from these intolerable conditions.

There is another injury—and it is not a small one—that results from their journeys. Because the Indians are now so few and the demands for their labor so numerous, each Indian is assigned many turns at compulsory labor. Moreover, contrary to what Your Majesty has ordered, the officials make the Indians go at the season when they should be sowing or weeding their fields, which are their sole wealth and means of support. The Indian must plant and weed his field within eight days or risk the loss of all his crops. If he returns from work when the time for seeding or cultivation is past, it does him little good to seed or cultivate, for he does not reap half the crop he would have, had each task been done at the proper time. Moreover, most of the Indians return sick or fall sick upon their arrival, and since they cannot cultivate or clear their fields, they harvest nothing or very little. As a result they suffer hunger all year long, and they and their families fall ill and die. On top of this, the officials fine them for not working their fields, though theirs is not the fault, and they are jailed and have to pay the costs.

Who shall tell the sum of the miseries and hardships these poor unfortunate people suffer, without help or succor from any quarter! Who does not turn his face against them, who does not persecute and vex them, who does not rob them and live by their sweat! Since I cannot tell all, but have told enough to make clear the need for a remedy, let me be silent concerning the innumerable crimes that I have personally seen and verified or that I have heard of from trustworthy persons.

The ancient kings and lords never ruled in this way, never took the Indians from their towns, never disrupted their way of life and labor. I cannot believe that Your Majesty or the members of Your Majesty's Council know or have been informed about what is taking place. If they knew of it, they would surely take steps to preserve Your Majesty's miserable vassals and would not allow the Indians to be entirely destroyed in order to gratify the wishes of the Spaniards. If the Indians should die out (and they are dying with terrible rapidity), those realms will very quickly become depopulated, as has already happened in the Antilles, the great province of Venezuela, and the whole coast of northern South America and other very extensive lands that have become depopulated in our time. The wishes of Your Majesty and his Royal Council are well known and are made very plain in the laws that are issued every day in favor of the poor Indians and for their increase and preservation. But these laws are obeyed and not enforced,[69] wherefore there is no end to the destruction of the Indians, nor does anyone care what Your Majesty decrees. How many decrees, cedulas, and letters were sent by our lord, the Emperor, who is in glory, and how many necessary orders are sent by Your Majesty! How little good have all these orders done! Indeed, the more laws and decrees are sent, the worse is the condition of the Indians by reason of the false and sophistical interpretation that the Spanish officials give these laws, twisting their meaning to suit their own purposes. It seems to me that the saying of a certain philosopher well applies to this case: Where there is a plenty of doctors and medicines, there is a plenty of ill health. Just so, where there are many laws and judges, there is much injustice.

We have a multitude of laws, judges, viceroys, governors, *presidentes*, oidores, corregidores, alcaldes mayores, a million lieutenants, and yet another million alguaciles. But this multitude is not what the Indians need, nor will it relieve their misery. Indeed, the more such men there are, the more enemies do the Indians have. For the more zeal these men display against the Indians, the more influence do they wield; the Spaniards call such men Fathers of their Country, saviors of the state, and proclaim them to be very just and upright. The more ill will such men show against the Indians and friars, the more titles and lying encomiums are heaped upon them. But let an official favor the Indians and the religious (who are bound together, one depending upon the other), and this alone suffices to make him odious and abhorrent to all. For the Spaniards care for one thing alone, and that is their advantage; and they give not a rap whether these poor and miserable Indians live or die, though the whole being and welfare of the country depend upon them.

God has closed the eyes and darkened the minds of these Spaniards, so that they see with their eyes what is happening, yet do not see it, so that they perceive their own destruction, yet do not perceive it, and all because of their callousness and hardheartedness. I have known an oidor to say publicly from his dais, speaking in a loud voice, that if water were lacking to irrigate the Spaniards' farms, they would have to be watered with the blood of Indians. I have heard others say that the Indians, and not the Spaniards, must labor. Let the dogs work and die, said these men, the Indians are numerous and rich. These officials say such things because they have not seen the Indians' sufferings and miseries, because they are content to sit in the cool shade and collect their pay. They also say these things to win the good will and gratitude of the Spaniards, and also because they all have sons-in-law, brother-in-law, relatives, or close friends among them. These friends and relatives are rich in farms, ranches, and herds; and the officials control a major part of this wealth. That is what blinds them and makes them say what they say and do what they do.

In the old days the Indians had few laws, so few that all knew them by heart, as is told of the Lacedaemonians and the Scythians, and none dared to break those laws. They were well governed, their numbers increased, and they lived happily and peacefully. They were masters of their poor little properties. They did not have to leave their native surroundings to support themselves, but enjoyed the company of their wives, children, and kindred by day and night. They paid their tribute without hardship or undue exertion.

I could say much more on this subject, but to tell it all would weary the reader. Indeed, I think it unnecessary, speaking to a Prince so upright, just, and Christian, to enlarge on what is so notorious and glaring that no man attached to the service of God and Your Majesty will deny it.

ARTICLE 11

You will inform yourselves how those who afterwards fixed the amount of tribute to be paid by the Indians to the Spanish encomenderos proceeded in this; whether they took care that it should conform to the tribute the Indians used to pay to their supreme ruler and other lords, or whether the assessment made was different from and greater than the tribute the Indians used to pay to their lords.

The first assessment was made by the Bishop of Mexico,[70] who came with the title of Protector of the Indians. He made very little inquiry into the matter, and it is said that he used to weep thereafter each time that assessment was mentioned, for he contented himself with reducing slightly the tribute the Indians paid under the "agreement" that they had made with the encomenderos. There were great frauds connected with this assessment, because many caciques and principales, fearing their encomenderos or wishing to please them, declared that the Indians could pay the amounts they were paying. Under pressure from their encomenderos, these caciques even overstated the amounts the Indians were paying, so that if some reduction were made, the assessment would remain what it had been.

Since that time the Audiencia and some visitadores have made other assessments. Because the first ones were so high, these officials thought they were doing the Indians a great favor by reducing the amounts slightly. As a result of failure to solve the problem once and for all, the Indians constantly clamor for relief from their heavy burdens. The Audiencia has sometimes lowered the assessments, sometimes raised them. In recent years the frauds and tricks practiced by the Spaniards have led to the increase or even doubling of the assessments, thus returning them to their former level or slightly below. This is the cause of the constant comings and goings of the Indians to and from the Audiencia, in which they waste their money and even lose their lives, but never obtain justice.

In recent years the encomenderos have used this gambit: One will claim that his Indians can pay more tribute than they are paying, because there are so many of them. The Audiencia then orders that a count be made of these Indians, and appoints someone to go and make it. The encomendero usually has ways and means of ensuring that the appointee is his choice. If his nominee is not selected, or if he is not pleased with the man, he persuades the Indians to challenge the appointee on his advice or that of some other Spaniard (for there are always some Spaniards clinging like leeches to the Indians), or he may get some third party to do the job. The encomendero does the same with the next man to be appointed, and so on until a person satisfactory to him is chosen. To make this man feel indebted to him, the encomendero lets him know that he owes his appointment to his efforts. This official brings along an interpreter and a notary, and all come attended by Negro, mestizo, and mulatto servants, and mounted on horses. They set about making the count. First of all they give notice thereof to the Indian governor, alcaldes, and regidores, whom the encomendero has already suborned and bribed in most cases. The count is made, and they take three, four, five, or ten, or even fifteen days for this, depending on the size of the town. During all this time they eat off the community. When they have finished and are handed an account of the provisions given by the town, they pay what they please and sometimes nothing at all.

The count having been made, it is submitted to the Audiencia, which makes a new assessment. Now the Indians come to protest that the count is incorrect and to petition for relief because the tribute imposed upon them is excessive. The encomendero is notified of their appeal, and the ensuing suit drags on for six months to a year, or longer. In the meantime the Indians pay tribute according to the new assessment, and must bear the costs of litigation to boot.

The Audiencia sends another official to count the Indians; and they spend on his maintenance and that of his aides, and on their suit, more than the amount of their tribute for one or two years. The Audiencia finally rules that the first count was correct, which is not strange, for the second count was marked by the same frauds and subornations as the first, and the Indian cause is always the weaker. So the Indians continue to suffer the same injuries as before, and they have used up their money to no avail. To cover their expenses the Indians assess themselves (for it is a most ancient custom among them to assess themselves for such contingencies). Each day that the count lasts they assess themselves to provide food for the person making the count and his aides, and to cover the incidental expenses that always attend such an affair.

Each tribute-payer pays as follows: A married man pays 8

reales and half a fanega of maize, and 1½ reales to his community; widowers, widows, and single men without parents but owners of land, pay half as much. This system has defects that I have mentioned, and many others that I shall describe. Never since the conquest of the land has care been taken that the tribute the Indians pay should conform to what they used to pay to their former lords. The Spanish officials are concerned only with the advantage of the Spaniards; if the Indians, their wives, and their children must perish in the process, so be it. The Indians pay incomparably more tribute now than in the old days, and suffer intolerable hardships not only in connection with the tribute but in all their dealings with the Spaniards.

This matter of a count is a novelty for the Indians. They never had such a thing formerly, nor was it necessary, for practically all paid tribute in the form of labor on designated fields. Moreover, from the age of five or six, almost all were inscribed in paintings kept by each town and barrio, and the names of those who died or were gone for any reason were erased. Therefore this count causes dismay among the Indians, save those who devote themselves to robbing their own people. These men, pretending zeal for the common good, assess the Indians so they can go to the Audiencia to ask for a new count; they would be happy to see these counts go on forever, for they are able to eat and travel about the country at others' expense. The Audiencia notifies the encomendero of the appeal, and this takes a good deal of time, especially if he does not live in the town where the Audiencia sits.

These Indians may ask for a recount every three months or whenever the fancy takes them; they will allege that many of their people have died or fled. To defray the expenses of going to the Audiencia they assess the townspeople; and in the course of this business they find it necessary to make a few other assessments. If a judge is sent to the town to make a new count, this requires an assessment, and still another is needed to provide his daily food. If the townspeople are to provide the judge with ten chickens or eggs daily, the unscrupulous Indian leaders will collect as many as there are people in the town, and keep the surplus for themselves. What the judge pays for the food they do not give to the people who supplied it, but again keep it for themselves.

They make other assessments for presents to be given to Spanish officials, and still others to defray their expenses in returning to the Audiencia with the new count, and for lawyers, attorneys, solicitors, and interpreters, so that all year long they levy assessments on the poor macehuales who toil to provide what they demand. Be it true or not what they say about the decline in the number of their people, *their* assessments go on endlessly, and thus the toil of the common people ever increases.

The men who levy these assessments are not natural lords, but macehuales who have made themselves bosses, alcaldes, regidores, or alguaciles, and so rob all they can while they hold office and power; and their successors do the same. Indeed, even some lords have lowered themselves to the same level. If the facts about such doings are known, they cannot be proved; and even if the facts are proved, these men have not the money to pay fines. So they are condemned to labor in the mines or to other servitude; and all redounds to the injury of the town and the common people, for the burden of the tribute falls on the shoulders of the few who remain.

Some encomenderos follow the practice of naming some principales of their towns, or of other towns, to go about as their representatives with the officials making a count. These principales, wishing to gain their encomendero's favor, or influenced by gifts or other means, do all they can to make it appear that there is a large number of people. Some encomenderos do the same on their own; and in the course of some

tours of inspection that I made I personally observed and established that these encomenderos import people from neighboring towns with the claim that these people have come to
live in their town, and so they reckon them as tribute-payers.
When the count is over, or when the tribute falls due, or
whenever the whim takes them, these people return to their
homes or go somewhere else, and their tribute obligations fall
on those who remain in the town.

The system of counts has another defect, which is that the
tribute is per capita. The number of Indians daily grows less,
but the tribute remains the same. To be sure, the law makes
provision for a reduction of tribute in such cases, but the law
is not complied with. The Indians, being generally a people
of great simplicity, do not know how to demand their rights
and so bear their woes in silence. If some of them, shrewder
than their fellows, and moved by zeal for the common welfare or by private interest, do complain in the name of all,
this leads to another evil, namely, that the Indians squander
their lives and money in suits, and all the while continue to
pay tribute according to the first count. In the end they never
obtain justice, for they drop the suit because they have run
out of money or the encomenderos have bribed their leaders;
or their leaders may have died; or they may be unable to
prove that some of their people have fled or died, or that
there was an error in the count. Meanwhile the number of
people in the town steadily declines, but tribute is collected
on the basis of the old count, and the living must pay for the
dead and the fugitives. One is tempted to say that the living
were better off dead, considering the woes they suffer.

Should the Audiencia order a new count, the Indians must
bear more costs. Even if they can prove a population loss, the
tribute of those who have died or fled is not abated by the
authorities, but must be paid by those who remain—something
that contravenes natural, divine, and human law. Whereas the

population goes on declining, tribute is collected on the basis of the old count, and since litigation and clamor for new counts never cease, the Indians expend greater sums than the sums they hope to save by having the tribute reduced. Needless to say, the encomendero always charges Indians who complain with being rebels; and he gets the cacique and principales to inform the authorities that the grumblers are lying, that their people are happy and quite able to pay the tribute. The encomendero will even request the Audiencia to send someone to find out what the townspeople actually think; the people questioned by this investigator have been well schooled in what they are to say. So all that the complainants get for their pains is to be called rebels, and to be held for months in jail, where they go mad with hunger, without a soul to intercede for them. At their trial the encomendero manages to prove all his charges against them, and they are sentenced to labor in chains in the mines or elsewhere for a year or longer. The judge also orders them to be flogged and to have their hair cropped, which is a great offense to Indians. Their time at forced labor is sold at public auctions, and at these auctions one sees them, in chains, sorrowful, unhappy, knowing not what to say or to whom they should complain. Accompanied by their wives and children, they are sent to distant regions. They lose their houses, lands, and belongings, grow vicious, and receive no religious instruction. It is considered a great favor to them if the judge orders that they receive wages, and even then they do not always get them.

When a count is ordered, the people of a town are summoned to the provincial capital, which may be a distance of 15, 20, and more leagues away; and there they must stay while the count is being made. All this time they neglect their farms and trades. The official making the count remains in the town as long as it suits him; he is in no hurry to leave, since the stay brings money into his pockets. Before he has finished and left the town, many of the people he counted have died, yet they are listed as tribute-payers, and the others must pay for them. If the Indian officials assess their people to cover this expense, the Spaniards punish them and strip them of their offices. If these officials do not assess their people, they must pay the tribute themselves or die in prison because of the shortage. For failure to make the tribute payments on time results in arrest of the cacique, governor, alcaldes, and regidores. Indeed, the main purpose of these offices is to extract tribute from the Indians. As for those unscrupulous Indians of whom I spoke before, they also serve as agents of wholesale robbery of their own people.

The Spaniards have found a way of getting rid of Indians who come to complain of excessive tribute; it consists in immediately asking these Indians if they bring a power of attorney. Since they are a very simple people, they do not understand what such a thing is. So these Indians, some of whom have come distances of 100 and more leagues, hang around for a few days, completely bewildered, and finally go home without being heard. If they do not go home, the encomendero runs to the governor and the principales to get them to say that they are not asking for any abatement of tribute. The result is that the protesters are seized and punished.

Sometimes a Spaniard who has no interest in the matter will ask the Indians why they have come to the Audiencia; the Indians, thinking the questioner is sympathetic to them, reply: To petition that the tribute be reduced. Thereupon the Spaniard warns them that other Indians who sought the same thing have been flogged and sent to the mines for their pains, and that the same will happen to them. Since the Indians, especially those who live a long way from the Spanish towns (and these Indians are the most heavily burdened because they do not know how to complain to the authorities), are a timid, miserable, and very simple people, they take fright at this and hastily depart. The wretch who is responsible for their flight is as joyful as if he had done some heroic deed.

Since the introduction of counts and assignments of tribute by heads, the practice has arisen of collecting tribute from cripples, blind and maimed persons, and other wretches who cannot work and even lack food; and they collect from minors and single young women without means of support. This is a cause of great offense to Our Lord. All these people were free from tribute in the time of their paganry. The principales have been told that such people are not to pay tribute, but they have no choice save to collect from them or go rot in prison. The only alternative is for the principales to sell their estates and pay the tribute themselves. As I have said, it is the principales who bear the brunt of all these evils.

The persons who make the count also contribute to this iniquity. Eager to show their diligence, and to prolong their stay as long as possible, these persons include in their census suckling infants, paupers, cripples, minors, and other ineligible persons, such as lords, caciques, principales, and mayeques. All these persons are required to pay the tribute quota of 1 peso and whatever else is set forth in the assessment. The officials declare that there are so many tribute-payers, and that number must stand for the life of the assessment. The principales assess the ineligible persons to make up the gaps caused by the death or flight of others; they declare that all were counted, and all must pay. The encomendero cares not what is done; his only concern is to collect every last penny of his tribute. If it becomes known and talked about that tribute was collected from ineligible persons, the encomendero casts guilt on the principales, saying they did it to steal money for themselves. The real cause is the encomendero's insistence on collecting all the tribute to which he lays claim. Thus all the offense, guilt, and punishment fall upon the Indians in one way or another.

Among the evils that flow from the system of counts, the following is not the least: The persons who make a count require the gobernadores, alcaldes and regidores, and *tequitlatos* (who are directly responsible for their barrios) to show them the census lists in their keeping and to swear that these lists are correct and true and that they will not conceal any tribute-payers. The officials swear to this effect. When the count is finished, they are again made to take such an oath, and almost invariably perjure themselves by permitting the inclusion of persons who should not have been counted. They do this from self-interest or to make up the deficit of tributes. No objections are raised because these principales allow the inclusion of the above persons, for the Spaniards are interested only in finding more tribute-payers. Very frequently, however, the statements made by the principales are perjured. Great perjuries also occur in the declarations concerning the yield and quality of lands and the number of people living on them that are made in connection with the counts both by encomenderos and Indians.

A religious of great authority told me that since the introduction of these counts he and other members of his Order, who are responsible for the religious instruction of the Mixe and Chontal Indians who live near Oaxaca, have learned that all the Indians had agreed not to have intercourse with their wives or other women, or else to seek to prevent conception or cause miscarriage in their women. As soon as he and the other religious learned of this, they labored earnestly to make the Indians see their error and the offense they were doing Our Lord. They replied that they could not pay tribute because many of their people were dying off and others were fleeing to the woods, that they had no reales nor any way of securing them, and that they did not want to have children who would suffer as they suffered; besides, they could not pay the tribute demanded of them and still support wives and children. So great was their dejection that nothing the religious said could induce them to abandon their design.

All these evils flow from the system of counts, from imposing money tribute on the Indians, and from assigning tribute by heads. I am aware that all these procedures conform to the law; but in order to do away with the present evils and avert those still to come, it would be better to abandon the system of counts and return to their ancient mode of paying tribute. How this should be done, I shall explain when I comment on Article 15.

ARTICLE 12

Item: You will inform yourselves how this assessment was made; whether the towns were summoned and gave their consent to the assessment; how the townspeople were assembled and what method was used to obtain their consent; and whether their consent was forced or freely given.

In my comments on Articles 10 and 11, I have already explained how the first assessments were made. At present, when a town is to be assessed, information is obtained from the encomendero and the Indians as to the quality and fertility of the land. Whatever the encomendero says the authorities accept, for the encomendero knows just how to phrase the report and how to manage the whole business. In other cases a count is made of the people. To this end the Audiencia summons the gobernadores, alcaldes, and regidores. These Indians do not know what they are being summoned for, and if they do know, they have no idea what they should say, or else they have been suborned to approve whatever is done. No effort is made to obtain the consent of the people. Even if they object, it does them no good, for all they get from objecting is expenses, suits, and their ruination.

I have already replied to the queries contained in this section in my comments on the other sections. I shall merely add that now and always the interest of the Spaniards has been the only concern. The people are summoned for the sole purpose of being counted; they are given no opportunity to present their views. When the count has been made, it is carried to the Audiencia, which makes the assessment without any consultation of the people. There is no question of obtaining their consent, for the whole business is carried out in an arbitrary way, and against their will. The only persons to whom notice of the assessment is given are the encomendero and some Indian principal or other who has no idea of what it is all about.

ARTICLE 13

*You will also inform yourselves whether in making this
assessment care was taken that the Indians be left with
enough to rear and marry off their children, support themselves and their children, help themselves in case of need
and illness, and prosper through their work and diligence;
or whether the assessment was made with regard only to
the amount of tribute the Indians could pay.*

The answer to the questions asked here is already clear: No
regard was given to the welfare of the Indians. Aside from a
very few principales and merchants, an Indian's whole estate
does not amount to the value of the tribute that he must pay.
Indeed, there are many whose total fortune does not come to
a peso; all these people have for their support is the labor of
their hands. As a result, they are not left with enough to
marry off a son or daughter; nor can they save the needed
money. Because of this many Indian boys and girls marry
clandestinely, and so spend their lives out of wedlock because
they and their parents lacked 4 or 6 reales. What the Indians
obtain from their fields barely provides them with their food,
for they have no other wealth or estate; they depend on their
lands for food, clothing, and the other necessities of life.

With great difficulty do the Indians keep body and soul together. A great many do not go to Mass or Sunday school because they cannot afford it. Many become so desperate because they cannot support themselves and their children and wives that they tire of it all and leave their families. If they become ill, they have no food and have nothing to fall back on; for if they cannot work, all is lost. In such case they cannot even keep warm. Since they have little clothing or bed furnishings, the fire is their shelter and a major element in their comfort. But if an Indian cannot go out to get fuel, he lacks a fire as well as everything else.

Once, on a tour of inspection of a certain region, I learned of some Indians who had hanged themselves after telling their wives and neighbors that they intended to do this because they could not pay so much tribute and support themselves. In Mexico City I learned that a daughter of Moctezuma, having contracted an illness of which she later died, was thrown out to lie on a mat on the ground. She was so poor that she would have had nothing to eat if the Franciscans had not sent her some food. Yet she was an Indian woman of high station. The misery and need of the Indians remain unknown to officials who never make a tour of inspection and will not listen to informed persons who could enlighten them about such things; these officials are content to sit at home and collect their pay and bask in the approval of the Spaniards. Indeed, these officials make fun of one who seeks to know and understand the misery of the Indians, and condemn his efforts as folly and vanity.

In short, the Indians are not assessed according to their ability to pay, nor is there any regard for their welfare. An Indian may be dying, but the tribute is collected from him just the same. Truly, it is a very great pity to see and hear about what is done in this matter and how contrary it is to Your Majesty's orders.

ARTICLE 14

Item: You will inform yourselves what kinds of people pay tribute to the Spaniards; whether peasants, or merchants, or artisans, or other sorts of people as well; whether those who pay tribute are poor or rich, what property they possess, and what is their capacity to pay.

I have already observed, especially in my comments on Article 4, that at present all classes of Indians pay tribute, and that the Spaniards have made tribute-payers of the lords and principales, who were free in the time of their heathendom, and to whom the commoners used to pay tribute. In short, all the Indians without exception are tribute-payers today, and but few escape from having to labor on the Spanish public works. As for the other queries in this section, I have already replied to them, especially in my comments on Article 13, wherein I declared that the Indians are a poor and wretched folk.

For a better exposition of the points raised in Article 15, I shall join the last part of Article 16 to it.

ARTICLE 15

Because it may aid the discharge of His Majesty's royal conscience to provide that the tribute be paid in another way, I command that after making the said inquiry you shall consult with the religious and other persons of honor and good conscience and send us your opinion as to what needs to be done, stating the quantity of tribute that you think necessary for the Indians to pay in order to keep them in peace and subjection, to provide them with instruction in our Holy Catholic Faith, to afford a decent maintenance to the Spaniards who are necessary for the defense of the land and for the enhancement and preservation of the Faith. You will also give your opinion as to the method to be followed in the apportionment of this sum among the towns, and its collection, with the least possible prejudice to the Indians.

ARTICLE 16

[Item: You already know what has been written to you touching the matter of tithes. Since it would be well were a solution found for this problem, I order you to discuss it again, for it would seem that some way could be found of avoiding illegal procedures and briberies in the collection of tithes. You will consider whether it would be advisable that Indian merchants who live by trade should pay a tithe on the value of the things they sell, and that artisans should pay a small per capita sum, so that all would contribute something for the benefit of all. But if you know some

other and better way, send us your opinion and the sup-
porting reasons[71]*], because it seems fitting that the tribute*
should be definite and fixed and not uncertain, as at pres-
ent, varying as it does with the capacity of the Indians to
pay; and because it seems unjust that they should pay all
the tribute they are able to pay, which makes them appear
to be slaves rather than freemen, against the intent of His
Majesty, whose laws make plain his wish that the tribute be
moderate and less than they paid in the time of their pa-
ganry.

These articles contain much matter for reflection, and much
reflection is called for in my reply. The holy zeal of Your
Majesty and his Royal Council is well known. I have said
enough to let it be understood how contrary to Your Majesty's wishes are the things that are being done in the assessment of the tribute paid by the Indians.

In what concerns Your Majesty's instructions to the oidores
to inquire into the matters that form the subject of this
cedula, taking information to this end from the religious and
other persons, I have done all I could to verify what I have
written here, and have informed myself in detail about each
topic. I did not take part in the inquiries conducted by the
Audiencia de los Confines and that of Mexico City, nor did I
join in framing the opinions they sent to Your Majesty, because I was absent at the time these things were done.

In my comments on Article 5, I related how the Indians
paid and collected tribute in the time of their heathendom. In
my comments on Article 11, I described the situation that
existed for some years after the Indians had become Your
Majesty's vassals and the evils that arise from the present order of things, especially from the system of counts. It seems

to me unjust that no difference should be made between rich and poor, and that all should be made to pay alike. To be sure, there is very little difference in wealth among the Indians.

Before I continue with my reply, let me briefly summarize what Your Majesty has decreed in the matter of Indian tribute. Your Majesty has ordered that the caciques and natural lords should receive the tribute and services they used to receive in the time of their heathendom, but that the tribute should not be excessive or imposed tyrannically; if it prove to be such, it should be appraised and lowered. On the other hand, Your Majesty orders that the tribute to be paid to the encomenderos should be fixed at such a rate that they may live comfortably, but without prejudice and harassment to the Indians, adhering in this to Your Majesty's provisions in the Indians' favor. Your Majesty has also ordered that the tribute be moderate and less than that which they paid in the time of their heathendom, so that they may know Your Majesty's desire to favor them. It appears to me that this implies a contradiction, for if they pay the caciques and lords what is due them, and if the encomenderos receive their due share of tribute, the total cannot be less than the amount they paid their caciques and lords in the time of their heathendom, but more than double as much.

Your Majesty has also ordered that assessments should be made, not on the basis of reports concerning the capacity to pay of the towns, but on the basis of personal observation and study of the character and capacities of each town, the fertility of its soil, and the like, in order that a just assessment may be made and each Indian may be made to understand precisely what he owes and is obliged to give, so much and no more. Your Majesty has also decreed that the Indians must not be compelled to pay tribute in things that they can give only at the cost of their destruction; instead they should give only

those things that are found in their native lands and regions
and that they can easily obtain, namely, the produce of their
fields or the products of their crafts, taking into account
the character and habits of each town. Moreover, the tribute
should consist of only two or three kinds of things, and no
more, and must not be indefinite; the precise quantity of each
thing must be declared. Your Majesty has also ordered that
the Indians must not be made to pay up to the limits of their
capacity, that they should be allowed to get richer and not
poorer, that they should be left with enough to take care of
their needs, cure their ills, and marry off their children, and
that they should enjoy rest and repose, with due regard for
their preservation, increase, and religious instruction. Moreover, Your Majesty has ordered that the oidores should in
turn continually tour the country, with instructions to regulate all assessments and reduce those that are excessive, and
has warned them that great care should be taken in all the
above as a thing of great service to Our Lord and Your Majesty.

Because the Emperor, our lord, held this matter to be of
such great weight, in one of his royal provisions he ordered
the persons to whom he committed the assessment of a province to join, before all else, in hearing a solemn Mass, that the
Holy Ghost might enlighten them and give them grace to
do well, justly, and righteously what they were charged and
ordered to do. Having heard the Mass, they were to promise
and swear solemnly before the officiating priest that they
would do all well and loyally. After taking the said oath, they
were to establish, through personal visitation and observation,
the number of Indians in each town and the nature of the
land wherein they dwelled. Having informed themselves as
to what the Indians could and should justly and conveniently
pay as tribute in virtue of the Emperor's lordship, they were
to declare, regulate, and reduce the assessment according to

the dictates of God and their consciences. From this it is clear how seriously the Emperor, our lord, took this business.

For the same reason, in certain other provisions he forbade that special commissioners (*jueces de comisión*) be sent to make assessments, and ordered that only the amount of tribute that was assessed should be collected, and no more. He further decreed that substitution of other commodities for the stipulated tribute should never be allowed, even if the Indians did this of their own free will. Many penalties, including loss of encomiendas, are prescribed for violation of these orders, but all of them together have not secured compliance.

On many occasions Your Majesty has ordered other things in his royal provisions, decrees, letters, ordinances, and instructions, directed to various regions. Many of these orders are in my possession, in addition to those that were printed in Mexico City. Above I gave the substance of the orders most pertinent to the subject under discussion, although all the orders are very just and necessary.

In considering the numerous and most needful prescriptions that Your Majesty orders to be kept, I have wondered how matters could be arranged so as to comply with all Your Majesty's wishes. Sometimes, when I perceived the defects that each and every possible solution presented, I should have been happy to find some way of avoiding giving the opinion that Your Majesty desires. For, although all that Your Majesty provides for in these articles is most saintly and necessary, it seems to me impossible to comply with all their provisions; however, wishing to carry out Your Majesty's orders and perform my obligations to your royal service, I shall give my opinion on these matters.

Throughout the Indies the natives are dying out and declining in number, though some assert that this is not so. Since the Indians are so heavily burdened with tribute payments that they cannot support themselves and their wives and children, they often leave them (although they love them dearly), and abandon their wretched little homes and their fields. They depart for some other region and wander about from place to place or flee to the woods, where jaguars or other beasts eat them. Some Indians have hanged themselves in desperation because of the great hardships they suffer on account of the tribute. I have personally verified such incidents on various tours of inspection.

Therefore it appears to me impossible to provide a system under which the tribute would be fixed and perpetual. On the contrary, it appears to me necessary to visit the Indian towns every year and reduce the tribute requirement, that the few Indians who remain should not have to pay for the many who were counted but have since died or fled. This matter will not brook delay.

As I said before, the Indians have little stamina. As a result, an Indian's planting is so small that his harvest will barely cover his needs for the year, for he cannot cultivate an area larger than the little plot that he and his wife and children (if he has them) can work. From this harvest half a fanega of maize is taken for tribute. This amount is taken in good and bad years alike, although Your Majesty has ordered they should not be made to pay tribute in bad years. The taking of this maize is a great injury to the Indians. One might think they would not miss half a fanega, but it is a great deal to them because of their small harvests. Maize is their staff of life, the source of their food and clothing, and if they do not grow it themselves, they have no means of obtaining it. Consequently, if the crop fails, they suffer from famine and eat herbs, roots, and fruit that rot their guts, giving them cámaras of which they quickly die. They have very little food other than maize, for in general they are all very poor. All they possess is the labor of their hands, though some have a piece of farm land around their houses. For the rest, an Indian has a very sorry mantle with which he covers himself, a sleeping mat, a stone to grind maize for his daily bread, and a few chickens—such is the extent of his fortune. The value of the whole may come to 10 pesos, and not all possess even this much. Consequently, the tribute they pay and the means to support themselves and their families come from their labor alone.

To ask the Indians for tribute in reales is also a great injury to them. Unless an Indian lives in a town not far from a Spanish town, or on a main traveled road, or raises cacao or cotton, or makes cotton cloth, or raises fruit, he does not receive money. There are regions where the Indians have never seen a real in all their lives, and do not even know what a real is. In order to earn money, therefore, they must quit their towns and homes, leaving their wives and children without means of support, and go 30, 40, and even more leagues to climates different from their own, where they sometimes lose their lives. Sometimes in their despair they prefer not to return home, or perhaps one will take to living with another woman and lead a depraved life, leaving all the burdens of supporting his family to his poor wife.

If an Indian cannot pay the money tribute because he lacks the means, or does not know where to go to earn reales, he goes to jail and his time at forced labor is sold to some Spaniard to cover the tribute and jailer's costs. He must toil for two, three, or four months or even longer, according to what he owes and what he is paid for his work, because he has no property that can be seized and sold by the authorities. The majority, or some, of the Indians to whom this happens do not even know why. It is the same thing with those who have some means, because the tribute is so excessive. The Spaniard who buys the time at forced labor of such Indians keeps priming them with money, clothing, or cacao; as a result they have to continue working for him all their lives long. Their encomendero does not worry himself about this because he does not lose any tribute; the remaining Indians must pay the entire assessment.

There is another great evil that arises from making the Indians pay tribute in money. The mines are gradually becoming worked out. Each year less silver is obtained from them, and much of this silver is sent to Spain. The Mint at Mexico City mints less silver than formerly.[72] A great part of what is minted is sent to Guatemala to pay for the cacao that merchants bring from there; much silver is also sent to Yucatán and other regions in exchange for wax and blankets. A considerable quantity also reaches Spain in every fleet and ship that goes there, both for Your Majesty and for the accounts of merchants and other private parties, not to speak of the silver that the ships' people carry on their own. Things are bound to come to such a pass that the Indians will not have a single real, for all their goods and services will be paid for in cacao. As a result they will have no way of getting reales to pay tribute or to use for any other purpose. What money they now have will soon be dispersed because of the great quantity of reales they pay in tribute each year, a quantity greater than the amount minted at the Mint of Mexico City. Thus they will be destroyed through the collection of what they neither possess nor have the means of getting. Besides, the trade with Guatemala and Yucatán will cease for lack of money. Since the people of those areas have no source of silver except Mexico, their tribute payments will also suffer.

The requirement that the Indians pay tribute in money has been a dreadful affliction because it affects all of them. This requirement contravenes Your Majesty's orders which provide that the Indians shall pay tribute in what they grow in their own towns. Not only is the money tribute excessive, and demanding of what they do not have to give; it does great injury to the Indian and Spanish communities alike, for in order to pay this tribute the Indians seek for labor that will give them reales, and thus they neglect the farm work that is necessary for Spaniards as well as Indians. This is why produce is so dear and agricultural production in decline. As a result, both Spaniards and Indians lose; and the only ones who gain are the encomenderos, because they get their tribute in reales and give not a rap about the general suffering caused by the dearth and high cost of all commodities.

These preliminary remarks are intended to make clear how urgent it is to remedy the existing state of affairs and keep the miserable Indians from dying out. They are the support of that land; and if they perish, it is the end of everything. That is what has happened in the islands, in the great province of Venezuela, and on the entire coast of the mainland. It is all a great injury to the service of Our Lord and of Your Majesty, and a great impediment to the conversion and religious instruction of the unhappy Indians.

In view of the above, and whereas Your Majesty orders that opinions be sent to him of the order that should prevail in the collection of tribute, with indication of the amount to be paid, and how this sum should be apportioned among the towns, and how collected, with the least possible injury to the Indians:

Let Your Majesty command, as a matter of great import for the service of Our Lord, for the general welfare of that land and its natives, and for the discharge of Your Majesty's royal conscience, that two, three, or more oidores (there are eight in Mexico City, and *alcaldes de corte* and corregidores besides) continually tour the country, visting towns, cattle ranches, farms, and textile factories. These oidores shall not hear cases or be burdened with any other business. Although there is a backlog of cases at present, soon there will be no suits to hear, nor even need for a court of justice.

Four oidores will suffice to inspect the towns, establish

the value of their land, their economic activities, the produce they grow and their markets for this produce, and the population of each town (this should be ascertained in the manner to be described, and not by counts, because of the disadvantages of this system). The oidores will also inform themselves of the trade and industry of each town, the importance of each line of trade and industry, and who are the natural lords, caciques, and principales, and what benefits they were wont to derive from their lordships and dignities. The oidores will also see that these lords and principales are maintained in their privileges, as Your Majesty has ordered.

These oidores will also ascertain what persons are free of tribute and will guard these persons in their ancient privilege and liberty. It is most important that this be done, even though it may take several days and cost some money. The oidores can easily establish the truth in this matter, for the facts are well known to the Indians, and if questioned, they will tell what they know with all candor. After the oidores have put these matters to rights, without allowing further delay to blur men's memories, the question of who is free of tribute will be settled once and for all.

The oidores will also assess the tribute each town must pay. To this end they will call on the people of each town, and on the encomendero, in the case of encomienda towns, or on Your Majesty's solicitor and the officials of your Royal Treasury, in the case of Crown towns, to name someone to represent them in the making of the assessment. This involves no cost, for these parties always name someone to go about with the officials sent to make an assessment. In this way the assessment will be made with the consent of the people who must pay the tribute, for they will be given an opportunity to discuss and reach an understanding as to the amount of tribute they can pay. In this way they can also be made to understand that the tribute must be paid punctually, without any delay.

If it please Your Majesty, let it be ordered that each assessment remain the same for four or five years. At the end of this period a new assessment will be made if it appears desirable, for this space of time is long enough to establish what tribute the town can actually pay, and whether the number of people is decreasing or increasing. If during this time they find it impossible to pay tribute because of crop failure or an epidemic, they should appeal to the Audiencia for relief, as Your Majesty has provided.

However, this arrangement has certain drawbacks, for the Indians must expend time and money in providing the Audiencia with the necessary information, in transmitting power of attorney, and in taking the other measures needed in support of their petition for a new assessment or an abatement of tribute. While these things are being done, the encomendero or Your Majesty's officials continue to collect tribute as before. This is a source of great injury and hardship to the Indians. It would be far better, therefore, if the *corregidor* or alcalde mayor, or the religious responsible for their instruction, were to give notice of crop failure or inability to pay tribute as soon as possible; this would be quicker, more certain, and less costly, and would impose no burdens on the Indians.

After the assessment of tribute has been made according to the characteristics and population of the town, but without assignment by heads, let the natural lords of the town apportion it among their people as they were wont to do, for they know best each man's ability to pay. If necessary, let these lords make a new apportionment every year. After the assignment of tribute has been made, let the lords turn the tribute roll over to the corregidor or *teniente* of the town, if it has one, and if not, let them turn it over to the corregidor nearest to the town. The corregidor will in turn send the tribute roll to the Audiencia. In the presence of the oidor who visited and assessed that town, let the Audiencia review the assignment and consider how it was done, whether injury was done to any person, or the assignment excessive to any person. If the assignment appears satisfactory, let the Audiencia approve it and order that it be retained; if not, let it be made anew. In assigning the tribute, care should be taken that if the tribute must be paid in money (although this has the drawbacks that I have described alone), a married tribute-payer should not pay more than 4 reales, a single man half as much. This is tribute enough, and should be paid in thirds or every three months. If this plan is carried out properly, it will provide more tribute for Your Majesty and the encomenderos than they now receive, and with less hardship to the Indians.

After the assignment of tribute has been made and approved, let the people assemble on a feast day in the church, and in the presence of the corregidor or teniente and the religious or priest who gives them religious instruction, let someone explain to them the total amount of tribute they must pay, and the amount that falls to the share of each, calling out the name of each man. And let it be explained to them that the whole amount must be paid by them every year whether their number declines or remains the same, unless there be some just cause for excusing them. If there is a surplus after the tribute is paid, let the surplus stay with the community; if there is a deficit, it must be made up by the community; and if the community is without resources, the Indians must cover the deficit by assessing themselves. Such an explanation is needed so that they will know what each one must pay and also so that they can avoid the evil of suits and counts, and the costs, assessments, and official visits they bring in their train. The Indians should also be told that in the event of an epidemic or crop failure they are immediately to notify the viceroy or Audiencia in order that suitable provision may be made.

Visits and assessments should be made only by oidores. To be sure, oidores also make mistakes; but there is reason to believe that they will do the job better, with more care and loyalty, than the private persons who are usually sent on such missions.

Counts should be avoided in making assessments, for the number of people in each town can easily be ascertained through the census lists maintained in each community by the ward collectors and by the religious or priests who instruct the Indians. This will prevent the delays, costs, and other nuisances that the counts produce. Assessments should be based on population, soil fertility, and similar considerations, with the assignment being made by the lord or cacique of the town.

The tribute should be stored in the *casa de la comunidad,* to which there should be three keys; if tribute is paid in money, there should be a money box with three keys in the same house. One key to the box should be in the possession of the *gobernador* or natural lord, another in that of an alcalde, the third in that of a regidor. The keys to the house should be kept by the other alcalde and the two majordomos commonly found in each town, each man having his own key. In the box there should be a book in which is set down who are the tribute-payers for each year, what the tribute comes to, what was taken in or taken out of the house and box, what was expended, and by whose order, and the like. The encomendero's share of tribute should come out of the house and box, and in the book should be set down the day payment was made, and to whom, and what it consisted of, and what remained after payment was made.

The encomendero should not be allowed to have other

interests or business in the Indian town. He or his agent should come there only at the time his tribute is paid, after receiving notice that it is ready, and then he should stay only three days. The people in charge of collecting the tribute should make sure it is ready by the appointed time; to this end they should give notice to the tribute-payers on two or three feast days, beginning fifteen days before the terminal day, so that each man will bring his quota. The encomendero should pay for the food he consumes during the time he is in town to collect his tribute. All the tribute should be brought to the provincial capital and there turned over to the encomendero; from there let him take it where he pleases at his expense, not that of the Indians. The encomendero who violates this rule should be punished.

An encomendero should never be allowed to come to an Indian town with all his household, as encomenderos now do, for this results in great offenses against the Indians. The encomenderos, their servants, and their Negro slaves trample the Indians' fields and fruit; they prevent them from selling their produce to whom they please and at their own price; they set the Indians bad examples and interfere with their religious instruction by occupying them in their own service. The encomenderos take the Indians' maize and vegetables, and force them to serve them, their people, and their horses, all without pay. They also sell the Indians wine and other unnecessary things.

The only way to end these evils is to forbid the encomenderos to stay among the Indians. At present these offenses are not divulged, for the Indians are afraid to complain and demand satisfaction for their injuries. The encomendero tells the Indians they are his property, and woe to them if they complain to the authorities; he will make them pay for it after the judge is gone. Actually, that is how matters turn out. The only remedy for the evil is to forbid the encomenderos to come to or stay in the Indian towns save at the time appointed for the collection of their tribute, under pain of heavy penalties effectively imposed.

In order to carry out Your Majesty's orders, restore the ancient mode of paying tribute to which the Indians are accustomed, end the evils that flow from the present system, and ensure that the country be abundantly provided with the necessities of life, the Indians should be made to pay tribute in the produce grown in each town. To this end, the officials should designate a certain extent of land which the natives will cultivate. This land should be divided into two parts, one to be cultivated one year, the other the next. The encomendero will supply them with seed of the things they are to grow; and if he does not do this at the proper time, the fault shall be his, and not that of the Indians. The Indians will be responsible for sowing and cultivating where irrigation is possible, for weeding and harvesting the fields, and for storing the crop in the house assigned by the encomendero for the purpose in the provincial capital. The crop will be stored there for him and at his risk, and he must not take an Indian's house for this purpose, but must rent a room or part of the casa de la comunidad.

Let the Indians plant maize where maize is the staple crop, and *chía*, beans, and chili peppers where they do well. There is a strong demand for these products, and all bring in money. Moreover, there would be an abundance of foodstuffs. Let the Indians be told how much land and seed they are to devote to each product, keeping in mind the number of people in each town. At the seasons for sowing, harvesting, and storing the crop the encomendero may send someone to observe what is done, or he may come to see for himself. But he must not demand that the Indians pay him a specified amount of tribute. They are to give him only what the land yields, be the harvest good or bad, be the amount collected large or small.

By making the Indians pay tribute in the form of labor on fields, as they did in the time of their heathendom, we should do away with assignment of tribute by heads and all the other annoyances I have described. The Indians would give in tribute only what the land yields, be that little or much. The Indians would find this system good, for they are accustomed to working together, old and young, men and women. They would not think this labor a hardship, for each would give only two or three days to each task that had to be done. There would be an end to the vexations connected with collection of tribute, and to the charges that the principales are robbing the Indians.

The whole land would be well provisioned, and Your Majesty, the encomenderos, and the Spanish and Indian populations alike would stand to gain. All products would sell at good yet moderate prices, for there is a market for all of them. This is well known to the persons who buy the tribute from the encomenderos and the royal officials for resale in their businesses. This, by the way, is a source of great harassment for the Indians, who are forced to serve as carriers for these traders. These persons also use their traffic as a pretext for staying in the Indian towns as long as they please, harassing the Indians and eating their food without pay. This evil would cease if Your Majesty's officials and the encomenderos themselves disposed of the tribute they receive.

Because the Indians now pay tribute in money, a dearth of provisions has arisen in New Spain. Maize, wheat, and other foods that the Indians used to grow are extremely dear, and all have taken to trafficking in order to get reales. As a result the supply of provisions must constantly diminish, with great hardship to the whole country. The encomenderos alone will be well off, for in addition to their money tribute the Indians give them maize. The encomenderos sell the surplus as they please, and their fellow citizens pay through the nose.

The Indians should not be made to grow wheat, for this causes them great hardship. They do not understand how wheat is grown, and do not have plows. As a result, they have to pay Spaniards to sow and cultivate the wheat fields for them; this is a great burden for the Indians. On the other hand, they grow maize very easily because they are familiar with it. Besides, there are already many Spanish farms where wheat is grown.

The encomendero should be notified of the days on which he or his agent is to come to observe the sowing, harvesting, and storing of the various crops. He must not stay beyond the allotted time, and must pay for the food he consumes during his stay.

Let the Indians be ordered to make another field of specified size to cover the expenses of the community. The crops from this field should be stored in the casa de la comunidad, and the details of the harvest should be recorded in a book to be kept in that house. From this harvest let the Indians pay the salaries of the gobernador, alcaldes, regidores, alguaciles, majordomos, and the persons who serve in the school, the monasteries and churches, and in other capacities. Let there be set down in the book the quantity of produce given to each person, and the date it was given. Every year let the Indians, two by two, carry to the Audiencia an account of receipts and expenditures, signed by the priest or religious in charge of the town. I do not suggest the use of legal officers, to avoid the expense that would ensue if they went over the accounts.

In order to look after the needs of the lords and caciques without hardship to the Indians, let the people of each town make another field of specified size for their lord or cacique.

They should work this field for him and store the crops in his house. They should also give him domestic service and bring him water and fuel, and fodder if he has a horse or mule, and they should perform this service by turns. The lord or cacique should be provided with the same amount of food or tribute that the Indians used to give him in their pagan days. Care should be taken that he receive enough for his support, for this is most important for the religious instruction and good order and government of the town, and to ensure that he be properly feared and obeyed.

In towns where cacao, cotton, or fruit is grown the tribute can be paid in money. The same is true of merchants, artisans, and Indians living within 15 or 20 leagues of a Spanish town or near mines or main traveled roads. Since these Indians are better off than others, it seems that a fair tribute would be 6 reales for a married man and 3 for widows and single men *sui juris*. These persons should not have to work on the fields cultivated for encomenderos, since they would pay tribute for themselves. They should, however, be obliged to labor on the fields set aside for the support of the communities and the lords, or provide substitutes. The payment of monetary tribute should not be assigned by heads, but should be imposed on the whole body of persons subject to it, with the apportionment left to the lord or gobernador.

The Indians should not be made to pay tribute in cloth, even though they make cloth, for it is a source of great hardship and offense to the poor and the women who make the tribute cloth and spoil many pieces because of the great pressure under which they work. It is otherwise with Indians who make cloth for themselves; they work slowly and at the time of their own choosing. Tribute cloth, on the other hand, must be delivered at a set time and must be of a specific measure and quality. Since each piece of cloth is worth much more than the tribute ordinarily required of Indians, there cannot be equality of treatment among them if tribute in cloth is imposed. Moreover, some women work harder than others, depending on the rate of output set by the persons in charge of the work and of collecting the tribute. It is no argument to say, as some do, that there will be a shortage of cloth if this tribute is not paid; it is better that there be a shortage of cloth than a shortage of people. Besides, there is always cloth available in those areas where the Indians are accustomed to make cloth; they make it for themselves and also take it to sell in places where it is not made. There are many cloth merchants, both Indians and Spaniards.

In the assessment of tribute, whether in produce or money, attention must be given to the needs of the lords and the problem of tithes, which I shall discuss at the close of my comment on Article 16. For this reason the tribute should on no account be increased. Indeed, the Indians cannot pay the tribute that is now levied upon them, and it is most urgent to reduce their burdens rather than increase them.

From my knowledge of the miserable state of these people, it is enough that each man pay the amounts I suggested above. The total of tribute payments should be divided into ten parts. A tenth should be applied for tithes for the Church, whereby, as Your Majesty has ordered, the Indians will not regard the tithe as a new imposition. Of the remaining nine parts, half should go to the encomendero and half to the natural lords. To provide this second half, it is most important that they make fields for their lords, as is their ancient custom. Since there are always many natural lords in each town, the share that each will receive of the half of the nine parts allotted to them will be very small. Nor should the Indians fail to render their lords personal service, for they owe it to these lords by very ancient custom.

Should the encomenderos grumble that what the lords and caciques get belongs to them, the lords could assert with bet-

ter right that what the encomenderos receive belongs by
rights to them. Be that as it may, the encomenderos are needed
(though not in such numbers as there are at present) to hold
the land and provide for its security. The tribute they receive
is given them by Your Majesty's grace and favor, and they
should be content with what they have; it is not for them to
pick and choose and say what they will or will not accept. Let
them take and keep the posts of honor and profit that Your
Majesty gives them. The half of the nine parts of tribute that
falls to their share should not be tithed, for it will have been
tithed already when a tenth of the total tribute is taken for that
purpose. Nor should there be charged to this half the salary
the encomendero pays the parish priest, the cost of the ornaments he provides for the church, and the various other
charges on his conscience.

The encomenderos should receive as much tribute as suffices for a decent living, and not what is needed to gratify
luxurious and extravagant tastes in clothing, food, household
service, and the like. If they wish for more, let them find some
way of earning the money, as is done in Spain.[73] [Besides, they
all have other estates and businesses from which they reap
large profits. In short, they are rich men, and would be richer
still if they reduced their extravagant scale of living. Once
good order is brought into the assessment of tribute, the encomenderos' share will be larger than it is now, yet the burden on the Indians will be lighter. The opportunities for
injuring and robbing the Indians that now exist will be removed, and there will be avoided the troubles that would result if the encomenderos had to collect the tithes themselves.]

In some places the repartimientos are excessively large.
Your Majesty has therefore ordered that they be reduced in
size, and that what is taken away be applied to provide a decent
living for conquistadores without Indians. It will serve Your
Majesty to command that this order be carried out; but to end

the delays in complying with the order it is necessary for Your Majesty to declare the maximum annual revenue in tribute to be left to each landowner. It seems to me that this maximum should be 3,000 ducats, with due regard to the station and merits of each man. The sum of 3,000 ducats is certainly enough to support a man in very honorable state, especially when it is recalled that all these people have other businesses, estates, and sources of revenue.

In addition to the men whom Your Majesty will reward in this way, and the Spaniards who now hold Indians in encomienda, there are others who came here poor, and as a rule after the land had been conquered and pacified, but today own mines and extensive estates and other resources. Thus there will be an abundance of people to see to the defense and security of the land. As for the other Spaniards in New Spain, it were well that Your Majesty order them to find gainful employment, or else deport them to Spain, for these men play the principal part in fomenting the riots and disorders of this land. Your Majesty should also order that no more people be allowed to come to New Spain; for there already are so many that it were better to send many packing home and not to allow new ones to come in.

Should it appear, because of the necessity of including in the tribute the tithes and the share of the natural lords, that the Indians must pay a little more, let Your Majesty order that each town give a certain number of native hens[74] and a certain number of hens of Castile. The assessment should be made, not by heads, but according to the kind of people in the town. Thus a married man would give one native hen, and a widow or bachelor would give one hen of Castile, which is worth half as much as the other. Where honey is made, instead of hens let the Indians give a certain number of gourds filled with honey, of the kind they use in trade. This should be done with due regard to the market value of a gourd of honey, so that a married man should not have to give more honey than 2 reales would buy, and the widower or bachelor half as much; it must be remembered that in addition to this they must pay tribute in produce, which is the most satisfactory arrangement, or in money, which has the disadvantages I have mentioned.

This supplementary tribute should not be assigned by heads. Instead, let the apportionment be made by the lord or gobernador. To the married men he will assign the native hens, to the bachelors the hens of Castile. All this tribute should be deposited in the casa de la comunidad of the provincial capital, and from there distributed to the persons who are to receive it, with the surplus remaining for the community.

In order that the Spanish towns may be supplied with all their needs, let each Indian town be ordered to send to a neighboring town a certain number of laborers for hire each week, and so many loads of fuel and vegetables each day. Wages and prices should not be fixed; let the Indians sell their labor and produce to all comers at whatever wages or prices they can get. The Indian lords and governors should see to the dispatch of these laborers and supplies. If the Indians pay tribute in produce, it will be unnecessary for them to bring maize for sale—as they now must do with great hardship to themselves—because it will be so plentiful.

The Indian towns should also be ordered to bring eggs and fish to neighboring Spanish towns on fish days and during Lent, but prices should not be fixed. There should also be designated a house to which the Indians can bring these things to sell. This is already the case at present. To avoid harassment of the Indians, let a person be named who will oversee the traffic and make sure that no force is used against the Indians (this is also done at present). This system will put an end to the harm they now sustain through being forced to sell their goods at fixed prices that are one-half of what they pay for them in their own towns.

This system will also put an end to the wrongs that are done to the Indians by forcing them to labor on Spanish public works and for private employers. The assignment of people for labor in the Spanish towns will be made with due regard for the needs of the Indian town in which they live and of the Spanish town where they are to work. I repeat that their wages should not be fixed; instead, they should hire themselves out by the day or week on the best terms they can get. The change will benefit the entire Spanish community. For at present the Indians who are brought to a repartimiento are assigned to private parties who pay these Indians a fixed low wage. Poor Spaniards, and all other persons, must make use of the Indian laborers who daily come to the Spanish towns to offer their services, but command a higher wage.

The reform I propose will mean the end of *visitas* and counts of tribute-payers, which are a waste of time and money. It will do away with harassment of Indians by the servants, Negroes, mestizos, mulattoes, and horses that the visitadores and their officials bring with them; and it will remove the burdens imposed on the Indian commoners, who must provide all these people with their daily food, and who are assessed to pay their salaries. No longer will the Indians be summoned for frequent counts in the provincial capitals. There they must stay for several days, away from their homes and usually in a strange climate, for almost all the provincial capitals are in the tierra fría, whereas their subjects live in the tierra caliente; this is especially true of the Indians who live near the coast. Meanwhile they neglect their farms and their trades.

This reform will also put an end to the suits of the Indians against their encomenderos and principales, their comings and goings to petition for visitas and counts, and the suits they bring against each other, for these arise from the commotions caused by the visitas and counts. It will remove the causes of the numerous perjuries that are committed at present, and eliminate the pretexts that are seized upon by the misleaders who have sprung up to rob the people and incite them against their lords. The lords will be cherished, obeyed, and feared, which is most necessary, for they will be responsible for seeing that the above reforms are carried out, that the Indians attend Sunday school, sermon, and Mass, and that each man does the duties of his office and works his field as he did of old. With the help of the lords, the Spanish and Indian communities will be supplied with all their needs without hardship to the natives, for the lord or governor will assign duties in such a way that no one will lose time from farming, and there will be an end to the wrongs done to the Indians who bring vegetables and other things to the Spanish towns. The lords themselves will be better off, for they will be relieved of the need, misery, and abasement in which they now live.

It may be said that the Indians should pay some money, in addition to giving tribute in produce, because their need of money for tribute would make them more willing to accept employment from Spaniards and to bring produce for sale in Spanish towns. If Your Majesty thinks this idea has merit (notwithstanding the disadvantages of making the Indians pay tribute in money), let Your Majesty order that each married man pay 2 reales, and a single man one real; the size of the tribute fields they must till should be reduced accordingly. However, the assessment of this money tribute should be made in the manner described above, and they should still till fields for the lords and for the community. The money tribute they should pay in two parts, twice a year, and the produce at harvest time.

Let Your Majesty also command that the visitas to be made by the oidores in rotation be made uninterruptedly, even if there is no need for assessments. These visitas are most necessary to ensure that justice be done to the Indians and that there be held residencias of the governors and of other judges, Indian as well as Spanish. The expense will be much less than that now incurred in sending private parties to do this work. The oidores will redress the wrongs done to the Indians, see that they obtain satisfaction for their injuries, and put an end to the encroachments of Spanish ranches and herds on their lands and the many other evils from which they suffer. It is not well to entrust such business to persons other than oidores, for such persons are interested only in their salaries, and there are situations in which they cannot, nay, dare not, do justice. It will be otherwise with oidores, for we may safely assume that they will have freedom of action, and that they will not allow their servants and officials and others of their party to commit any offense or take something without pay. The fines these oidores impose will be used to provide redress to injured parties, with the remainder entering Your Majesty's treasury. Your Majesty will order the salaries of these oidores to be paid in such manner as seems best to Your Majesty.

The oidores must not take with them any relative, servant, or friend as alguacil, escribano, interpreter, or in any other office, nor a relative, servant, or friend of any other oidor, or of the fiscal, viceroy, or *presidente*. In the residencia of each oidor let note be taken of the places he visited, and whether he observed Your Majesty's orders on these visitas. In conducting a residencia of an oidor, care should be taken that this is done in the form of a residencia and not a visita,[75] for experience has shown that many scandals and perjuries attend visitas of Audiencias. Neither an oidor nor any child or relative of his should be allowed to marry or own property in the province where such oidor holds office. This will remove all occasion for partiality or undue influence, since the motive of profit will be absent.

ARTICLE 17

If there are diverse opinions concerning all the foregoing, you will send all such opinions, with the supporting reasons given by each oidor. Because this is a very weighty matter and very necessary for the discharge of His Majesty's conscience, I command you to attend to the conduct of the said inquiry with all possible care and diligence, so that all replies come well documented and set forth in much detail, so that after due examination His Majesty may provide what seems best in the case. You will send this material by the first ships to depart for these realms after you have completed the inquiry. Done in Valladolid, December 23, 1553.

My reply to Article 15, detailing what I have done to comply with Your Majesty's order, will serve as a reply to this Article.

I have already explained why I delayed giving my opinion until now.

ARTICLE 18

You will also inform yourselves what tribute the Indians used to give in the time of their paganry to the Sun and to their temples, cúes, and sanctuaries, and what other properties and revenues they devoted to the worship of the Sun and the temples of their idols; and you will send a detailed account of all pertaining thereto. Dated as above. The Prince. By order of His Majesty, Juan de Sámano.

The Indians of Texcoco appointed fifteen principal towns and their subject towns, which were numerous and inhabited by a great number of people, to the service of their religion. These towns had charge of serving and repairing the temples and of providing the fuel for the fires which always burned in them. Father Toribio de Motolinía listed these towns in the book he wrote about New Spain, giving the sign of each town, so that its name might be known.[76] All these towns were in the territory of Texcoco. Your Majesty has ordered that Texcoco and its land, and other towns and provincial capitals, be vested in your Royal Crown, as appears from the second instruction that Your Majesty gave to the Audiencia of Mexico, dated Madrid, April 5, 1528, but the order has not been carried out. These rich and important towns, although part of the territory of Texcoco, are held in encomienda by private citizens of Mexico City. The same is true of other towns of the same rank.

I could not ascertain which towns served the temples of Mexico and other principal towns, but certainly they were numerous and very rich and populous.

Besides these towns, the Indians set aside much good land for the service of their religion. Lords and other individuals left these lands to the temples, and other persons rented them, or worked them for the temples out of devotion. At present these lands are distributed among the Spaniards. The boys, including the sons of lords and principales, who received their training in the Houses of Youth, served the temples. They harvested much maize, beans, chili peppers, chía, and other Indian foodstuffs from the temple fields, and all was stored in granaries and rooms of the temples that were designated for this purpose. From these granaries and rooms they took this food for the festivals and other ceremonies with which they honored their idols, and for the support of the numerous priesthood.

The Indians also gave many offerings, with the lords giving a certain part of their tribute. These offerings, which were voluntary, were stored with all the rest and used for the appropriate purposes.

I have now dealt with all the sections of Your Majesty's cedula except the first part of Article 16, which treats of the tithes; I propose to deal with this topic separately.[77] First, however, I wish to tell of the order of things that existed in the Valley of Matlalcinco, containing the towns of Toluca and Malinalco, which I touched on at the beginning of this relation. I also wish to tell of how it was in Utlatlán, which is the capital of a very large and important province of the same name, bordering on Guatemala. These important provincial capitals are also held in encomienda by private citizens.

Before Axayacatl,[78] Moctezuma's father, waged war on

the people of Matlalcinco, they had three lords. One was the principal lord, the second was somewhat below the first, and the third was of lesser rank than the first two. On the death of the principal lord, who in virtue of his dignity and lordship was named Tlatuan, his place was filled by the second lord, who was named Tlacatecatle, and into his vacant place entered the third lord, who was named Tlacuxcalcatl. The place of this third lord was filled by that son or brother of the first lord who appeared best qualified for the post. In this way none succeeded immediately to the place of his father, for the lords had to rise from rank to rank, with the last being chosen by the others. If the lord in the middle died, the third lord took his place, and was in turn replaced by a brother or son of the second lord; and if the third lord died, they chose a son or brother of his, always selecting the best qualified person.

Each of these lords had assigned to him certain towns and barrios that they called *calpules*, which rendered service to their acknowledged lord. This lord had in each town or *calpul* a principal or perpetual governor. If this man died, the community chose, to replace him, that son, brother, or close relative of his who seemed best qualified, and they announced their choice to the supreme lord for his confirmation, and this supreme lord informed the other two. If the election was properly held, it was approved; otherwise the lords ordered that it be held anew.

The tribute that these towns or calpules gave their lords was in the form of labor on specified fields. All able-bodied persons worked in these fields without recompense, and there was no shortage of workers. The harvest of maize, beans, and *huautli*,[79] which are the products of that valley, were stored and used as needed to satisfy the wants of a lord's household. When the governors or tequitlatos came to a lord's house, they brought with them many principales. The lord made them all welcome and provided them with food, lodging, and service all the time they stayed with him. Numerous slaves performed all the work of the lord's household.

These Indians always had large reserves of maize for use in time of crop failure; the men who gave me this account said that they had lived through four years of famine. During this time the lords asked for no tribute from their vassals. On the contrary, the lords ordered that there should be a distribution of food from the reserves of maize and beans, for they always had a large store of provisions in reserve. These Indians also told me that the lords treated their people and vassals with affection, calling them fathers, brothers, and sons, according to their age, and were always zealous for their people's welfare. Each lord endeavored to rule better than his predecessor, for it was the law that a lord who made himself a tyrant, be he a supreme or inferior lord, must be removed and replaced by another. The Indians who gave me this account told me that they saw one ruler removed because he governed badly and to the detriment of his vassals. The people worked tribute fields only for the supreme lords and the inferior lords who represented them in the towns.

Although each of the supreme lords had his particular towns, barrios, and jurisdiction, affairs of small importance were taken to the second or third lord, and dispatched by one or both of them. They referred a grave or important question to the principal lord, and all three resolved it jointly.

In the towns or calpules, each macehual prepared his field where he pleased or where he thought the land was best suited for planting, and he planted whatever he pleased. If the principal or governor fell ill, he asked the other people of the barrio to work his field for him, as for a needy person, and they did so.

When the supreme lord prepared to give a feast, the inferior lords asked the people in their charge to go hunting, and these people brought deer, rabbits, and other game that they were accustomed to eat as presents to the supreme lord. There was no pressure of any kind on them to do this, for they gave voluntarily what they caught, were it much or little.

In each town or calpulli the three supreme lords had their own lands. Since these lands were good, some peasants chose to rent them; but if they wished, they could farm on the lands of the community, without charge. The rent they paid for working land belonging to the supreme lords varied according to the agreement they made with the governors who had charge of such land. The rent usually consisted of several chickens or deer; in those days all such things cost little. These tenants were not obliged to labor on the tribute fields.

After Axayacatl had subjugated this land, he put the two inferior lords to death because they defied his authority in certain matters, and he took for himself their vassals and lands. The principal lord, whose proper name was Chimaltecutli, but who was called Tlatoané in virtue of his dignity and supreme lordship, was left all his dominion and land because he was very obedient to Axayacatl. When the vassals of Chimaltecutli rose up against him because he wore them out with toil in order to serve and please the Mexicans, Axayacatl invaded the land a second time and destroyed its people. Some, especially they of Zinancatepec, left their homes and went to Michoacán, to the place now called Tlaulan, and gave obedience to the lord of Mexico, who took their land for himself, renting some and distributing the rest, and he received tribute for this land. The people of Matlalcinco who remained had to make for the lord of Mexico a field that was 800 brazas long and 400 wide.

They stored the harvests from the tribute fields in granaries and used them for war and the needs of the state. This produce could not be used for other ends, and they rose up against a lord who tried to do so.

On the death of Axayacatl, he was succeeded by Tizoc,[80] who ruled in the manner of his predecessor. On the death of Tizoc, the electors chose his brother, named Ahuitzotl,[81] who ruled in the manner of his brother; and on the death of Ahuitzotl the electors chose a son of the elder brother, named Moctezuma,[82] who was ruling when the Spaniards invaded the land. Moctezuma showed much favor to distinguished warriors, honored them greatly, and gave them many gifts.

Before the Mexicans came to rule over the people of Matlalcinco, all the lands were held in common. One who had the good fortune to find a good piece of land worked it, as did his heirs after him. If a parcel of land was not good, the farmer sought another field among those that lay vacant, for land belonging to a man who worked it could not be taken from him. It was thus with the lands of each town or calpul, but not with the lands applied from ancient times to the use of the lords. This was very good land which was cultivated for the lords or which they rented out. These lands could not be alienated, for they went with their lordship and constituted entailed estates, as it were.

After the Spaniards had conquered the land, they divided the people and land among themselves. The Marqués [Cortés] took Toluca for himself and asked the people for tribute in maize, and this they gave him the first year. The next year he ordered them to cultivate a field for him, and this they did for many years. In addition, he sent them to work on the houses that he built in Mexico. Still later, he demanded slaves for the mines of Tletiztlac; the lords and principales gave him all the slaves, men and women, that they themselves had. On two occasions he took all those slaves away and branded them on the face, and ordered that they carry maize from his tribute field to the mines; he also demanded from the Indians fowls and eggs and food for the slaves and miners. When the mines of Taxco and Tzultepec were discovered, he demanded a perpetual grant of sixty Indians to mine silver there; he continued this practice for fifteen years, and the Indians were rotated every twenty days. Many died in the mines, and others were maimed or fell ill from the bad treatment they received there. They had to bring food from home because at the mines they received only 2 fanegas of maize to feed all sixty for a week. The Indians told me they had in writing the assessment made by Cortés, and this was in addition to the large field they cultivated for him in the town. Later on, in the time of Viceroy Antonio de Mendoza,[83] a money tribute was imposed on them, each Indian having to pay a tribute of 8 reales; this was in addition to the field on which they all worked.

Afterwards they were reassessed, and it was ordered that each Indian pay 4 reales, in addition to the field he had to work.

At another time, I was told by the men who gave me this account, Viceroy Antonio de Mendoza appointed as judge an Indian of Tula who was named Pablo González. This man distributed the lands among them, giving each Indian a parcel 100 varas in length and 20 in width (each vara contains 2 brazas, this being a measure used by the Indians), and he gave possession of the land to the persons to whom he had distributed it. He also ordered that in return for his parcel of land each man must pay 2 reales a year to the community.

The Valley of Matlalcinco and the neighboring Valley of Ixtlahuaca and Toluca form a very rich land because of the fertility of the soil. The Indians raise a great quantity of maize there, and it would be greater still were it not for the large herds of cattle that pasture there, doing much damage to their fields of grain and tuna[84]; this tuna is a very fine edible fruit that is widely grown and used by both Indians and Spaniards, and they make much profit from it.

Because the cattle are so numerous and wander about without herdsmen, the Indian cannot stop their foraging, although large numbers of the Indians take turns in watching their fields. As a result they suffer two serious injuries; a great many people waste their time in guarding against the cattle, to the detriment of their farm work and other tasks; and the cattle eat, trample, and otherwise damage their crops.

Moreover, the Spaniards made the Indians labor on the construction of an enclosure which was to keep the cattle from doing so much damage, but it was of little use. This was affirmed and proved by some Spaniards who had cattle there, in order to avoid paying their share of the cost. The enclosure is continually collapsing and is full of breaches, some made deliberately in order to let the cattle through to graze in the Indians' fields. The Indians who built the enclosure did not get their pay, because the money collected from the cattlemen was collected after much delay and litigation, and by the time it was gathered together the Spaniards had forgotten about the men who did the work.

Moreover, there was hatched a scheme that sounded very good, like all the schemes that are hatched in regard to the Indians and invariably result in injury, expense, and hardship to them. The plan was that all the money should be deposited with some one person who was charged with its collection, and this went on for a long time. This fellow had a good time with the money, and otherwise used it to his own advantage. On the pretext of waiting to distribute the money until it was all collected, he spent it in repairs on the enclosure, assessing the Indians to whom the money was due for the amount, as if the Indians were obliged to give their labor to and pay for the building of the enclosure—though this was the obligation of the scale owners—and on top of that to maintain and guard the fence! Because there are many bulls among the cattle, and because the Indians are afraid of being mistreated by the owners, the Indians dare not complain even when they see the cattle entering their fields.

The Spaniards have also taken a very great amount of land from the Indians to use as pasture for their cattle. Moreover, they drive their cattle to summer pasture prematurely and suddenly, at a time when much of the harvest from the Indians' grain and tuna fields remains to be gathered. The Indians also sustain much injury when the cattle are driven to Mexico City for weighing, because this valley is the route commonly followed by the drovers.

The same state of affairs, aside from the incident of the enclosure, exists in Petapan, which is a large town belonging to Your Majesty in the province of Guatemala. The cattle do very great damage to the grain fields and cacao plantations of that region. I found the same circumstances in Izcuntepetl, in the province of Chiapas, on a tour of inspection I made in that vicinity. The Indians came to me to complain that the cattle of their encomenderos ate up their crops and the crops of the tribute fields, yet they had to pay their tribute in its entirety. The same thing happens in all the other towns of that region.

I found the same state of affairs in Santa Marta and Cartagena when I visited there. When I visited the New Kingdom of Granada, there were as yet few cattle there, but since then a very large number of cattle has been brought in, and the same abuses will arise here as elsewhere. In short, I observed the existence of this evil in all the extensive regions to which I journeyed; it may be said to be general throughout the Indies.

I caused some cattle to be driven out of some Indian towns, but on my departure the cattle immediately returned, or rather were returned by their owners; this was done by the

encomendero of Mumustenango and the encomendero of Tec-
quepanquilco. In other places the cattle were so numerous that
it was impossible to drive them out. The damage done by the
cattle is irremediable. Even when the authorities order cattle owners to pay for the damage, on the few occasions
that the Indians complain about it, the order is never carried
out; and the Indians incur expenses greater than the compen-
sation they are to receive. I have known cases where it was
harder to wring the money out of the man who accepted
the fines for distrubution among the Indians than to collect
the fines from the men on whom they were imposed. Collection and distribution of the fines alike are always delayed
and involve litigation and trouble. In the end the Indians lose
the money and must swallow their losses and the costs they
have incurred, not to mention the time wasted in their
comings and goings to the Audiencia. What is more, the cattle
owners mistreat the Indians for having complained of them.
The only persons to profit by the whole business are the lawyers, prosecuting attorneys, notaries, solicitors, and the persons sent to verify the damage done by the cattle. In short,
all is show and pretense, with much giving of false, defective,
and lying testimony. Nothing that I might say would suffice to
expose the enormity of the things that are done.

The encomenderos also keep large herds of cattle and sheep
in towns that are suited for cattle raising. Here, too, the cattle do great damage to the farms and houses of the natives.

In this Valley of Matlalcinco are thirty-five towns, inhabited by fifty thousand Indians. Almost all these towns are
held in encomienda by private parties. This valley regularly
supplies Mexico City with maize, although some is brought
from other towns. There is in my possession a paper that
lists the towns, the persons who hold them in encomienda,
and the number of Indians in each town.

The province of Utlatlán borders on Guatemala. When I

was an oidor in Guatemala, I made a visit of inspection to this province. Through the services of a religious of the Dominican Order, a great servant of Our Lord and a very fine interpreter, a most learned and eloquent preacher who is now bishop,[85] I learned with the aid of paintings that they had which recorded their history for more than eight hundred years back, and which were interpreted for me by very ancient Indians, that in their pagan days they had three lords. The principal lord had three canopies or mantles adorned with fine featherwork over his seat, the second had two, and the third one.

I saw their lords at that time in the town of Utlatlán (from which the whole province takes its name). They were as poor and miserable as the poorest Indian of the town, and their wives fixed their tortillas for dinner because they had no servants, nor any means of supporting them; they themselves carried fuel and water for their houses. The principal lord was named Don Juan de Rojas, the second, Don Juan Cortés, and the third, Domingo. They were all extremely poor; they left sons who were all penniless, miserable tribute-payers, for the Spaniards do not exempt any Indians from payment of tribute.

The Indians' rule of succession and government was that each lord rose from grade to grade to the next dignity and insignia, and the lord who was always chosen anew was the third lord, whose insignia was one mantle. The election was made in the same way as in Mexico and in Matlalcinco. The principales chose the best-qualified son or brother of the lord who had died, and in the absence of such they chose a close relative of his. In short, it was done in the same way as in New Spain.

The lords appointed governors over their subject towns. If a governor died, the lord chose the best-qualified son or brother of the deceased to succeed him, and in the absence of such, some qualified relative. These governors were always principales and kindred of the lords.

The tribute these Indians gave their lords consisted of labor on maize fields and fields planted to the other things they eat. They also made a field for the governor in each town. All was done in very orderly manner, and the lords ruled their people wisely and meted out justice.

There were many large cúes or temples to their idols in Utlatlán. I saw some of them, and they were of marvelous construction, though in a very ruined state. Neighboring towns also had their cúes there, and the most important of these was the cúe of a town named Chiquimula. The Indians regarded this town of Utlatlán as a sanctuary, and that is why there were so many important cúes there. The lord of Chiquimula used to have many towns and vassals, but when I saw him, he was very poor and miserable.

I shall say no more about this, for if I were to treat the matters of each province in extensive detail I should never be done. It suffices for me to have given Your Majesty an account of the state of things in New Spain, for all the neighboring regions differed little from it in their rules of succession and modes of government.

Other Replies
to the Royal Cedula of
December 20, 1553

IN ADDITION to Zorita's *Brief Relation*, four other replies from New Spain to the royal cedula of December 20, 1553, have been published. Three of these reports are letters from religious; the fourth, prepared on the initiative of Viceroy Velasco and the *oidor* Antonio Rodríguez de Quesada of the Audiencia of Mexico, consists of sworn testimony by thirteen Indian *principales* concerning Indian tribute before and after the Conquest.

Because these reports, together with Zorita's *Brief Relation*, form a corpus of documents dealing with the same broad subject, I shall briefly summarize their contents.

I. "*Carta de Fray Nicolás de Witte a un ilustríssimo señor.*" *Metztitlán, August 21, 1554.*[1]

This letter is particularly valuable for the information it provides on Indian groups and states to the north and east of the Valley of Mexico not subject to the Aztec Empire, especially the important state of Metztitlán and the Huaxteca of Pánuco.

Fray Nicolás, of the Augustinian Order, prefaced his letter to Viceroy Velasco with the remark that he had lived and traveled

for twelve years among the Chichimeca and the Huaxteca of
Pánuco, and knew their languages. He had attended to both their
temporal and spiritual needs, for "these poor forsaken people
require help in everything."

Every part of ancient Mexico except Pánuco had its supreme
ruler, reported Fray Nicolás. Among the Huaxteca of Pánuco
each town was independent of the other, and these towns made
wars and formed alliances as they pleased, just like the states of
Italy. The Indians gave service and tribute to their supreme rulers,
but only once or at most twice a year. There was a great difference between the old Indian lords and the Spanish encomenderos; the appetites of the former were limited, but the greed of
the latter was infinite, which was the cause of the destruction of
the land. Fray Nicolás estimated that the tribute paid annually to
Moctezuma came to a value of 200,000 pesos de oro, but offered
no data in support of this estimate.

The supreme lord of Metztitlán ruled over a land thirty-five
leagues long and thirty leagues wide. He was ever at war with
three bordering states or peoples, Mexico, Tlaxcala, and the Huaxteca of Pánuco, and almost all the tribute he received was used for
war. When this ruler wished to hold a feast, he would ask the
people for tribute of capes and turkeys. The people also paid
tribute for the support of the temples, which were very numerous.
Fray Nicolás estimated that the annual value of the tribute given
to the ruler of Metztitlán came to no more than 10,000 pesos de
oro. Yet he was the supreme ruler of all the Chichimeca. When
Fray Nicolás, attended by Indians of Metztitlán, passed through
territory occupied by warlike Chichimeca, they received him well
and helped to pacify the land for him.

The Huaxteca of Pánuco had only local lords or caciques, but
now none was left, for a certain Spaniard had gathered them in a
corral, tied them up, and burned them to death. Once this had
been the most populous land on which the sun shone, wrote

Fray Nicolás, as proved by the ancient buildings that were found there, but now it was totally destroyed.

Except in Pánuco, in addition to giving tribute to the supreme ruler, each town served and gave tribute to its local lord. These lords also had slaves, both men and women, who made capes for them and performed most of the household service, so that the townspeople had little to do. The amount of tribute given by a town depended on its size. The value of the annual tribute received by a local lord may have come to 2,000 pesos de oro, or 1,000 pesos if it was a small town, taking into calculation the value of the personal service he received. Tribute of an equal value may have been given to the town's temples and priests.

Since the Spaniards had deprived the lords of their slaves, declared Fray Nicolás, the lords were as poor as the *macehuales*. With his own eyes he had seen the supreme lord of Metztitlán, digging stick in hand, going to work his land like the poorest *macehual* in the town. At the sight the eyes of Fray Nicolás had filled with tears, so that he could hardly speak to the unhappy lord.

The macehuales and the merchants alone used to pay tribute. The lords and the nobility were not only exempt from tribute but received service according to their rank. Using Spanish terminology, Fray Nicolás wrote that a hidalgo in charge of ten households had people assigned to cultivate a field for him and keep his house in repair. Among the Huaxteca of Pánuco the nobility were distinguished by certain marks or designs on their faces. Under the Spaniards, however, all Indians paid tribute.

Fray Nicolás testified that the Spaniards, in levying tribute, had taken no account of what the Indians used to give. The encomenderos thought only of securing silver, gold, and commodities that they could use in trade. "The Indians never used to give such large loads of *mantas*" [a *manta* was a piece of cotton cloth about 1 yard wide and 4 yards long], "nor had they ever heard of beds,

fine cotton fabrics, wax, or a thousand other fripperies like bed
sheets, tablecloths, shirts, and skirts. All they used to do was to
cultivate the fields of their lords, build their houses, repair the
temples, and give of the produce of their fields when their lord
asked for it."

None of the early tribute assessments had been made with the
consent of the Indians, for they dared not contradict their encomendero. As evidence, Fray Nicolás cited the reassessments
currently being made in the province of Metztitlán by the *visitador* Diego Ramírez.[2] He had reduced the first assessments to an
eighth of what they had been, and those made more recently to a
third. This clearly showed that the Indians had never been consulted or given their consent to these assessments. Until now the
Indians who lived some distance from Mexico City had regarded
themselves as slaves of the encomenderos; only now were they
beginning to awake to a sense of their rights.

Fray Nicolás proposed that a fixed tribute be established so that
the Indians might know exactly what they must pay; this would
eliminate the great robberies perpetrated by the principales and
tribute collectors. He suggested that a proper quota would be 1
peso de plata or its equivalent in kind, plus labor on a communal
field. This tribute would be divided between the Crown or encomendero, the cacique or *principal,* and the Church, each receiving a certain portion. This would do away with the unequal
burdens supported by different Indian towns and would end the
flight of Indians from one region to another, which was a major
cause of mortality and decline of the native population.

We may say that the tone and general conclusions of Fray
Nicolás' letter conform very closely with those of Zorita's *Brief
Relation.*

II. *"Carta parecer de Fray Toribio de Motolinía y de Fray Diego de Olarte a Don Luis de Velasco." Cholula, August 27, 1554.*[3]

This brief reply by two Franciscan friars opens with a discussion of the Indian tribute system before the Conquest. Towns conquered in war by the Triple Alliance of Tenochtitlán, Texcoco, and Tlacopan gave service and tribute to their rulers every eighty days, or, in some cases, once a year. They gave tribute in the produce of their lands. Towns that had submitted peacefully gave less tribute and aided their masters in war, in public works, and the like. The work parties sent by these towns received provisions from their supreme ruler, who also presented the principales who brought these parties with gifts of precious stones and fine mantles.

The rulers of conquered provinces and towns made great presents to their supreme rulers at certain feasts held every year; they did this in token of their vassalage. The principales or caciques of their own towns did the same for these vassal lords. Merchants and nobles who owned land also gave presents to the ruler, not as an obligation but because it was customary. All these presents were expended by the rulers in feasts and in gifts to warriors who had distinguished themselves in war.

The local lords and principales received tribute in their towns in the same way as the supreme rulers. Motolinía and Olarte make the interesting point that most of this tribute came from tenant farmers (*terrazgueros*), because "in many regions the greater part of the land belonged to the lords and principales."

Part of the text of this letter, criticizing the first Spanish tribute assessments and the reform efforts of Bishop Juan de Zumárraga, closely conforms in wording to parallel passages in Zorita's *Brief Relation.* I conclude that Zorita had access to this letter or some other document used by Motolinía and Olarte in the preparation of their report.

The friars asserted that since Zumárraga's time judges of the Royal Audiencia and other *visitadores* had made new and much more moderate assessments, but the reporters could not ascertain whether the consent of all the Indians had been obtained. Motolinía and Olarte knew, however, that many towns were now satisfied with their assessments.

In response to the questions of whether the tribute should be fixed, and how much each town should pay, the friars observed that this was a very difficult question. "Since the number of the Indians is declining, and they readily leave their huts and fields to go elsewhere, it would be proper to reduce the tribute almost every two or three years to make it correspond to their capacity, that the remaining few should not have to give what many used to pay, which leads to the destruction of all."

This statement is much more restrained in its optimism concerning the condition of the Indians than the more famous letter of Motolinía to Charles V.

III. *"Relación de Fray Domingo de la Anunciación acerca del tributo de los indios." Chimalhuacán, September 20, 1554.*[4]

Fray Domingo de la Anunciación of the Dominican Order, prior of the Convent of San Vicente de Chimalhuacán in the province of Chalco, had called together the principales and lords and elders of the towns of this province and had obtained information concerning Indian tribute from them.

Six aged principales of Chimalhuacán and its subject towns had traced the history of the tribute paid by these towns from the time of Moctezuma the Elder, who conquered the province of Chalco, to the coming of the Spaniards. During his lifetime the elder Moctezuma demanded no tribute from the Chalca, because he wanted them for friends rather than vassals. Under his successor, Axayacatl, the Chalca began to pay tribute. An Aztec majordomo was sent to see that this town of Chimalhuacán cultivated two maize fields, each 400 medias long and 80 medias wide. The Chalca gave Axayacatl no other tribute, but aided him in the conquest of other provinces. The tribute situation remained unchanged under Axayacatl's successors, Tizoc and Ahuitzotl. Indeed, these rulers presented the lords of Chalco with jewels of gold, rich mantles, and valuable necklaces and arms.

Following the accession of Moctezuma the Younger, new tributes were imposed on the Chalca. Moctezuma ordered the Chalca to come to Tenochtitlán two or three times a year to participate in dances and festivals. They also had to serve twice or three times a year in Moctezuma's military campaigns. In addition to the maize that they had given his predecessors, two or three times a year they had to bring stone, sand, and wood for building construction in Tenochtitlán. However, when the principales of Chalco came to the festivals in Tenochtitlán, Moctezuma presented them with many gifts of fine clothing, precious jewels, cacao, and turkeys.

When Cortés came to New Spain, the lords and principales of Chalco received him in peace and brought him food and provisions. On this account he had treated the Chalca well. After they had informed him what tribute they used to give Moctezuma, he ordered them to pay him 400 loads of maize and to assist him in the conquest of Mexico. Matters remained in this state until the coming of Beltrán Nuño de Guzmán, president of the first Audiencia of New Spain, who assigned to the Chalca the 8,000 fanegas of maize that they still paid at the time of this report. In addition, after the coming of Cortés they had to provide people for the public works of Mexico City and for the service of the Spaniards. This caused the Indians great hardship, for they spent two days going and two days returning from the city, but were paid for only two days of labor in the week, at the rate of 8 maravedís a day.

In the days before the Conquest the common people paid trib-

ute to their lords and principales according to the amount of land
they possessed; they also worked the fields of their lords and
built houses for them. Merchants and artisans paid tribute in the
products that they traded in or made.

The Indian elders declared that the lands they formerly possessed had been held in communal ownership by the towns and
the barrios into which they were divided. At an unspecified time
in the past certain principales sold part of this land to individuals
who left it to their descendants in the form of private estates.
Originally, however, these lands belonged to the towns (*alte-
petlalli*) or to the barrios (*calpulalli*). Lords and principales owned
other lands which their ancestors had received from former rulers;
these lands were called *tecutlalli*. These landowners received on
their estates men who fled from other towns and provinces. If
these men were satisfied with the treatment they received, they
agreed to serve and obey their new lords as tribute-payers.

With regard to the current tribute situation, the elders reported
that the tributes were not so excessive as they had been, because
the viceroy and Audiencia sent judges to count the number of
inhabitants of the towns. The towns visited by such judges usually paid no more tribute than the Crown Indians.

The elders also declared, however, that when they were pagans,
they had never paid such excessive tribute as they now paid, nor
had they borne so many burdens as they had had to bear since
becoming Christians. At present all Indians, peasants, artisans, and
principales, had to pay tribute. In this provincial capital (Chimalhuacán) the lords were exempt from tribute, but in other towns
the lords paid tribute like all the rest. Here Fray Domingo injected an impassioned comment on the extreme poverty and
misery of the Indians.

Fray Domingo declared that there must be an end to the
practice of making the surviving Indians pay the tribute of those
who had died, for this had been a major cause of the depopulation
of many towns, in the province of Chalco and elsewhere. He

cited, as one of many such cases, a town in his district called Teteoc, which had once exercised lordship in its own right and had a large population; now it was reduced to thirty-five households.

Fray Domingo also inveighed against the abuses committed by the *tequitlatos* or tribute collectors. These men went from house to house and collected from the Indians more tribute than they were obliged to give. Because of their ignorance the poor Indians did not know where or how they should complain of these outrages.

Fray Domingo's report agrees in point of view and in most of its statements of fact with Zorita's *Brief Relation*.

IV. *Información sobre los tributos que los indios pagaban a Moctezuma.*[5]

This *Información*, or report, consists of replies made in 1554 by thirteen principales of Tlatelolco, Cuautitlán, Atzcapotzalco, and Churubusco to selected questions from the cedula of December 20, 1553. In response to the first question concerning the amount and value of the tribute paid to Moctezuma, the witnesses gave itemized accounts of the tribute paid by the various provinces and towns in the Aztec Empire; the basis for their reports was a picture manuscript or tribute roll that may have dated from pre-Conquest times. Two of the depositions reveal some discrepancies that arose, in the opinion of the editors, F. V. Scholes and E. A. Adams, from differences of interpretation by the Indian elders of the picture manuscript before them. The remaining replies are exact copies of one or the other of these two reports.

Scholes and Adams have made a preliminary analysis of this important document, calling attention to some discrepancies between the *Información* of 1554 and two previously known tribute rolls, the Codex Mendoza and the Matrícula de tributos. Of special interest is the effort of the Indian witnesses to express the value of certain kinds of tribute in mantas, basing themselves on the calculation that the tribute manta was worth 4 pesos in 1554 and 1 peso before the Conquest. The total value of the tribute paid to Moctezuma each year is set at 1,962,450 pesos de oro común. Unfortunately, as Scholes and Adams indicate, it is difficult to reconcile this figure with the totals given for the individual provinces, suggesting negligence in the preparation or copying of the *Información*.

Scholes and Adams conclude that "the depositions made in 1554 offer new and interesting facts concerning the value of the tribute paid to Moctezuma," and point to the need for careful comparison of the *Información* with the Codex Mendoza and the Matrícula de tributos.

The Indian elders made briefer replies to other questions in the royal cedula. In the main these responses appear perfunctory and offer little new information. The first witness, Miguel Huecamecatl, a principal of Santiago Tlatelolco and seventy years of age, *más o menos*, evidently spoke for the rest, for their replies duplicated his without a change.

A flash of fire was elicited by the section asking whether the caciques held office by succession or by election. The old principal complained that very few caciques now held office by succession. Most had been nominated by the Indian commoners in the towns, and had been confirmed by the viceroy and Audiencia on the basis of false reports. The persons who were now being chosen as caciques were persons of low birth or boys reared in the churches and monasteries. As a result, the lawful caciques, their sons, and their heirs suffered great injury. The commoners also suffered, for in the old days the caciques had kept them from doing mischief to each other, punishing their misdeeds with death, exile, confiscation of goods, or slavery, as their offenses warranted.

This flattering appraisal of the role of the old Indian aristocracy agrees with Zorita's idealized portrayal of that role in his
Brief Relation. Mention of the rise of commoners or boys reared
in the churches and monasteries to positions of leadership con-
firms the indications in Zorita's work of a minor social upheaval
within the Indians communities in the period following the Conquest. [6]

Notes to Editor's Introduction

1. The word "Aztec" as applied to the people who expanded from their island redoubt of Tenochtitlán to form a great tribute empire in Central Mexico is technically incorrect; "Mexica" was the name by which they called themselves at the coming of the Spaniards. See R. H. Barlow, "Some Remarks on the Term 'Aztec Empire,'" *The Americas*, I (1945), 344-349; and *The Extent of the Empire of the Culhua Mexica* (*Ibero-Americana*, 28, Berkeley: University of California Press, 1949), p. 1. The name Mexica or Mexicans is not without ambiguity, however, whereas the word Aztec has the sanction of familiarity and long usage. I have therefore used it throughout this introduction.

2. E. R. Wolf, *Sons of the Shaking Earth* (Chicago: University of Chicago Press, 1959), p. 6.

3. *Ibid.*, p. 133.

4. Bernardino de Sahagún, *General History of the Things of New Spain*. Florentine Codex (translated from the Aztec into English, with notes and illustrations by A. J. O. Anderson and C. E. Dibble. Salt Lake City: University of Utah, and Santa Fe, New Mexico: School of American Research, 1950-), Book XII, *The Conquest of Mexico* (1955), p. 31.

5. S. F. Cook and Woodrow Borah, *The Indian Population of Central Mexico 1531-1610* (*Ibero-Americana*, 44, Berkeley: University of California Press, 1960).

6. Wolf, *Sons of the Shaking Earth*, p. 199.

7. "Opinion of the friars of the Order of St. Dominic of New Spain on the encomienda, May 15, 1544," cited in L. B. Simpson, *The Encomienda in New Spain* (Berkeley: University of California Press, 1950).

8. José Miranda, *El Tributo indígena en la Nueva España durante el siglo XVI* (Mexico: Colegio de México, 1952), carefully studies the evolution of

the tribute system and its impact on the economic and social life of the colony.

9. *Ibid.*, pp. 133-137; C. H. Haring, *The Spanish Empire in America* (New York, 1947), p. 283.

10. Charles Gibson, "The Aztec Aristocracy in Colonial Mexico," *Comparative Studies in Society and History* (The Hague, Netherlands), II, 2 (January, 1960), 169-196.

11. Cited in Haring, *The Spanish Empire in America*, p. 208 n.

12. *Ibid.*, pp. 62-63.

13. Gibson, "The Aztec Aristocracy in Colonial Mexico," p. 182.

14. Miranda, *El Tributo indígena*, p. 136.

15. Woodrow Borah, *New Spain's Century of Depression* (*Ibero-Americana*, 35, Berkeley: University of California Press, 1951), documents most skillfully the interrelations of population loss, economic decline, and institutional change.

16. L. B. Simpson, *Many Mexicos* (New York, 1941), p. 102.

17. W. H. Prescott, *The Conquest of Mexico* (Modern Library ed. [1843], p. 33 n.; François Chevalier, *La Formation des grands domaines au Mexique: Terre et société aux XVI e-XVII e siècles* (Paris, 1952), p. xxiii; Friedrich Katz, *Die sozialökonomischen Verhältnisse bei den Azteken im 15. und 16. Jahrhundert* (Berlin, 1956), p. 12.

18. Alonso de Zorita, *Historia de la Nueva España*, ed. by M. Serrano y Sanz (Madrid, 1909). Some of these documents are inserted in the editor's lengthy, useful, but carping if not hostile biographical sketch of Zorita, pp. vii-cx; others are grouped in a documentary appendix. The documents from which I have quoted extensively, without citation, are "Información de Servicios de Alonso de Zorita," pp. 438-470; "Carta del Dr. Zorita, a S. M., en la que después de exponer sus servicios, pide se le nombre Capitán para entrar a los Chichimecas," pp. 418-424; and "Parecer del Doctor Alonso de Zorita, sobre la enseñanza espiritual de los indios," pp. 502-524. Joaquín García Icazbalceta published a "Memorial de Don Alonso de Zorita" on Zorita's project for peaceful conquest of the Chichimeca in his *Colección de documentos para la historia de México* (Mexico, 2 vols., 1858-1866), II, 333-342.

19. Not "Zurita," the erroneous form used by García Icazbalceta in the preface to his edition of the *Brief Relation*, all the more strangely, as Serrano y Sanz observes, since the name "Zorita" or "Çorita" appears in all the texts cited by the Mexican scholar.

20. The *Soneto al Rey Nuestro Señor* of the poet Hernando de Acuña (1520?-1580?), cited in the translation by H. Warner Allen in F. D. Klingender, *Goya in the Democratic Tradition* (London, 1948), p. 26.

21. Fray Tomás de la Torre, *Desde Salamanca, España, hasta Ciudad Real, Chiapas, Diario del viaje, 1544-1545* (Mexico, 1945), cited in Benjamin Keen, ed., *Readings in Latin-American Civilization* (Boston, 1955), p. 104.

22. Gonzalo Fernández de Oviedo y Valdés, *Historia general y natural de las Indias* (Madrid, 4 vols., 1851-1855), I, 83-84.

23. H. H. Bancroft, *History of Central America* (San Francisco, 3 vols., 1883-1888), II, 359.

24. *Ibid.*

25. *Ibid.*

26. *Ibid.*, p. 367.

27. *Life in the Imperial and Loyal City of Mexico in New Spain . . . as Described in the Dialogues for the Study of the Latin Language Prepared by Francisco Cervantes de Salazar* [1554], ed. by M. L. B. Shepard with an introduction and notes by C. E. Castañeda (Austin: University of Texas Press, 1953), p. 38.

28. Bernardo de Balbuena (1561 or 1562-1627), poet and ecclesiastic, in *Grandeza Mexicana* (Mexico, 1954), p. 40. The work was written in Mexico between 1595 and 1603.

29. *Life in the Imperial and Loyal City of Mexico*, p. 41 n.

30. *Ibid.*, p. 44.

31. Miranda, *El Tributo indígena*, p. 109.

32. H. H. Bancroft, *History of Mexico* (San Francisco, 6 vols., 1883-1888), II, 584-585.

33. Identified by Pascal de Gayangos, editor of *Cartas y relaciones de Hernán Cortés al emperador Carlos V* (Paris, 1866), p. 196, as modern Oaxtepec, Morelos.

34. *El Libro de las tasaciones de pueblos de la Nueva España*, prólogo de Francisco González de Cossío (Mexico, 1952), pp. 199-200.

35. Cedulas of November 27, 1560, and August 4, 1561.

36. For the opinions of Zorita and other royal officials, see F. V. Scholes and E. B. Adams, eds., *Documentos para la historia del México colonial* (Mexico, 6 vols. to date, 1954-1959), V, *Sobre el modo de tributar los indios de Nueva España a Su Majestad, 1561-1564* (1958), pp. 19-35.

37. Miranda, *El Tributo indígena*, p. 133.

38. Gerónimo de Mendieta, *Historia eclesiástica indiana* (Mexico, 1870), pp. 347-352.

39. Serrano y Sanz, in his introduction to the *Historia de la Nueva Espána*.

40. Joaqúin Ramirez Cabañas in his preface to Zorita's *Breve y sumaria relación de los señores de la Nueva España* (Mexico, 1942), p. xv.

41. *Colección de documentos para la historia de México*, II, 534.

42. García Icazbalceta, ed., *Nueva colección de documentos para la historia de México* (Mexico, 5 vols., 1886-1892), II, 248-249.

43. "Carta de Fr. Jacinto de San Francisco al Rey Felipe II," in *Nueva colección de documentos para la historia de México*, II, 235-247.

44. "Memorial de Don Alonso de Zorita," in *Colección de documentos para la historia de México*, II, 333-342; "Carta del Dr. Zorita . . . en la que

. . . pide se le nombre Capitán para entrar a los Chichimecas," in *Historia de la Nueva España*, pp. 418-429.

45. P. W. Powell, *Soldiers, Indians, and Silver. The Northward Advance of New Spain, 1550-1660* (Berkeley: University of California Press, 1952), is a definitive account of the Spanish-Indian struggle on the silver frontier.

46. Haring, *The Spanish Empire in America*, p. 297.

47. *Ibid.*, pp. 65-66, 58.

48. Coatzacoalcos, a province taking its name from the Coatzacoalcos River, in the present state of Veracruz.

49. *Historia de la Nueva España*, pp. 9-28.

50. B. Sánchez Alonso, *Historia de la historiografía española* (Madrid, 3 vols., 1941-1950), II, 240.

51. Robert Ricard, "Remarques bibliographiques sur les ouvrages de Fr. Toribio Motolinía," *Journal de la Société des Americanistes*, N. S., XXV (1933), 139-151.

52. For a discussion of problems connected with Olmos' compilation, see A. M. Garibay K., *Historia de la literatura nahuatl* (Mexico, 2 vols., 1953-1954), I (1953), Ch. 8, "Discursos didácticos," pp. 401-448.

53. Miranda, *El Tributo indígena*, p. 162.

54. For Motolinía's views, see his letter to Charles V in *Colección de documentos para la historia de México*, I, 253-277, partially translated in Simpson, *The Encomienda in New Spain*, pp. 234-243. The context of Motolinía's optimistic appraisal of the status of the Indians is a bitter personal attack on Las Casas; one may seriously doubt his objectivity. The letter contains the remarkable statement that "cattle have been removed from every place where they did damage," so contrary to other evidence that Professor Simpson observes that "Motolinía's optimism leads him astray." Simpson cites the complacent opinion of Francisco de Ceynos, *oidor* of the Audiencia of Mexico from 1530 to 1546, and from 1558 to 1565, in *The Encomienda in New Spain*, pp. 152-153. For the letter from which this opinion is taken, see *Colección de documentos para la historia de México*, II, 237-243.

55. Simpson, *The Encomienda in New Spain*, p. 152.

56. *Cartas de Indias* (Madrid, 1877), pp. 93-96.

57. "Carta al Rey Felipe de los provinciales de las órdenes de San Domingo, San Francisco, y San Agustín," Mexico, February 25, 1561, in *Cartas de Indias*, pp. 147-151.

58. *Instrucciones que los virreyes de Nueva España dejaron a sus sucesores* (Mexico, 2 vols., 1873), I, 57-58

59. Sherburne F. Cook and Woodrow Borah, "The Rate of Population Change in Central Mexico, 1550-1570," *Hispanic American Historical Review*, XXXVII (November, 1957), 463-470.

60. Miranda, *El Tributo indígena*, p. 168.

61. *Ibid.*, p. 115.

62. Gibson, "The Aztec Aristocracy in Colonial Mexico," pp. 178-182;

Chevalier, *La Formation des grands domaines au Mexique*, pp. 273-274.
63. *Ibid.*, p. 274.
64. *Historia de la Nueva España*, p. xcvi.
65. García Icazbalceta, in his introduction to Zorita's *Breve relación*, in *Nueva colección de documentos para la historia de México*, III, xx.
66. The literature on this theme is voluminous. Lewis Hanke has illuminated the subject, and especially the role of Las Casas, with a series of studies that include *The Spanish Struggle for Justice in the Conquest of America* (Philadelphia: University of Pennsylvania Press, 1949), and *Aristotle and the American Indians* (New York, 1959), a broadly conceived and thought-provoking book. However, Hanke's failure to take into account the clash of political and economic interests that underlay the dispute over the Indian gives his writings a curiously abstract air and leads to such hyperboles as the claim, in his *Aristotle and the American Indians,* that "no other nation made so continuous or so passionate an attempt to discover what was the just treatment for the native peoples under its jurisdiction, as the Spaniards." For a vigorous critique of Hanke's approach, and an effective attempt to place the Indian question in its political, social, and economic context, see Juan Friede, "Las Casas y el movimiento indígena en España y América en la primera mitad del siglo XVI," *Revista de Historia de América* (Mexico), XXXIV (1952), 339-411. For the attitudes of the influential Gerónimo de Mendieta, a close friend of Zorita's, see John Leddy Phelan, *The Millennial Kingdom of the Franciscans in the New World: A Study of the Writings of Gerónimo de Mendieta (1525-1604)* (Berkeley: University of California Press, 1956).
67. Juan Ginés de Sepúlveda, *Tratado sobre las justas causas de la guerra contra los indios,* cited in Keen, *Readings in Latin-American Civilization,* p. 91.
68. Francisco Cervantes de Salazar, *Crónica de la Nueva España* (Madrid, 1914), pp. 30-32.
69. See, on the shaping of this convention, the illuminating first chapter in H. N. Fairchild, *The Noble Savage: A Study in Romantic Naturalism* (New York, 1928).
70. *Ibid.*, p. 21.
71. G. C. Vaillant, *Aztecs of Mexico* (New York, 1941), p. 280.
72. Sahagún, *General History of the Things of New Spain*, Book III, *The Origin of the Gods* (1952), pp. 6-7.
73. Fernández de Oviedo y Valdés, *Historia general y natural de las Indias,* cited in Keen, *Readings in Latin-American Civilization,* pp. 17-18.
74. A sling formed by a strap slung over the forehead or chest, used by Indians for carrying a pack on the back.
75. Sahagún, *General History of the Things of New Spain*, Book VII, *The Sun, Moon, and Stars, and the Binding of the Years* (1953), p. 23.

Notes to the *Brief Relation**

1. Varius Geminus, Roman rhetorician cited by Seneca the Elder and St. Jerome for his oratorical talent.

2. The Spanish official Vasco de Puga first published this cedula of Charles V, dated December 20, 1553, in his compilation, *Provisiones, cedulas, instrucciones de su Majestad . . . para la buena expedición de los negocios, y administración de los negocios, y administración de justicia, y gobernación de esta Nueva España* (Mexico, 1563; reprinted, Mexico, 2 vols., 1878, and Madrid, 1945). This work is generally known as the *Cedulario de Puga.* A corrected text of the cedula of December 20, 1553, based on a manuscript copy in the Archivo General de Indias (Seville) of the order sent to the Audiencia de los Confines, differing slightly from that sent to the Audiencia of Mexico, is given in F. V. Scholes and E. A. Adams, eds., *Documentos para la historia del México colonial* (Mexico, 6 vols. to date, 1954-1959), IV, *Información sobre los tributos que los indios pagaban a Moctezuma* (1954), pp. 18-23. This text does not vary materially from that given in Zorita's *Relación.*

3. Audiencia de los Confines. The name originally assigned to the Audiencia of Guatemala, established by a royal order of November 25, 1542, with its seat at Valladolid de Comayagua. Transferred successively to Gracias a Dios, Guatemala City, and Panama, in 1568 it was re-established definitively in Guatemala City.

4. "The exact status of Mexican hieroglyphics," observes F. A. Peterson,

* A few notes entered by Joaquín García Icazbalceta in his edition of Zorita's *Brief Relation* (*Nueva Colección de documentos para la historia de México*, Mexico, 5 vols., 1886-1892, Vol. III, 1891) are merged with my notes. I have placed his notes in brackets with his name.

"has never been satisfactorily treated. The present-day arrangement into pictographic, ideographic, and phonetic symbols, is crude and does not fit Mexican circumstances. Mexican writing consists of highly conventionalized abstractions and meaningful symbols. Most of it is classified somewhere between the ideographic and the phonetic, because much of it is probably of an incipiently phonetic nature." *Ancient Mexico* (New York, 1959), p. 235. Indian picture writing was done on paper made from a variety of barks or an animal parchment. A picture writing or codex consists of a single long sheet of paper or animal parchment, folded like a screen so that two pages confront the user wherever he opens it, with thin slabs of wood or skin glued on each end to serve as binding. Only a small number of pre-Conquest codices remain; they contain principally annals or genealogies, and calendrical, ritual, religious, and divinatory material.

5. Zorita's three Franciscan sources: Fray Toribio de Benavente Motolinía (1495?-1565?). Born in Benavente, province of Zamora, Spain, Motolinía was one of twelve Franciscans who came to Mexico in 1524 in response to Cortés' request for missionaries. In New Spain Fray Toribio adopted the Indian name "Motolinía," meaning "poor man" (compare St. Francis' title of *poverello*). Motolinía combined strenuous missionary activity with intensive study of Indian languages, customs, and history. Although critical of Spanish misdeeds and eulogistic of Indian virtues, he defended the encomenderos against the attacks of the famous Dominican Bartolomé de Las Casas in an angry letter to Charles V (for a partial English translation, see L. B. Simpson, *The Encomienda in New Spain*, Berkeley: University of California Press, 1950, pp. 234-243). Two of his major works have been published. His *Historia de los indios de Nueva España*, composed in 1541 and first published by Joaquín García Icazbalceta in 1890, is available in two English translations: E. A. Foster, Motolinía's *History of the Indians of New Spain* (The Cortés Society, 1950), and F. B. Steck, O.F.M., *Motolinía's History of the Indians of New Spain* (Academy of American Franciscan History, 1951). His *Memoriales* was published by García Icazbalceta's son, Luis García Pimental (Mexico, 1903). For the relation between these two works, and their possible relation to a putative lost work of Motolinía's, which may have been the one utilized by Zorita, see my introduction.

Francisco de Las Navas (?-1578). Fray Francisco came to New Spain in 1538. He is said to have baptized more than twelve thousands Indians and to have known the Mexican or Nahuatl language perfectly. He died Guardian of the Convent of Tlatelolco, July 29, 1578.

Andrés de Olmos (c. 1491-1571). Fray Andrés, born near the village of Ona, province of Burgos, Spain, entered the Franciscan convent at Valladolid at the age of twenty, and is said to have distinguished himself there for his knowledge and piety. In 1528, Juan de Zumárraga, named to the bishopric of Mexico, chose him as his aide. Having mastered the most important Indian languages of Mexico, Olmos launched on a missionary career that continued for forty-three years. His writings include a Nahuatl grammar, translated by Rémi Siméon, *Grammaire de la langue Nahuatl ou Mexicaine* (Paris, 1875); a collection of Aztec didactic discourses or *huehuetlatolli,* some of which Zorita used in Spanish translation; and a work on Mexican antiquities, now lost.

6. The Dominican, Franciscan, and Augustinian Orders.

7. Zorita applies the name "Mexico" both to the Aztec capital of México-Tenochtitlán and to the Spanish city that rose on its ruins.

8. The following table, adapted from a table in John Fiske, *Discovery of America* (Boston, 2 vols., 1892), II, 225, shows the relationships of the eleven Mexican rulers or *tlacatecuhtli* ("chiefs-of-men"):

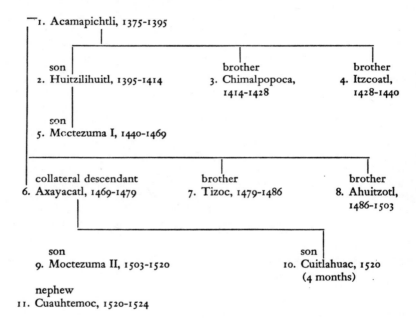

1. Acamapichtli, 1375-1395

son
2. Huitzilihuitl, 1395-1414

brother
3. Chimalpopoca, 1414-1428

brother
4. Itzcoatl, 1428-1440

son
5. Moctezuma I, 1440-1469

collateral descendant
6. Axayacatl, 1469-1479

brother
7. Tizoc, 1479-1486

brother
8. Ahuitzotl, 1486-1503

son
9. Moctezuma II, 1503-1520

son
10. Cuitlahuac, 1520 (4 months)

nephew
11. Cuauhtemoc, 1520-1524

9. The material on this and the following pages closely parallels the more detailed account of investiture ceremonies in Motolinía's *Memoriales,* pp. 282-284. The *Memoriales* indicates that the ceremony of investiture described at this point was used with the ruler of Tenochtitlán.

10. The version of this speech appearing in Motolinía's *Memoriales,* p. 283, differs from the version given by Zorita in details of wording and especially in the greater clarity with which Motolinía's text brings out the pagan essence of the discourse by its forthright references to human sacri-

fice, the Sun God, and the Goddess of Earth, which do not appear in Zorita's text. For purposes of comparison, I offer a partial translation of Motolinía's version:

"My Lord: Consider the honor your vassals have done you. Now that you are confirmed as ruler you must take great care of them and regard them as your sons; you must see to it that they be not offended and that the greater do not mistreat the lesser. You see that the lords of your country, your vassals, are all here with their people. You are their father and mother, and as such you must protect and defend them and treat them justly; for the eyes of all are upon you, and you are the one who must govern them and keep order among them. You must be very diligent in affairs of war. And you must see to it that the sun and the earth continue on their courses; (which means, in plain speech), consider, Lord, that you must toil in order that the sun god should not lack his sacrifice of blood and food, that he may continue on his course and shed his light on us; and you must do the same for the earth goddess, that she may give us provisions; and you must watch over and punish and slay the wicked, lords as well as councilmen (*regidores*). . . ."

11. Motolinía's *Memoriales*, p. 298, gives more details of this computation: "They considered an even-numbered day, such as four, six or eight, a bad sign or bad house; and because they always counted from the number of the day on which he [the ruler] was born, if he had been born on an even-numbered day, they sought an odd-numbered day for the festival, because even and odd always make odd, which was regarded as a good sign." Gerónimo de Mendieta, who consulted the same work of Motolinía's that Zorita drew upon, adds this detail: "And, on the contrary, if he had been born on an odd-numbered day or house, they chose an even-numbered day for the festival, that all together they might be odd" (*Historia eclesiástica indiana*, Mexico, 1870, p. 159). The Spanish sources are not in agreement as to whether good or bad luck was associated with the number of a day or with the complete day sign or formula, composed of a number and the name of the day. For the Aztec-Maya calendar, see César Lizardi Ramos, "El calendario maya-mexicano," *Esplendor del México antiguo* (Mexico, 2 vols., 1959), I, 221-242.

12. Firmianus Lactantius (?-A. D. 325 or 326). Church father and theologian; his principal extant work is the *Institutiones Divinae* in seven books, composed about A.D. 320, in defense of Christianity.

13. Sogamoso. In pre-Conquest times, sacred city of the powerful Muisca people of the highlands of Colombia and famed for the splendor of its temple, said to have been covered with plates of gold.

14. Perhaps Fray Tomás Casilla, bishop of Chiapas (1550-1567), who corresponded with Zorita.

15. Probably Fray Andrés de Olmos. This and other speeches in this book are examples of a type of Aztec literature known as *huehuetlatolli* or

"Speeches of the Ancients." These were didactic discourses or homilies pronounced on special or solemn occasions—marriage, the election of a ruler, the birth of a child, and the like. Their language is typically florid and metaphorical, with much use of conventional formulas or phrases. For a discussion of the genre and its Nahuatl and Spanish sources, see A. M. Garibay K., *Historia de la literatura nahuatl* (Mexico, 2 vols., 1953-1954), I (1953), Ch. 8, "Discursos didácticos," pp. 401-448. Father Garibay believes that the speeches collected by Olmos come from the region of Texcoco and its domain, whereas the speeches compiled by Bernardino de Sahagún in Book V of his *Historia general de las cosas de la Nueva España* were more likely collected in Tenochtitlán and Tlatelolco.

16. Spanish versions of this and some other speeches cited by Zorita, taken from Juan de Torquemada, *Los Veinte Libros riutales y Monarquía indiana* (1723), are given side by side with Zorita's texts in Antonio Peñafiel, ed., *Huehuetlatolli: Traducción de las antiguas conversaciones o pláticas por Fray Juan de Torquemada y el Dr. D. Alonso de Zurita* (Mexico, 1901). More faithful to the pagan originals, Torquemada's texts use "gods" where Zorita's versions speak of "God." There are other differences of wording which suggest translation or editing by different hands.

17. Zorita's "Suma de los tributos," one of the works he wrote in retirement, now lost.

18. Rather, *calpulalli* ("lands of the *calpulli*").

19. The controversy over the nature and role of the Aztec *calpulli*, closely connected with the dispute over the nature of Aztec society and government in general, has not yet ended. The pioneer American anthropologist, Lewis Morgan, flatly rejected Spanish accounts of Aztec royal palaces, kings, and nobles as full of "contradictory assertions, gross exaggerations, and fabulous statements." For Morgan, the so-called Aztec Empire was only a confederacy of tribes dwelling in pueblos, governed by a democratically elected council of chiefs, and collecting tribute from neighboring towns. Morgan's disciple, Adolf Bandelier, continued his work. In two papers based on intensive but tendentious research ("On the Distribution and Tenure of Land, and the Customs with Respect to Inheritance among the Ancient Mexicans," "On the Social Organization and Mode of Government of the Ancient Mexicans," *Peabody Museum Reports*, II (1878-1879), 385-448, 557-699, Bandelier sought to prove that the unit of Aztec social organization was the *calpulli*, a patrilineal, exogamous clan which did not recognize private property in land. He held that the supreme government of the Aztecs, essentially democratic in character, was vested in a tribal council composed of twenty members, one for each of the twenty Aztec clans.

Even in the nineteenth century, Bandelier's notions had aroused skepticism among historians impressed by evidence in Spanish and Indian sources of a highly stratified and complex social order among the Aztecs. In 1931 appeared the important revisionist work of Manuel Moreno, *La Organización política y social de los Aztecas*. Moreno, restudying the sources used by Bandelier, came to diametrically opposed conclusions. For Moreno, the *calpulli* was not a clan or kinship group at all, but a mere territorial division, one of the wards into which Tenochtitlán was divided for administrative purposes, and completely subservient to the central government. Moreno dismissed the whole conception of Aztec "tribal democracy," arguing that the evidence proved the existence of an Aztec state which wielded power for the benefit of "a few aristocratic and privileged classes to the prejudice of the rest of the people."

Arturo Monzón, *El Calpulli en la organización social de los Tenochca* (Mexico, 1949), takes an intermediate position. Monzón regards the *calpulli* as a clan which was ambilateral with respect to the rule of descent, and endogamous or with a tendency toward endogamy as concerns the regulation of marriage. The Aztec clans, however, were not the egalitarian, democratic groups of the Iroquois type, but were strongly stratified internally and in relation to each other, with indications that there existed one principal clan to which belonged all the chiefs of the whole tribe. In short, according to Monzón, Aztec society combined kinship organization with a strongly aristocratic character. However, according to this writer, technical advance and labor productivity had not yet reached the point where kinship bonds dissolve and true social classes emerge. Among recent works, E. R. Wolf, *Sons of the Shaking Earth* (Chicago: University of Chicago Press, 1959), appears to favor Monzón's intermediate position.

A recent text, Harold Driver, *Indians of North America* (New York, 1961), observes that the Aztec *calpulli* was apparently an endogamous deme. Driver defines an endogamous deme as "a community (village or band) which is not further segmented by unilineal descent and which is small enough so that all members are aware of their bilateral genetic relationship to all or most other members of the group. Such genetic relationship is often not traceable in cultures without writing, but if the members regard themselves as being genetically related, that is sufficient to label their group a deme. Marriage within the endogamous deme is the rule, providing the bride and groom are not too closely related" (pp. 306-307).

It should be noted that the foregoing discussion deals with the Aztec *calpulli* alone, and has no necessary application to the *calpulli*, or its counterpart under other names, in other parts of Middle America. Hugo G. Nutini cautions that "the term calpulli, as it is found throughout Mesoamerica today, does not possess a unitary meaning, as several anthropologists seem to have assumed. Calpulli means different things in different regions. It can be either a territorial unit or a kinship unit; it can be endogamous, exogamous, or have no marriage regulatory functions; it can be localized, non-localized, or semilocalized; and membership can be hereditary, residential, or by choice

"Clan Organization in a Nahuatl-Speaking Village of the State of Tlaxcala, Mexico," *American Anthropologist*, LXIII (February, 1961), 62-78.

What is true of the *calpulli* today was doubtless true of the *calpulli* of pre-Conquest times.

20. At this point Zorita's Nahuatl terminology becomes sadly confused. The confusion arises from misuse of two words: *calpulli*, pl. *calpultin*, meaning "clan"; and *calpulle* or *calpulleh*, pl. *calpulleque*, meaning "clan elder" or "clan administrator." I owe this clarification to the courtesy of Professor Arthur J. O. Anderson of San Diego State College.

21. Biscay: one of the four provinces composing the Basque region of northeastern Spain. Montaña: the mountainous region of the Spanish provinces of Burgos and Santander. The *parientes mayores* were town elders who played leading roles in the municipal and regional life of these provinces.

22. The notion of the *señor natural* or "natural lord" played a significant role in Spanish political thought of this period. The Crown utilized it to maintain a privileged class of Indian nobles who served as intermediaries between the Spanish rulers and Indian tribute-payers. The pro-Indian party, especially the regulars, often championed the cause of the Indian *señores naturales* as part of their anti-encomendero campaign. R. S. Chamberlain defines the concept of *señor natural* in Spanish political thought as "a lord who by inherent nature of superior qualities, goodness, and virtue, and by birth of superior station, attains power legitimately and exercises dominion over all within his lands justly and in accord with divine, natural, and human law and reason, being universally accepted, recognized, and obeyed by his vassals and subjects and acknowledged by other lords and other peoples as one who rightfully possesses his office and rightfully wields authority within his territory." "The Concept of the *Señor Natural* as Revealed by Castilian Law and Administrative Documents," *Hispanic American Historical Review*, XIX (May, 1939), No. 2, 130-137.

23. Nezahualcoyotl, ruler of Texcoco (1418-1472), architect of the Triple Alliance of Tenochtitlán, Texcoco, and Tlacopan, and a noted poet, law-giver, and philosopher who made Texcoco the cultural center of ancient Mexico. For an attractive evocation of Nezahualcoyotl and his times, based on careful study of Spanish and Indian sources, see Frances Gillmor, *Flute of the Smoking Mirror: A Portrait of Nezahualcoyotl, Poet-King of the Aztecs* (Albuquerque: University of New Mexico Press, 1949).

24. Nezahualpilli, ruler of Texcoco (1472-1516), son of the above, and also noted for administrative ability. In alliance with Ahuitzotl of Tenochtitlán, made a successful campaign into northern Oaxaca. His last years were troubled by growing friction with Tenochtitlán.

25. "Every ten or twelve days." Motolinía, *Memoriales*, p. 305.

26. Nezahualpilli.

27. Nezahualcoyotl.

28. Nezahualpilli (?).

29. Maxiscatzin, one of the four lords of Tlaxcala at the time of the Spanish Conquest. Urged alliance with Cortés against the Aztecs, and stood by the Spaniards at the time of their flight from Tenochtitlán. Died of smallpox (1521).

30. The "wine" was pulque.

31. [The material in brackets is written on the margin of the manuscript in a different hand. García Icazbalceta.]

32. [Interest was taken in many places. (Note in a different hand.) García Icazbalceta.]

33. [For the rulers they always sought older women, not girls. (Note in a different hand.) García Icazbalceta.]

34. [When a son or daughter was born to a ruler, the child was assigned a house and apartments, lands and people to work them; and when a daughter married (as a general rule she married outside her own town), she remained in possession of the said lands and people. (Note in a different hand.) García Icazbalceta.]

35. I have substituted a literal translation of the Aztec name *telpochcalli* (House of Youth) for the word "community" (*comunidad*), applied by Zorita to the school maintained by each *calpulli* for the training of the children of commoners. Temple schools, reserved for the sons of rulers and nobles, were called *calmecac*.

36. Probably Fray Andrés de Olmos.

37. That is, the girl's nurses.

38. Cortés is referring to the advanced Moslem culture of North Africa.

39. A rectangular platform ascended by four staircases, one on each side.

40. The mark of silver was equal to 8 ounces.

41. Eulalia Guzmán observes that this figure is incorrect. The distance from Tenochtitlán to the west bank of the lagoon was much less than 2 leagues, while the distance from the city to the east bank was as much as 6 leagues, and even more. *Relaciones de Hernán Cortés a Carlos V sobre la invasión de Anáhuac. Aclaraciones y rectificaciones por la profesora Eulalia Guzmán* (Mexico, 1958), p. 291.

42. H. R. Wagner comments on Cortés' statement: "No brass, lead, or tin to my knowledge has ever been found in the excavations in Mexico. . . . The question whether tin existed is much debated." *The Rise of Fernando Cortés* (The Cortés Society, 1944), pp. 232-233.

43. Turkeys.

44. *Metl*, in Nahuatl. Maguey is a term imported from the West Indies.

45. "Glazing was unknown. What appeared to be such to Cortés was the perfect polish given to the tile." Eulalia Guzmán, *Relaciones de Hernán Cortés a Carlos V.*

46. Temples.

47. The material quoted above is from the Second Relation of Cortés to the Emperor Charles V. I have used the corrected text edited by Eulalia Guzmán, *Relaciones de Hernán Cortés a Carlos V*, pp. 141, 147-152, 291-295, 297-326.

48. The above paragraph is almost identical with a passage in Motolinía's *Memoriales*, p. 186.

49. Fray Toribio de Benavente Motolinía.

50. The following quotation from Motolinía parallels, with some variations, the text of Motolinía's *Historia de los indios de Nueva España*, in Joaquín García Icazbalceta, ed., *Nueva colección de documentos para la historia de México* (Mexico, 5 vols., 1886-1892) III, 141-143. These passages are not found in Motolinía's *Memoriales*.

51. The phrasing of the *Historia* makes the meaning clearer: "They do not have the bother of dressing or undressing." A. E. Foster, *Motolinía's History of the Indians of New Spain*, p. 98.

52. Probably Fray Andrés de Olmos.

53. Tezcatlipoca, head of the Aztec pantheon, was the pardoner of sins to whom Aztecs did penance and offered prayers for forgiveness.

54. "When Israel went out of Egypt, the house of Jacob from a people of strange language."

55. "And Solomon's wisdom excelled the wisdom of all the children of the east country, and all the wisdom of Egypt."

56. Probably of the *Institutiones Divinae*.

57. "As in the title on eunuchs and in the title concerning the things the Romans should not export"; "concerning the refinements of the Latin language"; "barbarian because foreign, alien, strange."

58. "Maccus translated it into a foreign tongue: if one examines closely the meaning of this word *barbare*, it becomes clear that it means nothing more than Roman, to the Greeks, who considered not only Scythians but Latins foreigners; this explains why elsewhere Plautus refers to Naevius as the foreign poet."

59. "Egypt was occupied by Scythians or Indians or some such folk, that is, by foreign neighbors." Henri Ternaux-Compans, translator of the French edition of Zorita's work, *Rapport sur les différentes classes de chefs de la Nouvelle Espagne* (Paris, 1840), comments in a note: "This passage is probably from Lactantius, who spoke of Mercurius Trismegistus. The copyist doubtless omitted at the beginning of this phrase some words that belonged here: 'Lactantius in speaking of Mercurius Trismegistus.' "

60. "Let us pray for our most Christian Emperor, that God may bring under his sway all the barbarian nations."

61. Sayago. A region of the province of Zamora, Spain, situated between the rivers Duero and Tormes. The *Enciclopedia Universal Ilustrada* asserts that "the people of Sayago are unjustly famed as being uncouth (*rudos*);

this reputed uncouthness may be due to the dialectal differences between this district and the rest of the country, which cause the speech of these people to sound crude in the ears of strangers."

62. See above n. 20.

63. In point of fact, Tenochtitlán probably supplied a good part of its own food needs through *chinampa* agriculture, the so-called "floating gardens," consisting of platforms made by filling woven reed baskets with earth and anchoring them in the shallow waters of the lake. "The Tenochcas and their neighbors thus converted great sections of otherwise unproductive marsh, flooded in the rainy season, into a grid of canals and fields, the fertility of which is equaled only by the river-flooded lands of the Nile." George C. Vaillant, *Aztecs of Mexico* (New York, 1941), p. 125.

64. For the development of the system of *cuentas* and *visitas*, see my introduction.

65. Fray Toribio de Motolinía.

66. Texts of the above quotations from Motolinía are found in the *Historia de los indios de Nueva España* and the *Memoriales*. However, these texts differ in details of phrasing from each other and from the version found in Zorita.

67. The voyages outfitted by Cortés had as their object the discovery of the East Indies and of a strait connecting the Atlantic with the Pacific. His northward navigation led to his discovery of Lower California (1536).

68. Before and after the Spanish Conquest, Mexico City was exposed to great inundations as a result of flooding of the lakes during the rainy season. After Tenochtitlán had almost been destroyed by flood in 1440, Moctezuma I, assisted by Nezahualcoyotl of Texcoco, had a great dike erected around the rim of the city to prevent invasion by the waters of the lake. Following the great flood of 1553, the viceroy Luis de Velasco ordered a similar dike built to prevent recurrence of the disaster. Neither his efforts nor those of his successor, Martín Enríquez, proved successful. In the seventeenth and eighteenth centuries attention was focused on construction of a great canal designed to drain the Valley of Mexico and thus prevent the inundation of the city. Large numbers of Indians were forced to work on this project under dangerous and unsanitary conditions that caused the death of thousands.

69. A reference to the famous formula employed by Spanish officials to shelve a royal order that was inconvenient or impossible to execute: *Obedezco pero no cumplo.*

70. Juan de Zumárraga (1486-1548). Franciscan friar, appointed first bishop of Mexico, December 12, 1527, receiving at same time title and office of Protector of the Indians. Displayed great zeal in work of conversion and defense of Indians' rights. Died eight days after receiving the bull which raised his see to an archbishopric.

71. The bracketed portion of this article was omitted by Zorita.

72. Now, it is said, more silver is minted than formerly. [Note of Zorita.]

73. [It is interesting to note that the rest of the paragraph represents a revision by the author, who crossed out the following, as if he had repented of having written it: "Never have services been better repaid than those of the conquistadores and settlers of the Indies. Yet they never cease complaining, for nothing that is given them will suffice to make them stop their complaining and their inveterate, ingrained custom of saying they deserve much more than this." García Icazbalceta].

74. Turkeys.

75. The *residencia* and the *visita* were both procedures of judicial review of an official's conduct. However, the *residencia* was held in public, and opportunity was given to all to present accusations or give evidence. The procedure in the *visita*, on the other hand, was supposed to be secret, presumably giving the investigated official opportunity to use undue influence to secure his exoneration.

76. Motolinía's *Memoriales*, pp. 353-356, lists sixty-six towns belonging to the ruler of Texcoco; fourteen towns are named that were assigned to construction and maintenance of the houses of the ruler and the temples. The painting of the glyphs or signs of these towns, however, originally included in the manuscript, had disappeared, according to its editor, by the time it was published.

77. Zorita did not carry out this intention.

78. Axayacatl, ruler of Tenochtitlán (1469-1479). He extended Mexican domination into the Matlazinca country and south to Oaxaca and Tehuantepec. His campagn against the Tarascans, however, met with a crushing defeat, the first such reverse until the coming of the Spaniards in 1519.

79. Sesame.

80. Tizoc, ruler of Tenochtitlán (1479-1486). He began reconstruction of the great temple to Huitzilopochtli, the war god, and Tlaloc, the rain god; he also commemorated his conquests by having carved the so-called Sacrificial Stone, an immense vessel for burning human hearts. His military exploits seem to have been confined to previously conquered and lost towns.

81. Ahuitzotl, ruler of Tenochtitlán (1486-1503). In his reign, reconstruction of the great temple of Huitzilopochtli was completed. For the proper dedication of this temple, Ahuitzotl and his ally Nezahualpilli, ruler of Texcoco, made a two-year campaign into northern Oaxaca, amassing twenty thousand prisoners, who were sacrificed. His campaigns extended south into Guatemala and as far north as the Huaxteca in Veracruz. He was constantly engaged in putting down revolts by subject towns. According to one account, he was killed in an accident while engaged in supervising restoration of dikes wrecked by the great flood of 1503.

82. Moctezuma II, surnamed Xocoyotzin (the Younger), ruler of Tenochtitlán (1503-1519). Fought unsuccessful war against the Tlaxcalans. In 1516, on the death of Nezahualpilli, he appointed his successor as ruler of Tex-

coco without recognizing the choice of the Texcocan council. The rejected candidate, Ixtlilxochitl, revolted, and the alliance between Tenochtitlán and Texcoco was seriously strained. In the face of the Spanish invasion Moctezuma pursued a wavering policy composed of threats and blandishments, but finally admitted Cortés into his capital. Taken prisoner and held as hostage by the Spaniards, Moctezuma died in 1519, killed by stones hurled by his own people, according to the Spanish accounts; strangled by the Spaniards, in the Indian versions.

83. Antonio de Mendoza (1485-1552). First viceroy of New Spain (October 1535–November 1549), and viceroy of Peru (1551-1552). An able administrator, Mendoza stabilized political conditions in New Spain, sought to regulate and reform the Indian tribute and labor system, and promoted settlement and exploration to the north and northwest (Coronado's expedition). Had differences with Cortés, who unsuccessfully sought to engineer Mendoza's ouster. A standard work on Mendoza is Arthur S. Aiton, *Antonio de Mendoza, First Viceroy of New Spain* (Durham: Duke University Press, 1941.)

84. The prickly pear; *opuntia*.

85. Perhaps Fray Tomás Casilla, bishop of Chiapas (1550-1567).

Notes to Appendix

1. Mariano Cuevas, ed., *Documentos inéditos del siglo XVI para la historia de México* (Mexico, 1914), pp. 221-228.

2. For the frustrating experiences of Diego Ramírez, see W. V. Scholes, *The Diego Ramírez Visita* (Columbia, Missouri, 1946).

3. Cuevas, ed., *Documentos inéditos del siglo XVI para la historia de México*, pp. 228-232.

4. *Ibid.*, pp. 235-242.

5. Vol. IV (1954) of *Documentos para la historia del México colonial*, ed. by F. V. Scholes and E. A. Adams (Mexico, 6 vols. to date, 1954-1959).

6. Of interest, in this connection, is the statement in a Franciscan document that some negligent religious had given an education to sons of peasants and other lower class persons that caused them to rise to leadership ("se han alzado a mayores"). As a result, these plebeians now governed in many towns, supplanting and abasing the *principales* who were their absolute lords before they received the Faith. "El Orden que los Religiosos tienen en enseñar a los indios de Doctrina . . . ," in *Nueva Colección de documentos para la historia de México,* (Mexico, 5 vols., 1886-1892), II, 62.

A Glossary of Spanish and Nahuatl Terms

Terms glossed or defined in the text are not, with some exceptions, included in this list. Only senses applicable to this book are covered. Monetary units are also discussed at the end of the Editor's Introduction.

alcalde. A magistrate or mayor of a Spanish or Indian town who in addition to administrative duties possessed certain judicial powers as a judge of first instance; the number of alcaldes was one in a small town or pueblo, elsewhere invariably two.

alcalde de corte. One of a number of magistrates uniting administrative and judicial powers, each having jurisdiction over a district of colonial Mexico City.

alcalde mayor. A provincial governor exercising political and judicial authority within his district.

alguacil. A municipal officer charged with maintenance of public order, apprehension of criminals, and similar duties: constable.

almud. A variable dry measure (from 2 to 21 liters).

audiencia. The highest royal court of appeals within a jurisdiction, serving at the same time as a council of state to the viceroy or captain general, having a limited degree of legislative power, subject to ultimate royal approval, and presided over by a viceroy or a captain general, or by a president of its own, in the case of subordinate audiencias.

barrio. (1) *Calpulli;* especially one of the *calpullis* or territorial divisions composing a pre-Conquest Indian town. (2) Ward of a colonial town or city: quarter.

braza. A measure of length (5.48 ft.).

cacique. Indian hereditary chief.

calpisque. Calpisqui.

calpisqui, pl. *calpixque.* Indian tribute collector: steward.

calpul. Calpulli.

calpulle or *calpulleh,* pl. *calpulleque.* Chief clan elder or administrator.

calpullec. Calpulleque.

calpulli. See p. 298, n. 19.

cámaras. A usually fatal epidemic disease characterized by diarrhea.

casa de la comunidad or *casa de comunidad.* A public building in an Indian town used for the transaction of official business, the storing of public property and moneys, and the like.

chía. Lime-leaved sage (*Salvia hispanica L.*) from the seeds of which the natives prepared a beverage.

chinancalle or *chinancalleh,* pl. *chinancalleque.* Chief elder or administrator of a *calpulli,* especially of a small *calpulli.*

chinancalli, pl. *chinancaltin. Calpulli;* especially a small *calpulli.*

comendador. Knight commander of a military order in Spain.

corregidor. A provincial governor exercising political and judicial authority within his district.

cuartillo. A small coin, being the fourth part of a real.

cúe. An Indian temple.

ducado. The standard gold coin of Castile after 1497, valued at 375 maravedís.

encabezamiento. A Spanish tax system under which a general tax on individuals was collected by the different cities of the realm, which in turn were responsible for paying definite sums to the Crown.

encomendero. The holder of an encomienda.

encomienda. See p. 8.

escribano. Notary or scribe.

escribano de gobernación. A notary attached to the governor of a province.

estado. A measure of length (1.85 yards).

fanega. A grain measure (about 1.6 bushels).

fiscal. Crown attorney charged with the defense of the king's interests especially in cases affecting the Exchequer, the Church, and the rights of the Indians, and with giving legal advice to the viceroy or governor in matters of administration.

gobernador. Governor.

macehual (*macegual, maceual*), pl. *macehualtin.* Indian commoner: peasant.

manta. An essential article of Indian dress in pre-Conquest times and the early colonial period, consisting of a plain blanket of maguey fiber or coarse cotton, in the case of commoners, or of an elaborate, richly decorated mantle in the case of nobles or rich merchants, that hung under the left arm and was knotted on the right shoulder; the tribute *manta* was a piece of cotton cloth about 1 yard wide and 4 yards long.

maravedí. A Spanish copper coin of the value of $.007 in U. S. pre-1934 gold dollars.

mayeque. A peasant of ancient Mexico, resembling the serf of medieval Europe, who was bound to the soil, worked the land on shares for the lord, and owed his lord personal service. Called also *tlalmaitl.*

media. A land measure (about three-fourths of an acre).

milpa. A maize field.

oidor. A member of an Audiencia: judge.

pariente mayor. Chief elder of a Spanish community.

peso. A silver coin equal to 8 reales or 272 maravedís.

peso de minas also *peso de plata.* An uncoined silver unit valued at 450 maravedís.

peso de oro also *peso de oro de minas.* An uncoined gold unit valued at 450 maravedís.

peso de oro ecomún. An uncoined gold unit worth about 300 maravedís.

peso de oro de tipuzque. An uncoined monetary unit consisting of gold mixed with copper, valued at about 272 maravedís.

pilles. Hispanized plural of *pilli.*

pilli, pl. *pipiltin.* A noble through descent from an Aztec ruler: knight, grandee.

pipiltzin. Reverential form of *pipiltin.*

presidente. The president of a subordinate Audiencia, usually appointed governor of the area under the Audiencia's jurisdiction, subject to the supervision and direction of the viceroy in matters of policy.

principal. A member of the Indian aristocracy.

real. A silver coin valued at 34 maravedís.

regidor. Councilman.

repartimiento. (1) *Encomienda.* (2) The periodic conscription of Indians for labor useful to the Spanish community. (3) A group of Indians drafted for such labor.

residencia. Judicial review of an officer's conduct at the end of his term of office, usually made by a specially designated commissioner (*juez de residencia*) with public notice given of the day and place when the *residencia* would open so that residents of the district could come forward and present evidence or accusations, and a time limit set for conclusion of the *residencia,* at the end of which the judge prepared his report, pronounced sentence, and remitted it to the Council of the Indies (if the official had been appointed by the Crown) or to the local Audiencia, review being made by the appropriate body.

tecquiuac. Tequiuaque.

tectecutzin. Tetecuhtzin.

tecuhtli (*tecuitli, teccutli*), pl. *tecuhtin* (*tecutin*); reverential *tecuhtzin,* pl. *tetecuhtzin* (*tetecutzin, tetecuhtzitzin*). An individual who had acquired nobility through special services, usually in battle, to the Aztec state, and had land and peasants assigned for his support.

teniente. Lieutenant.

tequitlato, pl. *tequitlatoque.* Steward or majordomo charged with assignment of tribute or labor to vassals of an Indian lord.

tequiua, pl. *tequiuaque.* A brave warrior who had captured four prisoners of the bravest enemy cities and was thus qualified to form part of the Aztec war council and to hold high military and governmental office.

teules. Hispanized plural of *tecuhtli.*

tierra caliente. The hot coastal lowland zone of Mexico.

tierra fría. The temperate highland zone of Mexico.

tlatoani, pl. *tlatoque.* Supreme lord: ruler, king.

tlatocamilli. Land set aside in each *calpulli* or town for the support of the ruler and other general purposes.

tlatoques. Hispanized plural of *tlatoani.*

tomín or *tomín de oro.* Smallest division for gold of the mark, the basic unit of monetary weight, consisting of 12 grains (0.575 grams).

vara. A variable unit of length.

visita. 1. An investigation of an official's conduct, usually supposed to be secret, and typically instituted because of complaints of mismanagement or misconduct, made by a *visitador* appointed by the Council of the Indies (in the case of officials appointed by the Crown) or by the viceroy or president in consultation with the Audiencia.

2. A triennial tour of inspection of a province, made by one of the *oidores* chosen by the viceroy or president, usually in turn, with the object of making a searching inquiry into eco-

nomic, social, and judicial conditions, treatment of the Indians, and the like.

3. An official visit (as for the purpose of determining the capacity of an Indian town to pay tribute) made by an *oidor* or other agent at the direction of the viceroy and Audiencia.

visitador. An official entrusted with the conduct of a *visita.*

NOTE ON THE DECORATIONS

Most of the decorations in this book are derived from two celebrated Aztec or neo-Aztec picture writings. These are the Codex Borbonicus and the Codex Telleriano Remensis, both published in facsimile with commentaries by E.-T. Hamy in Paris in 1899.

The history of the Codex Borbonicus is obscure. It was long thought to be pre-Conquest, but Robert Barlow has recently cast doubt on its antiquity by noting that the blank spaces in the manuscript were probably left to allow for the insertion of interpretations in Spanish. In Barlow's opinion, the codex was made immediately after the Spanish Conquest.

From the Biblioteca de San Lorenzo of the Escorial, where it was in the sixteenth century, it was carried to France in the time of Napoleon's invasion of the Peninsula. Early in the nineteenth century it was acquired by the library of the French Chamber of Deputies (Bibliothèque du Palais-Bourbon) in Paris. Today it is in the Bibliothèque Nationale.

The Codex Borbonicus contains a Tonalpohualli, a religious calendar of two hundred and sixty days used by priests for purposes of divination. It also depicts the eighteen seasonal festivals of the Aztecs.

The Codex Telleriano Remensis was composed after the Conquest, apparently with the aid of native informants, but clearly reveals European influence. It is named after a former owner, Charles Maurice Le Tellier, Archbishop of Rheims. It was later acquired by the Bibliothèque Nationale.

The Codex Telleriano Remensis consists of three parts: a section dealing with the great seasonal ceremonies; a Tonalpohualli or sacred almanac; and a picture chronicle terminating with the year 1562. The author of the codex appears to have been the Dominican Pedro de los Ríos.

i, 79   The Great God Tezcatlipoca, shown as presiding god of the Feast of Panquetzaliztli (Flags) in the fifteenth month of the Aztec solar calendar. Codex Telleriano Remensis.

iii, 186   Tezcatlipoca, Great God, shown as a presiding god of the day hours in the Tonalpohualli of the Codex Borbonicus. Beside him, his asociated bird, the horned owl.

1, 275   Tepeyollotl, Heart of the Mountain, Jaguar God or Earth God, one of the forms or guises of the great creator god Tezcatlipoca. Codex Telleriano Remensis.

17, 219   The Spanish conquistador Nuño de Guzmán shown departing for the conquest of Jalisco. Entry for the year 1529 in the picture chronicle of the Codex Telleriano Remensis.

39   Mexico City drawn in Zorita's time by the Flemish artist and geographer Joris Hoefnagel. Published in *Civitates orbis terrarum* compiled by Georgius Braun and Franz Hohenberg. First edition, Cologne, P. Gallaeum, 1572.

52, 235   Tlaltecuhtli, Lord of Earth, the Earth Monster, shown as a presiding god of the day hours. Above, his associated bird, green hummingbird. Codex Borbonicus.

58, 197   Teoyaomiqui, God of Dead Enemy Warriors, a specialized death god, shown as a presiding god of the day hours. Above, his associated bird, the screech owl. Codex Borbonicus.

61, 191 Xochipilli, the Prince of Flowers, God of Pleasure and Feasting, shown as a presiding god of the day hours. Above, his associated bird, the butterfly. Codex Borbonicus.

63, 229 The day sign Seven Vulture, with its associated night god. Codex Borbonicus.

83, 198 The day sign Two Jaguar, with its associated night god. Codex Borbonicus.

84, 195 The day sign Twelve Lizard, with its associated night god. Codex Borbonicus.

88, 263 A corpse bundled on its funeral litter, a ritual figure representing the Feast of Xocotlhuetzi (the Dead) in the tenth month of the Aztec solar calendar. Codex Telleriano Remensis.

103, 192 Tonatiuh, the Sun God, shown as a presiding god of the day hours. Above, his associated bird, the quail. Codex Borbonicus.

112, 200 The day sign Three Eagle, with its associated night god. Codex Borbonicus.

122, 231 The day sign Thirteen Serpent, with its associated night god. Codex Borbonicus.

153 Title page of *Túmulo Imperial de la Gran Ciudad de México* by Francisco Cervantes de Salazar. Mexico, Antonio de Espinosa, 1560. The foreword to this work describing the religious ceremonies held in Mexico following the death of Charles V was written by Alonso de Zorita, then oidor in Mexico.

162, 261 Tlaloc, God of Water or Rain, shown in association with the Feast of Tlaxochimaco (Birth of Flowers) in the ninth month of the Aztec solar calendar. Codex Borbonicus.

174, 233   The day sign Nine Alligator, with its associated night god. Codex Borbonicus.

180, 234   Ritual figure of an Aztec noble, representing the Feast of Hueitecuhilhuitl (Great Rulers) in the eighth month of the Aztec solar calendar. He is dressed in a fine mantle, has rich featherwork on his shoulders, and his lower lip is pierced with a labret, the sign of his dignity. Under his extended right hand appears the hieroglyph for the word *ilhuite,* "feast." Codex Telleriano Remensis.

190, 260   The Great God Quetzalcoatl, God of Learning, shown as a presiding god of the day hours. Beside him, his associated bird, the turkey cock.

Index

ABOUT THE AUTHOR

Benjamin Keen, professor of history at Northern Illinois University, was graduated from Muhlenberg College and received his M.A. degree from Lehigh University and Ph.D. from Yale University. He is one of the few American scholars who is devoted to translating literary materials from other languages. He is also deeply interested in the Aztec civilization, and is a frequent contributor to the *Hispanic American Historical Review*. This is his third translation for the Rutgers University Press: *The Life of the Admiral Christopher Columbus by His Son Ferdinand*, 1959, and *The Spain of Ferdinand and Isabella*, 1961, both of which were History Book Club Selections.